Lecture Notes in Computer Science　　13010

More information about this subseries at http://www.springer.com/series/8851

Ngoc Thanh Nguyen · Ryszard Kowalczyk ·
Anna Motylska-Kuźma ·
Jacek Mercik (Eds.)

Transactions on Computational Collective Intelligence XXXVI

Springer

Editor-in-Chief
Ngoc Thanh Nguyen (iD)
Wroclaw University of Technology
Wroclaw, Poland

Co-Editor-in-Chief
Ryszard Kowalczyk
Swinburne University of Technology
Hawthorn, VIC, Australia

Guest-Editors
Anna Motylska-Kuźma
WSB University Wroclaw
Wroclaw, Poland

Jacek Mercik
WSB University Wroclaw
Wroclaw, Poland

ISSN 0302-9743   ISSN 1611-3349 (electronic)
Lecture Notes in Computer Science
ISSN 2190-9288   ISSN 2511-6053 (electronic)
Transactions on Computational Collective Intelligence
ISBN 978-3-662-64562-8   ISBN 978-3-662-64563-5 (eBook)
https://doi.org/10.1007/978-3-662-64563-5

This Springer imprint is published by the registered company Springer-Verlag GmbH, DE
part of Springer Nature
The registered company address is: Heidelberger Platz 3, 14197 Berlin, Germany

Preface

It is our pleasure to present to you volume 13010 of LNCS Transactions on Computational Collective Intelligence (TCCI). In autumn 2020 (November 27) the WSB University in Wroclaw, Poland, hosted the sixth seminar on "Quantitative methods of group decision making". Thanks to the WSB University in Wroclaw we had an excellent opportunity to organize and financially support the seminar. This volume collates extended and revised versions of papers presented at this seminar. During the seminar we listened to and discussed over 13 presentations from participants representing 10 universities. The XXXVI issue of TCCI contains seven high-quality, carefully reviewed papers.

The first paper "*A Theoretical Examination of the Ranked Choice Voting Procedure*" by Hannu Nurmi and Rachel Perez Palha is devoted[1] to the analysis of Ranked Choice Voting (RCV). Over the past couple of decades Ranked Choice Voting (RCV) has been advocated in the USA as a substitute for the current first-past-the-post (FPTP) electoral system. While its entrance to the electoral system of the USA is yet to be seen, it has found strong support among numerous voter groups, activists, and voting theorists. The authors discuss the proposed voting method in some detail, evaluating it in the light of standard social choice criteria of performance. They conclude that while RCV certainly represents an improvement over FPTP in terms of richness of voter input, it falls short of satisfying several important, even essential, conditions for a satisfactory voting method. A modification of, and an alternative to, RCV is discussed as well.

In the second paper entitled "*A Game Theoretic Model of Searching for a Unique Good from a Large Set of Offers*" by David Ramsey, the author studies a game theoretic approach to the number of offers being placed on the short list with two players who have symmetric roles. Consumers can nowadays easily access information via the Internet about a wide range of offers on the market. For example, a family looking for a new flat can find basic information on offers via an Internet site. Much of this information is of a quantitative nature (e.g. price, size of the flat), which is very useful in determining a set of potentially very attractive offers. However, many of the traits associated with the attractiveness of a flat are qualitative in nature and can only be assessed by physically viewing an offer (e.g. view from the balcony, attractiveness of the immediate location). This necessitates physically viewing a number of offers before making a final decision. Since the costs of physically viewing a flat are much greater than the costs of finding data about flats on the Internet, consumers often use information from the Internet to form a short list of offers to be viewed. Since the decision to buy such a product is often made collectively, e.g. by a couple or family, the author considers a game theoretic approach to such a problem with two players who have symmetric roles. The one possible asymmetry considered is that one player might

---

[1] Hereafter descriptions of the papers are taken directly from summaries prepared by their authors.

exhibit a higher level of altruism than the other. Although short lists are often used in practice, there is little research on determining, for example, how many offers should be placed on the short list according to the parameters of the problem and the relations between the players. This model indicates that altruism between the players and coherent preferences are important factors in facilitating the search. When the players neither have coherent preferences nor feel altruism towards each other, a situation similar to the battle of the commons exists, which leads to a large number of offers being placed on the short list.

In the third paper "*Operation Comfort of Multistate System vs. The Importance of Its Components*" by Krzysztof Szajowski and Małgorzata Średnicka considers the analysis of the significance of complex system components. When examining the reliability, Birnbaum (1968) proposed measures of element significance. This direction of research into mathematical models of systems has led to many alternative analyses. The aim of their article is to further expand the diagnostic capabilities of systems through a specialized analysis of their mathematical models. They propose, using the methods of game theory and stochastic processes, functionals that measure the structural reliability of the system and the operational performance related to maintenance. This allows for the construction of a new measure of significance, using knowledge of system design, reliability, and wear to optimize repair and maintenance. The considerations of their work are aimed at showing the ways of applying this approach to multi-state systems.

The fourth paper "*Implicit Power Indices for Measuring Indirect Control in Corporate Structures*" by Jochen Staudacher, Linus Olsson, and Izabella Stach deals with measuring indirect control in complex corporate shareholding networks using the concept of power indices from cooperative game theory. They focus on the approaches by Mercik-Lobos and Stach-Mercik which measure the control power of all firms involved in shareholding networks with algorithms based on the raw Johnston index. They point out how these approaches can be generalized by replacing the raw Johnston index with various other power indices in a modular fashion. They further extend the algorithmic framework by investigating more than one regression and present requirements for software and modeling. Finally, they test the new framework of generalized implicit power indices for a network with 21 players and discuss how properties of the underlying power index like efficiency or null player removability influence the measurements of indirect control.

In the fifth paper entitled "*1% Tax in Public Benefit Organizations: Determinants of Its Share in Organizations' Total Revenues – Analysis of 3rd Sector in Poland*" Hanna Pyrkosz and Anna Motylska-Kuźma identify variables which influence the share of 1% of income taxes in total revenues of Public Benefit Organizations. Their methodology is based on statistical analysis of the data, which have been obtained from (comprehensive) technical reports from the year 2018 of 100 Public Benefit Organizations. The organizations were selected from the official list of Public Benefit Organizations published by Director of the National Institute of Liberty. Using analysis of the correlation and hierarchical regression, they examined the relations between the 1% tax revenue share in total revenue with such factors as location, legal form, website use, campaigning, area of activity, and age of organization. The analysis shows the importance of the legal form and experience of organizations in attracting the funds from the 1% tax mechanism and does not confirm the general opinion about the importance of the promotion and visibility of the PBOs. The research shows also over prioritization of the size of the organization as the factor which could significantly attract the possible donors.

In the sixth paper *"Reformulation of Some Indices Using Null Player Free Winning Coalitions"* Izabella Stach and Cezarino Bertini present a new representation for some power indices in a simple game using null player free winning coalitions. Analogously to a set of winning coalitions and minimal winning coalitions, a set of null player free winning coalitions fully captures the characteristics of a simple game. Moreover, expressing indices by winning coalitions that do not contain null players allows them to show the parts of the power that are assigned to null and non-null players in a simple game in a transparent manner.

The last paper is an invited paper entitled *"Analysis and Modelling of Activity-Selection Behaviour in Collaborative Knowledge-Building"*. A preliminary version of this paper was published as a poster in The Web Conference 2020 and was presented in the proceedings of the 12th International Conference on Computational Collective Intelligence (ICCCI) 2020. Anamika Chhabra, S. R. S. Iyengar, Jaspal Singh Saini, and Vaibhav Malik analyse people behavior in their social lives. People neither behave uniformly in their social lives nor is their behavior entirely arbitrary. Rather, their behavior depends on various factors such as their skills, motives, and back-grounds. The authors' analysis shows that such behavior also prevails in the websites of Stack Exchange. They collected and analyzed the data of over 5.3 million users from 156 Stack Exchange websites. In these websites, users' diverse behavior shows up in the form of different activities that they choose to perform as well as how they stimulate each other for more contribution. Using the insights gained from the empirical analysis as well as classical cognitive theories, the authors build a general cognitive model depicting the users' interaction behavior emerging in collaborative knowledge-building setups. Further, the analysis of the model indicates that for any given collaborative system, there is an optimal distribution of users across its activities that leads to the maximum knowledge generation.

We would like to thank all authors for their valuable contributions to this issue and all reviewers for their opinions which helped to ensure the high quality of the papers. Our very special thanks go to Ngoc Thanh Nguyen who encouraged us to prepare this volume and who helped us to publish this issue in due time and in good order.

July 2021

Anna Motylska-Kuźma
Jacek Mercik

Transactions on Computational Collective Intelligence

This Springer journal focuses on research in applications of the computer-based methods of Computational Collective Intelligence (CCI) and their applications in a wide range of fields such as semantic web, social networks and multi-agent systems. It aims to provide a forum for the presentation of scientific research and technological achievements accomplished by the international community.

The topics addressed by this journal include all solutions of real-life problems for which it is necessary to use CCI technologies to achieve effective results. The emphasis of the papers published is on novel and original research and technological advancements. Special features on specific topics are welcome.

Contents

A Theoretical Examination of the Ranked Choice Voting Procedure

Hannu Nurmi[1]([⊠]) [iD] and Rachel Perez Palha[2] [iD]

[1] Department of Philosophy, Contemporary History and Political Science,
University of Turku, Turku, Finland
hnurmi@utu.fi
[2] Department of Civil and Environmental Engineering,
Universidade Federal de Pernambuco, Recife, Brazil
rachel.palha@ufpe.br

Abstract. Over the past couple of decades Ranked Choice Voting (RCV) has been advocated in the U.S. as a substitute for the current first-past-the-post (FPTP) electoral system. While its entrance to the electoral system of the U.S. is yet to be seen, it has found strong support among numerous voter groups, activists and voting theorists. We discuss the proposed voting method in some detail evaluating it in the light of standard social choice criteria of performance. We conclude that while RCV certainly represents an improvement over FPTP in terms of richness of voter input, it falls short of satisfying several important, even essential, conditions for a satisfactory voting method. A modification of and an alternative to RCV is discussed well.

Keywords: Voting procedures · No show paradox · Profile restrictions

1 Introduction

The voting procedures used in various parts of the world have been designed for apparently the same general purpose, viz. to combine the views of the voters into a collective decision outcome actionable in various specific ways, be it composing a collective decision making body, deciding which policy to pursue, electing a single person to act on behalf of the population, etc. Every now and then the existing voting procedures are subject to changes. These may be due to forces that seek to increase their influence over collective choices or due to general belief that the prevailing systems are unsatisfactory from the normative point of view. Upon closer inspection all systems based on aggregating individual votes are based on some fairly specific desideratum that is primarily being pursued. Thus, for example, the plurality voting rule – also known as first-past-the-post (FPTP) – is based on the idea that whichever alternative (candidate, policy alternative,

The perceptive, thoughtful and thought-provoking comments of two referees are gratefully acknowledged.

N. T. Nguyen et al. (Eds.): TCCI XXXVI, LNCS 13010, pp. 1–16, 2021.
https://doi.org/10.1007/978-3-662-64563-5_1

law proposal) is considered the winner has to be supported by more voters than any of its competitors. Similarly, the plurality runoff procedure can be seen as a pursuit for an outcome that is supported by more than half of the electorate. Various Condorcet extensions (a.k.a. Condorcet consistent voting methods) can be similarly motivated. To wit, Dodgson's rule explicitly aims at an outcome that – if not the Condorcet winner *ab initio* – is as close as possible to being the Condorcet winner in the preference profile of the electorate. Copeland's rule, in turn, transforms the election into a majority tournament between alternatives considered in pairs and elects the alternative that beats more of its competitors than any other alternative.

Much of the drama surrounding voting theory stems from the observation that the primary desiderata of voting rules conflict with other similar desiderata, perhaps individually not as important as the primary ones, but taken together serious enough to cast doubt on the procedure under scrutiny. Our focus in this article is one procedure vigorously advocated by elections reformers in the United States and its improvement by eminent social choice theorists. This article continues the critique presented in [29] by providing a more detailed account of the shortcomings of the proposed system and more detail on the Ranked Choice Vote (RCV) voting procedure is given in the third section of this article.

Since this is a theoretical article, we are using theoretical examples to illustrate various properties of voting rules. In those examples, the views of the voters are expressed as preference relations over the alternatives under scrutiny. Some concepts and properties, especially the Condorcet winner and monotonicity, are easily observable if the preference rankings of the voters are available. In everyday elections they are not. This is because the voters are not always permitted to report their opinions in this manner. Given that we shall refer to some of those in real-life unobserved concepts and properties, one could ask[1] what relevance they have for the voters pondering upon the voting procedures. For example, if there is a Condorcet winner alternative in an electorate, but it will – under the procedure being used – not be elected, how would they know about this, much less worry about this? Barring quite obvious circumstances, there is no other way to find out that the Condorcet winner was not elected than by finding out the distribution of voters over the preference rankings. The same goes for finding out whether a monotonicity failure has occurred. However, rather than counting the frequency of various anomalies related to voting rules our interest is in the possibility or impossibility of those anomalies. If an anomaly is impossible under a given rule, then it can never be encountered in practice, while if it is possible, we might ask the question of how often and in what circumstances might this anomaly occur. A rich and growing literature strives for giving answers to this question [9,19]. Ours is not a contribution to this research. Rather we look upon voting procedures as tools for finding plausible outcomes with plausibility seen in relation to the expressed views of the voters. Now, if the presence or absence of an anomaly cannot be determined (because we do not have enough data on voter rankings) in a given setting, this does not mean that it has or has

---

[1] as one of our referees does.

not occurred. However, the results we are referring to next pertain to impossibility or possibility of such anomalies. We deem such results relevant for the choice of rules fully cognizant of the fact that probability and simulation models can essentially augment the information obtained from impossibility or incompatibility results. The number of theoretical concepts, anomalies and paradoxes discussed in the literature is vast, but our focus here is on a small subset of those. The oft-mentioned desiderata of Condorcet consistency and monotonicity are our primary focus.

2 Two Peculiar Features of the U.S. Electoral System

The U.S. presidential election system has occasionally produced results that have raised the eyebrows of large segments of the electorate: the elected president may have less popular votes than some other candidate. It is easy to see the reason for this apparent anomaly: the primary actors in the choice between candidates are the states of the union and their votes are (in a vast majority of states) determined by the plurality of votes. To put it bluntly, all votes cast in favor of a candidate that does not command more votes than each of his/her competitors are in a sense wasted. Yet, a candidate that loses in all states might well be the winner in the national vote count. Table 1, where we have three candidates and two states each with 10 voters, illustrates.[2]

Table 1. National FPTP winner can lose in all states

Candidate	Votes in state 1	Votes in state 2	National votes
Brown	4	4	8
Jones	6	0	6
Smith	0	6	6
Winner	Jones	Smith	Brown

Here candidate Jones gets, not just the plurality, but a majority of votes in one state and the same is true of Smith in the other state, while Brown does not garner even a plurality in either state. Yet, Brown gets more national votes than either of his/her competitors. This may seem surprising, even paradoxical. Similar phenomena have been known for a long time. In dichotomous settings – i.e. where just two candidates or alternatives are being focused upon – Ostrogorski's and Anscombe's paradoxes as well as multiple election and referendum paradoxes all deal with opinion aggregations that lead to inconsistent outcomes

---

[2] This is of course a highly simplified example. To attach more realism to it, one could multiply the number of voters in each state by the same number. States with varying populations could also be added to make the same point. A more realistic example is discussed in [28, pp. 13–16].

under a fixed distribution of voter opinions over two alternatives. For more information, see [2,5,27,34]. Ranked choice voting (RCV) addresses another anomaly of the U.S. elections system, viz. the possibility that the winning candidate under FPTP might be a candidate that is worse than another in the sense of losing a pairwise majority comparison with the latter. In fact, the FPTP winner may be so bad in the binary sense that it would lose all such comparisons. This extreme eventuality is know as Borda's paradox after the 18'th century French mathematician and measurement theorist. A version of the paradox in presented in Table 2 where seven voters make a choice from the set of three candidates, viz. A, B and C.

Table 2. Borda's paradox

3 voters	2 voters	2 voters
A	B	C
B	C	B
C	A	A

Borda's main point was that the candidate winning the FPTP vote – A in this example – may be defeated by all other candidates – i.e. B and C – in pairwise majority contests. This would make A the Condorcet loser in modern terminology.

3   RCV as a Special Variant of STV

The advocates of the ranked choice voting (RCV) argue that a voting system that operates on more detailed preference information could provide ways of addressing this problem. Their favorite among such systems, RCV, has quite a long history (briefly discussed in [13, p. 13]) and has been known as the alternative vote, Hare's system and – most recently – the instant runoff voting (IRV). The following quote is from the FairVote website [32]:

> Ranked choice voting (RCV) makes democracy more fair and functional. It works in a variety of contexts. It is a simple change that can have a big impact. RCV is a way to ensure elections are fair for all voters. It allows voters the option to rank candidates in order of preference: one, two, three, and so forth. If your vote cannot help your top choice win, your vote counts for your next choice. In races where voters select one winner, if a candidate receives more than half of the first choices, that candidate wins, just like in any other election. However, if there is no majority winner after counting first choices, the race is decided by an "instant runoff". The candidate with the fewest votes is eliminated, and voters who picked that candidate as 'number 1' will have their votes count for their next choice. This process continues until there's a majority winner or a candidate won with more than half of the vote.

RCV is, in fact, a special case of the more general single-transferable vote (STV) procedure that has long been in use in Ireland in parliamentary elections with multiple-member constituencies. In a k-member constituency a candidate needs to be ranked first among the remaining candidates in d ballots where d is Droop's quota computed as follows:[3]

$$d = \lfloor \frac{V}{k+1} + 1 \rfloor \tag{1}$$

Here V equals the number of valid votes cast in the constituency. If there are ballots in which a candidate's first rank count exceeds d, the surplus ballots (i.e. those exceeding d) are distributed proportionally to the candidates ranked second in those ballots. The process is continued until all k seats have been distributed among the candidates. Thus, RCV can be seen as an application of STV to single-member constituencies.[4]

4   The Performance of RCV on Standard Criteria

4.1   Arrow's Conditions

Arrow's [3] impossibility theorem demonstrates the incompatibility of the following conditions for all social welfare functions:[5]

1. unrestricted domain (U)
2. independence of irrelevant alternatives (IIA)
3. Pareto (P)
4. non-dictatorship (D)

Of these conditions RCV, as many other voting procedures, satisfies all but one, viz. IIA. It will be recalled that IIA amounts to the requirement that whenever two candidates, say x and y, are identically positioned *vis-à-vis* each other in individual preference rankings in two preference profiles, their respective ranking in the ensuing collective rankings also remains the identical. IIA is often aptly called binary independence condition. The following two profiles presented in Table 3 demonstrate that RCV fails on IIA. In the left-hand panel, A wins once C has been eliminated. The right-hand panel is obtained by preserving the individual preferences regarding A and B exactly the same as in the left panel, but lifting C above A and B in one voter's preference. In the resulting profile 2, A is eliminated first whereupon B emerges as the winner. Clearly, the collective ranking between A and B changes from profile 1 to profile 2.

---

[3] The bracket-like symbols '$\lfloor$' and '$\rfloor$' signify that the expression between them be rounded down to the nearest integer. Formally, $\lfloor r \rfloor := max\{n \in N | n \leq r\}$, where N is the set of natural numbers [31, p. 45].

[4] The first-named author of this article has aired his views on some properties of multi-winner STV in [26].

[5] A social welfare function assigns to each n-tuple of connected and transitive individual preference relations a (collective)connected and transitive preference relation.

Table 3. RCV does not satisfy binary independence

Profile 1			Profile 2			
2 voters	2 voters	1 voter	1 voter	1 voter	2 voters	1 voter
A	B	C	C	A	B	C
B	A	A	A	B	A	A
C	C	B	B	C	C	B

4.2   Condorcet Criteria

Performance criteria of voting procedures that are associated with Condorcet play an important role in the theory of voting. Two basic criteria are particularly often discussed, the Condorcet winning criterion and the Condorcet losing criterion. The former states that the voting outcome under a procedure should always coincide with the Condorcet winner whenever one exists in the profile.[6] In addition to these, there are several Condorcet-related criteria discussed in the literature [17,36], but our focus here is on the two Condorcet-related criteria just mentioned.

It is well-known that RCV fails on the Condorcet winning criterion [37, pp. 23–25]. A simple example is provided by the right-hand panel of Table 3. In this 5-voter profile, A is the Condorcet winner, but B wins under RCV.

When it comes to the Condorcet loser criterion, the verdict is clear whenever there is a singleton choice set under RCV. To wit, to become the single winner in RCV, the candidate, say x, has in the final count to be ranked first by more than 50% of the voters. Clearly, x is then a Condorcet winner in the set of the remaining (non-eliminated) candidates. In other words, in this subset x defeats all the others, while a Condorcet loser would have to lose in all pairwise contests. Thus, x cannot be the Condorcet loser.

In case RCV ends up in a tie between several candidates, the exclusion of the Condorcet loser can no longer be guaranteed. Let us define a stronger Condorcet loser criterion and call it the strong Condorcet loser exclusion, as follows: a procedure satisfies the strong Condorcet loser exclusion if its choice set never includes the Condorcet loser. Table 4 demonstrates that RCV fails on this stronger criterion: the choice set consists of A, B and C. In fact, the failure is radical: RCV elects a choice set that includes an absolute loser, i.e. a candidate ranked last by more than 50% of the voters. In the example A is the absolute loser. It is worth noticing that in Table 4 there is also Condorcet winner (D) which, however, is eliminated.

4.3   Choice Set Variability Criteria

Another family of criteria for comparing voting procedures pertains to the changes of voting outcomes resulting from certain types of changes in the pref-

---

[6] This is known as the Condorcet principle [17, p. 471].

Table 4. RCV ends with a tie including the absolute loser

3 voters	2 voter	3 voter	1 voter
A	B	C	D
D	D	D	B
C	C	B	C
B	A	A	A

erence profiles. Typically, some changes in outcomes are considered plausible, rational or natural, given some types of changes in profiles. Should a profile exist where such plausible changes in outcomes are not associated with the profile changes, the procedure under investigation fails on the criterion.

Consistency refers to a combination of two preference profiles, say R and R', each associated with disjoint voter groups over the same set A of candidates. We assume that in both profiles the procedure singles out the same choice set, say A_0. The procedure satisfies consistency if, under these circumstances, it always results in A_0 in the combined electorate [39].[7]

The inconsistency of RCV has been established by Doron in 1970's [10]. Table 5 presents a 30-voter, 3-candidate example somewhat simplifying Doron's 42-voter, 4-candidate one. Under RCV A wins in profile 1 (after C has been eliminated) and in profile 2 (after B has been eliminated), but in the combined electorate C emerges as the winner (after B has been eliminated).

Table 5. Inconsistency of RCV

Profile 1			Profile 2		
5 voters	6 voters	4 voters	5 voters	7 voters	3 voters
A	B	C	A	C	B
B	C	A	B	A	A
C	A	B	C	B	C

Consistency is but one property in the class of choice set variability criteria. Another similar performance criterion is monotonicity. Its basic content is that additional support for a candidate does no harm to it in the sense of electoral success. This intuitively plausible criterion takes on several specific definitions depending on the context in which the additional support is studied. The standard notion of monotonicity is related a fixed electorate, i.e. one consisting of a

---

[7] Cf. the positive involvement property of Saari [33, p. 216]: 'a procedure is positively involved if when c_j is selected for a profile and when a group of new voters, all of the same voter type with c_j top-ranked, join the group, c_j remains the selected candidate.' For discussions on this and other properties related to consistency, see [24, 30, 39].

fixed number of voters. In this context monotonicity means that an improvement of the winning candidate's position in the individual preferences, *ceteris paribus*, never makes it a non-winner [17, p. 476]. Procedures failing on this criterion are obviously somewhat suspicious since adding the support of one's favorite is supposed to be the main point of voting and electoral competition. If additional support may turn winners into losers, the electoral campaigning may occasionally turn into a bizarre game of strategy where campaign organizers may have to encourage some supporters of a party or candidate not to rank their favorite candidate first or not to participate in the election at all. Yet, such procedures exist and are even widely used [13,36]. As will be seen shortly RCV is one of them.

It should be mentioned at this point that additional support can take on several meanings in the electoral context, two of which are of special interest. To wit, additional support can mean – as above – that some voters rank a given candidate higher in their reported preferences than originally. However, it can also mean that the electorate is augmented by some voters ranking a given alternative first. The latter occurs in variable electorates, while the former in fixed ones.[8]

The non-monotonicity, i.e. failure on monotonicity, of RCV has been known for more than four decades. Doron and Kronick provide the example reproduced in Table 6. In this 17- voter profile A wins once C has been eliminated. Suppose now that the two voters with the BAC preference increase the support of the winner A by ranking A first, *ceteris paribus*. In the resulting profile B is first eliminated, whereupon C wins. So, additional support turns the winner into a non-winner. This profile contains a majority cycle that would, *prima facie*, seem to restrict the possibilities of monotonicity violations. Upon closer inspection, this is not the case, i.e. RCV can violate monotonicity even in the Condorcet domain, i.e. in the subset of profiles with a Condorcet winner [7]. An example demonstrating this is reproduced in Table 7. In the table C is the Condorcet winner and A the absolute loser. C is first eliminated whereupon B defeats A and becomes the RCV winner. Suppose now that a group constituting 4% of the total number of voters switches from the ACB ranking to the BAC one, *ceteris paribus*, thus adding the support of the winner B. In the ensuing profile A is eliminated and C becomes the RCV winner violating monotonicity. A recent study of Brandt et al. [6] gives lower bounds on the number of candidates (3) and voters (17) that make monotonicity violations possible in profiles with a Condorcet winner.

Turning now to monotonicity in variable electorates, the concept of no show paradox should be briefly addressed. In the literature it has been given two different meanings. Historically the first one, due to Fishburn and Brams, is spelled out in the following definition:

---

[8] The title of Smith's path-breaking article [36] may be confusing in this regard. It is clear, however, that what he dealt with were electorates of fixed size, but of variable profiles. The concepts related to monotonicity in electorates of variable size were yet to be introduced at the time Smith's article was published.

Table 6. Non-monotonicity of RCV [11, p. 309]

6 voters	2 voters	4 voters	5 voters
A	B	B	C
B	A	C	A
C	C	A	B

Table 7. Non-monotonicity of RCV in a profile with Condorcet winner [27, p. 57]

34% of the voters	35% of the voters	31% of the voters
A	B	C
C	C	B
B	A	A

Definition 1. *The addition of identical ballots with x ranked last may change the winner from another candidate to x* [18, pp. 206–207].

Pérez [30, pp. 605–606] calls the above paradox the negative strong no show paradox (negative SNSP). The paradox is a particularly unpleasant surprise to voters who, by voting according to their preferences, 'cause' an outcome that they deem the very worst, while with their abstaining, *ceteris paribus*, some other – in their opinion more preferable – outcome would have emerged. This technical definition of the no show paradox devised by Fishburn and Brams has, however, not become standard in the literature. Indeed, in their article they use the concept also in a wider sense as referring to all forms violating participation, i.e. the principle that abstention *ceteris paribus* never leads to a more preferable outcome than voting according to one's preferences. In the wider sense, then, the no show paradox occurs when a voter or a group of unanimous voters gets a preferable outcome by abstaining than by voting according his/her/their preferences.

A monotonicity failures in the opposite direction have also been discussed. One especially dramatic type of such upward monotonicity failure refers to counterintuitive changes in the set of winning candidates: winners may become nonwinners when their support is increased by augmenting the preference profile with new ballots all ranking the original winner first.[9]

Definition 2. *Assume that x wins in a profile and then a group of voters with identical preferences where x ranked first joins the electorate, ceteris paribus. If in the ensuing new profile x is no longer the winner, we have an instance of the positive strong no show paradox (positive SNSP). A procedure in which such an instance cannot occur is immune to the positive strong no show paradox* [30, pp. 605–606].

---

[9] For a discussion on various notions of non-monotonicity in fixed and variable electorates, see [13,16,23,30,38].

Positive SNSP frustrates those voters who voted – in accordance with their preferences – for their favorite and by so doing turned him/her from a winner into a non-winner, certainly an unpleasant prospect as well. Both positive and negative SNSP are extreme cases of failure on participation, but due to their dramatic nature perhaps of special interest. Are the voters, then, expected to do the calculations needed to ascertain whether these failures have in fact occurred in a given election? Probably not, but political activist groups certainly are. And they are likely to alert the constitution designers of the anomaly they encountered and of the fact that what they uncovered flies in the face of the basic rationale of voting.

It turns out that RCV fails on participation. More specifically, it is not immune to the negative SNSP. Table 8 – a modification of an example devised by Felsenthal and Maoz [12, p. 119] – provides an illustration. It represents a setting where RCV leads to the negative SNSP in a procedure-specific sub-domain of the Condorcet domain, viz. DSF domain.[10] This domain consists of profiles where a Condorcet winner exists and coincides with the choice resulting from the procedure under study. Obviously for the Condorcet extensions, the Condorcet and DSF domains are identical. In general, if a given type of paradox can occur in the DSF domain, it is *eo ipso* possible in the Condorcet and unrestricted domains as well, since DSF is a sub-domain of the latter two.

Table 8. RCV is vulnerable to negative SNSP in the DSF domain

3 voters	1 voter	2 voters	3 voters	3 voter	3 voters	2 voters
A	A	B	B	C	C	A
B	C	A	C	A	B	B
C	B	C	A	B	A	C

In Table 8 the six left-most columns denote the original 15-voter profile where RCV ends up with the Condorcet winner, B, being elected (once A has been eliminated). Thus the profile is in the DSF domain. This profile is then augmented with two voters with the ABC ranking. In the augmented profile B is eliminated whereupon C, the last ranked candidate in the two entrants' ranking, wins under RCV. Thus we have an instance of the negative SNSP.

While the present authors have not been able to construct an example showing the vulnerability of RCV to the positive SNSP, the multi-member constituency version of RCV, that is STV, is vulnerable to this dramatic form of the violation of participation. The example devised by Fishburn and Brams [18, pp. 212–213] shows that additional support in terms of adding a set of voters ranking one of the original winners first, turns this winner into a non-winner. This possibility stems from the fact that in multi-winner STV, the quota d that guarantees the election of a candidate is (much) smaller than 50% of the votes.

---

[10] The letters refer to the initials of Dan S. Felsenthal who introduced the concept.

The less dramatic form of upward monotonicity failure in variable electorates whereby a set of voters improves upon the outcome by abstaining (but does not make it a winner) is a well-known weakness of RCV. The following example [28, pp. 94–95] shows that the portion of the electorate that can benefit from abstention, *ceteris paribus*, can be nearly as large as a half of the electorate (Table 9). In this profile A becomes the RCV winner after C is eliminated. Suppose now that the group constituting 47% of the electorate abstains. Then B is eliminated, whereupon C becomes the RCV winner. In other words, nearly a half of the electorate is better off abstaining.

Table 9. RCV is vulnerable to NSP

26%	47%	2%	25%
A	B	B	C
B	C	C	A
C	A	A	B

Would a profile restriction to Condorcet domains make RCV invulnerable to the weaker form of the no show paradox, as argued by Felsenthal and Nurmi [15, p. 21], [14, Sect. 5.4]? No. This has been demonstrated by Brandt et al. [6]. Table 10 reproduces their example. Here A is the Condorcet winner and is elected under RCV (once C and D have been eliminated). Thus we are in the DSF domain. Suppose now that the two right-most voters abstain. Then D is the first to be eliminated, followed by A, whereupon B wins. Thus the two voters benefit from the abstention, *ceteris paribus*.

Table 10. RCV is vulnerable to NSP in DSF domain [6]

5 voters	4 voters	3 voters	2 voters	2 voters
B	A	C	D	D
A	B	A	C	B
D	D	B	A	A
C	C	D	B	C

If RCV's performance with respect to monotonicity-related criteria is poor, this is also the case when a candidate set modification criterion known as the subset choice condition (SCC) is focused upon.[11] It characterizes procedures guaranteeing that whichever candidate wins in a set of candidates, wins also in all proper subsets of candidates it belongs to. It is a rare property among

---

[11] This criterion has many names, e.g. the hereditary condition [1, p. 27], individual choice postulate 4 [8] and property α [35, p. 17].

voting rules and it is therefore not surprising that RCV fails on it. A minimal
– in terms of the number of candidates and voters – example is presented by
Brandt et al. [6] and reproduced in Table 11. The first three columns represent
the preferences of 5 voters over three candidates and the two right-most columns
the restriction of those preferences over a two-element subset. Applying RCV to
the former profile, A wins, but applying it to the subset $\{A, C\}$, C becomes the
RCV winner. Thus, SCC is violated.

Table 11. RCV fails on SCC [6]

2 voters	2 voters	1 voter	3 voters	2 voters
B	A	C	C	A
C	C	A	A	C
A	B	B		

As said, SCC is very uncommon property among voting rules. Perhaps a
restriction to the DSF domain might lead to RCV choice that are consistent
with SCC. Alas, this is not the case, as shown by Table 12. In this 31-voter
profile A is the Condorcet and RCV winner which means that we are in the DSF
domain. In the subset $\{A, C, D\}$, however, A is first eliminated whereupon C
narrowly beats D becoming the RCV winner. Hence RCV can violate SCC also
in the DSF domain.

Table 12. RCV fails on SCC in DSF domain [15, p. 71]

3	3	2	3	5	6	1	2	6
A	A	A	B	B	C	C	D	D
B	C	D	C	D	A	B	C	A
C	B	B	A	A	D	A	A	C
D	D	C	D	C	B	D	B	B

5   Modifying RCV

Given the poor showing of RCV in terms of important social choice criteria,
two of the most prominent social choice theorists of our time have proposed
modifications of the system to make it a more defensible alternative to the FPTP.
Maskin and Sen – two winners of the Nobel Memorial Prize in Economic Sciences
– have in two opinion pieces [21] and [22] published in The New York Times taken
a firm stand against FPTP and in one of those articles explicitly related their
proposal to RCV [22]. The crux of the proposal is to take advantage of the
information contained in the ranked choice ballots and elect on the basis of this
information the eventual Condorcet winner. So, the proposal parts company with

RCV at the very outset by making the proposed system a Condorcet extension, something that RCV is not, as was shown in the preceding. But what if there is no Condorcet winner?

Here the proposal is not quite explicit, but judging on the basis of the 2016 article some kind of runoff is envisaged. In the examples discussed the number of runoff contestants is two, but the number is left open for contests with more than three competitors. In [29] the possible interpretation that only two contestant with the highest support in terms of the plurality votes be included in all cases was discussed. Here another possibility is briefly dealt with. Namely, the 2016 contribution mentions as an attractive possibility 'a runoff between the two candidates who win the most aggregate support in the pairwise comparisons'. This cycle-breaking step would make the proposed system completely non-positional.

The idea of accepting two candidates with largest aggregate support makes the proposal a Borda elimination system of sorts. In fact, in three-candidate races it is identical with the Borda elimination which counts Borda scores of each candidate and eliminates the one with the smallest score. The process is repeated until the winner is found or there is a tie between several candidates. This is known as Baldwin's rule [4]. This and similar score elimination rules are analyzed in [20]. It is a Condorcet extension as is its predecessor, Nanson's method [25]. In three candidate races Baldwin's and Nanson's methods are equivalent. The question left open in the Maskin-Sen proposal is how many candidates to qualify for runoff in races involving more than three candidates. It is not difficult to concoct examples where the Condorcet winner would not be among the two candidates with the highest Borda scores. Table 13 shows that even the strong Condorcet winner may not survive the elimination if only two candidates are elected for the runoff. This is, of course, not a weakness of the Maskin-Sen proposal since the runoff kicks in only after it is found that no Condorcet winner exists. Yet, it would be tempting to interpret the proposal as suggesting the adoption of Nanson's method. This would certainly be in the spirit of what Maskin and Sen write. Moreover, it would make the whole business of looking for an eventual Condorcet winner redundant: it is known that Nanson's method necessarily elects the Condorcet winner when one exists and provides an outcome in profiles where no such winner is to be found. The drawbacks of this proposal are those that characterize all Condorcet extensions. Some of those have been touched upon in the preceding.

Table 13. The strong Condorcet winner gets eliminated under Maskin-Sen elimination rule

7 voters	4 voters	2 voters
A	B	D
D	D	B
B	C	C
C	A	A

6 Concluding Remarks

RCV is analyzed above in terms of some important and well-known social choice desiderata. As all voting rules, it has its flaws, but it is fair to say that those are unusually many. While not a Condorcet extension it suffers from the main weaknesses associated with the Condorcet extensions. Perhaps its main virtue is the encouragement it provides to the voters who are afraid of wasting their vote by revealing their true preferences. If their favorite has a small support in the terms of first rank counts, their second ranked candidate in a way steps in and motivates the voters to go to the polls. This is not a minor virtue, but hardly offsets the numerous weakness. The voter encouragement property of RCV is counterbalanced with monotonicity-related properties of many positional systems, including RCV's primary contestant, FPTP. If the proposal of Maskin and Sen amounts to Nanson's rule, one of the main flaws of FPTP is thereby rectified and to the pleasure of those inspired by Condorcet's vision of winning, the Condorcet winners get elected. In all, the Maskin-Sen proposal represents an improvement of both the FPTP and RCV, but all the flaws – especially the monotonicity-related ones – remain unsolved. In future research, the impact of these flaws on voters might be evaluated in a behavioral study where the group is queried on their perception regarding those flaws in elections or in the evaluation of a commercial product.

References

1. Aleskerov, F.T.: Arrovian Aggregation Models. Kluwer, Dordrecht (1999)
2. Anscombe, G.E.M.: On frustration of the majority by fulfillment of the majority's will. Analysis **36**, 161–168 (1976)
3. Arrow, K.J.: Social Choice and Individual Values, 2nd edn. Wiley, New York (1963)
4. Baldwin, J.M.: The technique of the Nanson preferential majority system. Proc. R. Soc. Victoria **39**, 42–52 (1926)
5. Brams, S.J., Kilgour, D.M., Zwicker, W.S.: The paradox of multiple elections. Soc. Choice Welfare **15**, 211–236 (1998)
6. Brandt, F., Matthäus, M., Saile, C.: Minimal voting paradoxes. Manuscript, Technische Universität München (2020)
7. Campbell, D.E., Kelly, J.S.: Anonymous, neutral, and strategy-proof rule on the Condorcet domain. Econ. Lett. **128**, 79–82 (2015)
8. Chernoff, H.: Rational selection of decision functions. Econometrica **22**, 422–443 (1954)
9. Diss, M., Merlin, V. (eds.): Evaluating Voting Systems with Probability Models. Springer, Cham (2021). https://doi.org/10.1007/978-3-030-48598-6
10. Doron, G.: The Hare voting system is inconsistent. Polit. Stud. **XXVII**, 283–286 (1979)
11. Doron, G., Kronick, R.: Single transferable vote: an example of a perverse social choice function. Am. J. Polit. Sci. **XXI**, 303–311 (1977)
12. Felsenthal, D.S., Maoz, Z.: Normative properties of four single-stage multi-winner electoral procedures. Behav. Sci. **37**, 109–127 (1992)

13. Felsenthal, D.S., Nurmi, H.: Monotonicity Failures Afflicting Procedures for Elect-
    ing a Single Candidate. Springer, Cham (2017). https://doi.org/10.1007/978-3-
    319-51061-3
14. Felsenthal, D.S., Nurmi, H.: The no-show paradox under a restricted domain. Homo
    Oeconom. **35**, 277–293 (2019)
15. Felsenthal, D.S., Nurmi, H.: Voting Paradoxes Under a Restricted Domain.
    Springer, Cham (2019). https://doi.org/10.1007/978-3-030-12627-8
16. Felsenthal, D.S., Tideman, N.: Varieties of failure of monotonicity and participation
    under five voting methods. Theor. Decis. **75**, 59–77 (2013)
17. Fishburn, P.C.: Condorcet social choice functions. SIAM J. Appl. Math. **33**, 469–
    489 (1977)
18. Fishburn, P.C., Brams, S.J.: Paradoxes of preferential voting. Math. Mag. **56**,
    207–214 (1983)
19. Gehrlein, W., Lepelley, D.: Elections, Voting Rules and Paradoxical Outcomes.
    Springer, Berlin (2017). https://doi.org/10.1007/978-3-319-64659-6
20. Lepelley, D., Moyouwou, I., Smaoui, H.: Monotonicity paradoxes in three-candidate
    elections using scoring elimination rules. Soc. Choice Welfare **50**(1), 1–33 (2017).
    https://doi.org/10.1007/s00355-017-1069-1
21. Maskin, E., Sen, A.K.: How majority rule might have stopped Donald Trump. The
    New York Times, 28 April 2016 (2016)
22. Maskin, E., Sen, A.K.: A Better Electoral System in Maine. The New York Times,
    10 June 2018 (2018)
23. Miller, N.R.: Closeness matters: monotonicity failure in IRV elections with three
    candidates. Public Choice **173**, 91–108 (2017)
24. Moulin, H.: Condorcet's principle implies the no show paradox. J. Econ. Theory
    45, 53–64 (1988)
25. Nanson, E.J.: Methods of elections. Trans. Proc. R. Soc. Victoria **19**, 197–240
    (1883). Also. In: McLean, I., Urken, A.B. (eds.) Classics of social choice. University
    of Michigan Press, Ch. 14, pp. 321–359 (1995)
26. Nurmi, H.: It's not just the lack of monotonicity. Representation **34**, 48–52 (1996)
27. Nurmi, H.: Voting Paradoxes and How to Deal with Them. Springer, Heidelberg
    (1996)
28. Nurmi, H.: Voting Procedures under Uncertainty. Springer, Berlin-Heidelberg
    (2002). https://doi.org/10.1007/978-3-540-24830-9
29. Nurmi, H.: Electoral reform and social choice theory: piecemeal engineering and
    selective memory. Trans. Comput. Collect. Intell. **XXXIV**, 63–73 (2019)
30. Pérez, J.: The strong no show paradoxes are a common flaw in Condorcet voting
    correspondences. Soc. Choice Welfare **18**, 601–616 (2001)
31. Pukelsheim, F.: Proportional Representation. Apportionment Methods and Their
    Applications. Springer, Heidelberg (2014). https://doi.org/10.1007/978-3-319-
    03856-8
32. Ranked Choice Voting 101. https://www.fairvote.org/rcw#where_is_ranked_
    voting_used. Accessed 25 Dec 2020
33. Saari, D.G.: Basic Geometry of Voting. Springer, Heidelberg (1995). https://doi.
    org/10.1007/978-3-642-57748-2
34. Saari, D.G., Nurmi, H.: Connections and implications of the Ostrogorski paradox
    for spatial voting models. In: Van Deemen, A., Rusinowska, A. (eds.) Collective
    Decision Making. Theory and Decision Library C (Game Theory, Mathematical
    Programming and Operations Research), vol. 43, pp. 31–56. Springer, Heidelberg
    (2010). https://doi.org/10.1007/978-3-642-02865-6_3

35. Sen, A.K.: Collective Choice and Social Welfare. Holden-Day, San Francisco (1970)
36. Smith, J.H.: Aggregation of preferences with variable electorate. Econometrica **41**, 1027–1041 (1973)
37. Straffin, P.: Topics in the Theory of Voting. Birkhäuser, Boston (1980)
38. Woodall, D.R.: Monotonicity of single-seat preferential election rules. Discret. Appl. Math. **77**, 81–98 (1997)
39. Young, H.P.: Social choice scoring functions. SIAM J. Appl. Math. **28**, 824–838 (1975)

A Game Theoretic Model of Searching for a Unique Good from a Large Set of Offers

David M. Ramsey[✉]

Department of Operations Research, Wrocław University of Science and Technology,
Wrocław, Poland
david.ramsey@pwr.edu.pl

Abstract. Consumers can nowadays easily access information via the Internet about a wide range of offers on the market. For example, a family looking for a new flat can find basic information on offers via an Internet site. Much of this information is of a quantitative nature (e.g. price, size of the flat), which is very useful in determining a set of potentially very attractive offers. However, many of the traits associated with the attractiveness of a flat are qualitative in nature and can only be assessed by physically viewing an offer. (e.g. view from the balcony, attractiveness of the immediate location). This necessitates physically viewing a number of offers before making a final decision. Since the costs of physically viewing a flat are much greater than the costs of finding data about flats in the Internet, consumers often use information from the Internet to form a short list of offers to be viewed. Since the decision to buy such a product is often made collectively, e.g. by a couple or family, we consider a game theoretic approach to such a problem with two players who have symmetric roles. The one possible asymmetry considered is that one player might exhibit a higher level of altruism than the other. Although short lists are often used in practice, there is little research on determining e.g. how many offers should be placed on the short list according to the parameters of the problem and the relations between the players. This model indicates that altruism between the players and coherent preferences are important factors in facilitating search. When the players neither have coherent preferences nor feel altruism towards each other, a situation similar to the battle of the commons exists, which leads to a large number of offers being placed on the short list.

1 Introduction

The rapid development of information technology has enabled consumers to rapidly obtain data about a wide range of offers. When a consumer is searching for a non-unique good (e.g. a book or CD), then it may well be sufficient to find the cheapest offer. However, when a consumer is looking for a valuable, unique good (e.g. a flat or second-hand car), then information from the Internet is not sufficient to make an informed decision. In such situations, forming a short list of

© Springer-Verlag GmbH Germany, part of Springer Nature 2021
N. T. Nguyen et al. (Eds.): TCCI XXXVI, LNCS 13010, pp. 17–43, 2021.
https://doi.org/10.1007/978-3-662-64563-5_2

offers to physically view is a natural heuristic that enables decision makers (DMs) to choose an attractive offer, while limiting the search costs. Since the decision to purchase such goods is often made by a household, rather than an individual, one should consider group decision procedures or game theoretic approaches.

This article presents a game theoretical model in which two DMs (denoted DM1 and DM2) search for a unique, valuable resource by applying the short list heuristic. It is assumed that based on initial information, both DMs can define their own full linear ranking of offers. On the basis of their rankings, they independently choose a number of offers to physically view. Each of the selected offers is then jointly observed by the DMs. Furthermore, it is assumed that both of the DMs can define their own full linear ranking of the offers on the short list (the i-th most attractive offer according to a DM is ascribed a rank of i). The offer on the short list associated with the minimum sum of the ascribed ranks after the second round of inspection is then accepted. If there are several offers for which this minimum sum is attained, then one offer is selected at random from this set. Due to the nature of the search process, it is assumed that the costs of physically viewing an offer are much greater than the costs involved in processing the information available from a data base.

Due to constraints on cognition and time, DMs often use heuristic approaches to decision problems. A heuristic should be well adapted to both the structure of the information available about offers and the cognitive abilities of DMs. A short list is appropriate when some useful information about offers can be obtained at relatively little cost, but relatively expensive close inspection is required to accurately compare offers (see Simon [1955; 1956], Todd and Gigerenzer [2000], and Bobadilla-Suarez and Love [2018]). In recent years, there has been a significant amount of research on the theoretical properties of short lists in terms of economic rationality (see Masatlioglu *et al.* [2012], and Lleras *et al.* [2017]). Short lists may be useful when offers can be categorised into different types (Armouti-Hansen and Kops [2018]), while Borah and Kops [2019] consider search procedures in which DMs form short lists based on information from peers. However, little work has been addressed to the question of appropriate lengths of short lists according to the structure of the information and search costs. Moreover, models involving several DMs would also be interesting. The research presented here addresses such questions.

The model presented here is somewhat similar to the one considered by Analytis *et al.* [2014]. According to their model, In phase one (parallel search) a DM ranks offers on the basis of initial information. In phase two (sequential search), the DM closely inspects offers, starting with the highest ranked offer from phase one. The DM purchases the first offer whose value exceeds the expected reward from future search. In order to realize such a strategy, the DM must observe the values of offers, while in order to derive the optimal strategy, the distribution of the values of offers given the signal from first phase must be known.

The model presented here is adapted from the model of a single DM using online and offline information to search for a good presented by Ramsey [2019]. On the basis of online information, the DM selects k offers to be inspected more closely. After this round of closer inspection the highest ranked offer from the short list, based on all the available information, is accepted. It is assumed that the signals observed in these two phases are described by a pair of random variables (X_1, X_2) from a continuous joint distribution. The DM cannot measure these signals precisely, but is able to rank offers on the basis of the signals observed so far. By assumption, the DM's payoff is given by a function of these signals minus the search costs incurred. In order to realize such a strategy, the DM has to be able to rank offers according to the signals observed so far. In order to derive the optimal strategy, knowledge of the signal's joint distribution is required. This paper presents a game theoretic version of such a search problem where the DMs have symmetric roles. One important aspect is an analysis of how the coherence of the DM's preferences and their level of altruism affect behavior at equilibrium and the effectiveness of search.

A group decision procedure for selecting such a good was presented in Ramsey [2020a]. The same author also considered a game theoretic version of such a decision procedure (Ramsey [2020b]). In that model the roles of the players are clearly asymmetric. One of the DMs selects the short list, while the other DM makes the final choice from the offers on the short list.

Section 2 presents the original model of the search process with one DM. A game theoretic model of joint search by two DMs is considered in Sect. 3. Some theoretical results for an optimization problem and game theoretic problem obtained by slightly simplifying this game is presented in Sect. 4. This is done in order to gain some insight into the expected behavior of DMs in the game considered here. In Sect. 5, a method for solving this game via the use of simulations is described. A description of the numerical results obtained is given in Sect. 6. Section 7 gives some conclusions and directions for future research.

2   A Model of Search with an Individual Decision Maker

This model was first described by Ramsey [2019]. A DM wishes to choose one of n offers. Each offer is characterized by a pair of random variables from a continuous joint distribution. These two variables can be interpreted as signals of an offer's value. The DM initially observes (in parallel) the first signal corresponding to each offer. The DM cannot precisely measure the realization of this variable, but can assign ranks to these initial signals from 1 (the best) to n (the worst). This will be called the initial ranking. The strategy of the DM is defined by the choice of the length of the short list, k, where $1 \leq k \leq n$. When $1 < k < n$, in the second round, the DM observes the second signal of the values of the k best offers according to the initial ranking. When $k = 1$, the DM chooses the best offer according to the initial ranking without observing the second signal of any offer. When $k = n$, then the DM automatically observes both signals for all of the offers before making a decision. It is assumed that if the DM observes both signals for all the offers, then he/she can construct a linear ranking of these offers based on the combined information. This will be called the overall ranking. However, after the second round of inspection, the DM is only able to rank the k offers on the short list. This will be called the DM's partial ranking. By assumption, the partial ranking is fully consistent with the overall ranking, i.e. offer i is ranked below offer j in any partial ranking containing those two offers if and only if offer i is ranked below offer j in the overall ranking.

Let the j-th signal corresponding to the i-th offer be denoted by $X_{i,j}$, where $1 \leq i \leq n$ and $j = 1, 2$. By assumption, the pairs of signals $(X_{1,1}, X_{1,2}), \ldots, (X_{n,1}, X_{n,2})$ are statistically independent and identically distributed realizations from a continuous joint distribution, i.e. by assumption, information about one offer does not give any information about any other offers. Hence, the two signals describing an offer may be correlated with each other, but signals describing different offers are independent of each other. The value of offer i, V_i, is a function of these two signals satisfying the following conditions:

1. V_i is strictly increasing in both $X_{i,1}$ and $X_{i,2}$.
2. When $x < y$ the distribution of V_i given $X_{i,1} = x$ is stochastically dominated by the distribution of V_i given $X_{i,1} = y$.

The DM cannot observe the precise values of these variables, but can perfectly compare any pair of offers based on the signals observed, i.e. form perfect linear rankings of the (expected) values of offers based on the available information. The DM wishes to maximize the expected reward from search, which is defined to be the value of the selected offer minus the search costs. The costs of search are split into:

1. The costs of initial inspection, denoted by $c_1(k, n)$.
2. The costs of inspecting the short list, denoted by $c_2(k)$.

The total search costs, $c(k, n)$ are given by $c(k, n) = c_1(k, n) + c_2(k)$. It may be reasonably assumed that $c_2(k)$ is linearly increasing in k. This is due to the fact that after inspecting the first offer on the short list, it suffices to compare each successive offer to the best of the previously inspected offers. The costs of initial inspection are strictly increasing in both the number of offers available and the length of the short list. These costs reflect the effort needed for initial inspection of the offers and control of the short list. Due to the increasing demands on memory and processing as the size of the short list increases, it is assumed that the difference $C(k, n) = c_1(k + 1, n) - c_1(k, n)$ is non-decreasing in k, i.e. the marginal increase in the search costs resulting from increasing the size of the short list from k to $k + 1$ is non-decreasing in k. In other words, the search costs are convex in k.

Intuitively, a short list of length k should consist of the k highest ranked offers from the initial ranking. This is due to the fact that the distribution of the reward obtained by choosing from these offers stochastically dominates the reward obtained by choosing from any other set of k offers given the initial ranking.

Let $M(k, n)$ be the marginal increase in the expected value of the offer ultimately selected when the length of the short list increases from k to $k + 1$.
From Ramsey [2019] the optimal length of the short list satisfies the following
condition:

**Theorem 2.1. Suppose that $M(1, n) > C(1, n)$. The optimal size of the
short list, k^*, is the smallest integer k, such that $k \leq n$ and $M(k, n) <
C(k, n)$.**

The proof of this theorem is omitted, since it is simpler and similar to the
proof of Theorem 4.2, which gives the form of the solution to an optimization
problem based on the game presented in Sect. 3.

Theorem 2.1 corresponds to the intuitive statement that the size of the short
list should be increased if and only if the marginal increase in the value of the
offer ultimately selected exceeds the marginal increase in the search costs. When
the condition $M(1, n) > C(1, n)$ is satisfied, it is better to form a short list of
length two than automatically accept the most highly ranked offer according to
the initial inspection.

It should be noted that when $M(k, n) = C(k, n)$, then the DM is indifferent
between using a short list of length k and using a short list of length $k + 1$. The
condition given above assumes that when the optimal length of the short list is
not unique, then the smallest length from the set of optimal lengths is used.

Numerical results indicate that when n is relatively large the optimal size of
the short list is almost independent of the total number of offers available.

3   A Game Theoretic Model

Assume that two DMs acting in conjunction wish to choose one of n offers using
a procedure based on forming a short list. The following procedure describes a
possible approach to such a problem: DM1 observes the first signal for each of
the offers and selects a short list of potentially attractive offers to be inspected
more closely. After closer inspection of the offers, DM2 then makes the final
selection of the offer. Such a model was presented by Ramsey [2020b].

This paper considers the following game. DMj, $j \in \{1, 2\}$ independently
selects k_j offers to inspect more closely on the basis of initial information, where
$1 \leq k_j \leq n$. Note that the DMs also select the values k_1 and k_2 independently.
After the second round of inspection, the DMs then present a linear ranking of
the offers on the short list based on all of the information gained. The offer for
which the sum of the assigned ranks is smallest is the one ultimately selected.
When several offers achieve the same minimum sum of ranks, then an offer is
selected at random from this set.

Suppose a player can express preferences more subtly than a simple linear
ranking, e.g. state that two initial signals are of very similar attractiveness. In
this case, it might be reasonable to adapt the number of offers placed on the
list to a player's appraisals, e.g. if two offers are initially appraised to be very
similar, then they are either both placed on the short list or neither is placed on

the short list. Assuming that preferences are expressed via a linear ranking, it is reasonable to assume that the number of offers selected for the short list by a player is purely adapted to such a ranking. Hence, it is assumed that player j selects the number k_j before the initial signals are observed. In general, the value of k_j can be selected from a discrete distribution, say of the variable K_j. When $P(K_j = m) = 1$ for a specific value of m, then the strategy of player j is said to be a pure strategy. Otherwise, such a strategy is said to be mixed. In this case, let $P(K_j = m) = p_{m,j}$ for $m = 1, 2, \ldots, n$.

Simulations are used to estimate the utility matrix of the game when both players use a pure strategy. Let $U_j(k_1, k_2)$ be the expected utility of player j when player 1 selects k_1 offers for the short list and player 2 selects k_2 offers. The utility matrix of a game is given by

	$k_2 = 1$	$k_2 = 2$	$\ldots$	$k_2 = n$
$k_1 = 1$	$[U_1(1,1), U_2(1,1)]$	$[U_1(1,2), U_2(1,2)]$	$\ldots$	$[U_1(1,n), U_2(1,n)]$
$k_1 = 2$	$[U_1(2,1), U_2(2,1)]$	$[U_1(2,2), U_2(2,2)]$	$\ldots$	$[U_2(2,n), U_2(2,n)]$
$\ldots$	$\ldots$	$\ldots$	$\ldots$	$\ldots$
$k_1 = n$	$[U_1(n,1), U_2(n,1)]$	$[U_1(n,2), U_2(n,2)]$	$\ldots$	$[U_2(n,n), U_2(n,n)]$

A pure Nash equilibrium (k_1^*, k_2^*), where k_1^* and k_2^* are constants, satisfies

$$U_1(k_1^*, k_2^*) \geq U_1(k_1, k_2^*), \quad \forall k_1, 1 \leq k_1 \leq n \tag{1}$$

$$U_2(k_1^*, k_2^*) \geq U_2(k_1^*, k_2), \quad \forall k_2, 1 \leq k_2 \leq n. \tag{2}$$

In other words k_1^* must be the best response to k_2^* and vice versa.

A mixed Nash equilibrium (K_1^*, K_2^*), where K_1^* and K_2^* are random variables, satisfies

$$U_1(K_1^*, K_2^*) \geq U_1(k_1, K_2^*), \quad \forall k_1, 1 \leq k_1 \leq n \tag{3}$$

$$U_2(K_1^*, K_2^*) \geq U_2(K_1^*, k_2), \quad \forall k_2, 1 \leq k_2 \leq n. \tag{4}$$

Note that the expected utilities of the players when they use mixed strategies can be derived by calculating their expected utilities with respect to the joint distribution of (K_1, K_2), the numbers of offers placed on the short list by the two DMs. For further information on Nash equilibria see Maschler *et al.* [2020]. In particular, when k_1 belongs to the support of the mixed strategy of DM1 at equilibrium, then Eq. (3) is satisfied with equality, otherwise the inequality is strict.

Suppose that the DMs use pure strategies, i.e. the number of offers they place on the short list is deterministic. It should be noted that the sets of offers placed on the short list by the DMs might not be mutually exclusive. Hence, the total number of offers placed on the short list, K, is a random variable. Assume that the number of offers selected by the DMs is relatively small, in particular $k_j \leq 0.5n$, $j \in \{1, 2\}$. Let $\tilde{k} = \max\{k_1, k_2\}$. The random variable K has support on the set of integers $\{\tilde{k}, \tilde{k} + 1, \ldots, k_1 + k_2\}$.

Since such procedures often involve DMs who are bound by emotional ties (or professional ties, when two managers are searching for a new employee), then such a model should take into account the common interest between the DMs. Such common interest may result from two sources: a) one DM may show altruism (good will) towards the other, b) the values of offers to the individual DMs may be correlated, i.e. they can have similar preferences.

In addition to the assessments of a single signal by the two DMs being correlated (according to the coherence of their preferences), the two signals describing an offer as observed by a single DM may be correlated. The assessment of the i-th signal by DMj is denoted by $X_{i,j}$. Define $\mathbf{X} = (X_{1,1}, X_{2,1}, X_{1,2}, X_{2,2})$ to be the signals corresponding to an offer observed by the DMs. In general, the structure of the correlations between these signals may be complex. Hence, to ensure that this correlation structure is simple to interpret, the following assumptions are made:

1. The coefficient of correlation between the two signals describing an offer as observed by a single DM is ρ_1 (for both DMs).
2. The coefficient of correlation between observations of a single signal by the two DMs is ρ_2 (regardless of the signal).
3. Given the observation of the first signal by a DM, the observation of the second signal by this DM is conditionally independent of the observation of the first signal by the other DM.
4. Analogously, given the observation of the second signal by a DM, the observation of the first signal by this DM is conditionally independent of the observation of the second signal by the other DM.
5. The joint distributions of $(X_{1,1}, X_{2,1})$ and $(X_{1,2}, X_{2,2})$ are identical, i.e. the distribution of the signals describing an offer is the same for both DMs.

Given a pair of signals $(X_{1,j}, X_{2,j})$, the value of an offer is $f(X_{1,j}, X_{2,j})$ (independently of the DM). It is assumed that

1. $f(X_{1,j}, X_{2,j})$ is increasing in both arguments.
2. $E[f(X_{1,j}, X_{2,j})|X_{1,j} = x]$ is increasing in x.

In other words, large signals are associated with attractive offers.

The matrix of correlations between these signals is given by

$$\rho = \begin{pmatrix} 1 & \rho_1 & \rho_2 & \rho_1\rho_2 \\ \rho_1 & 1 & \rho_1\rho_2 & \rho_2 \\ \rho_2 & \rho_1\rho_2 & 1 & \rho_1 \\ \rho_1\rho_2 & \rho_2 & \rho_1 & 1 \end{pmatrix}. \tag{5}$$

The correlation structure describing the association between these assessments is illustrated by Fig. 1.

By definition, the costs incurred in the first round of search by DMj, $c_1(k_j, n)$, are convex in k_j. The costs incurred by each player in the second round of inspection are identical and linear in the total number of items placed on the short list.

The individual payoff of a DM is assumed to be the value of the ultimately selected offer to the DM minus the search costs incurred. As the DMs may show

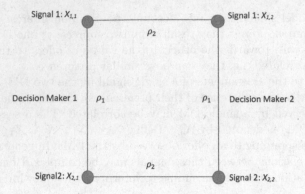

Fig. 1. Correlation structure describing the association between assessments of an offer according to the decision makers.

altruism towards each other, the utility obtained by DMj is assumed to be a weighted average of the payoffs obtained (see Fehr and Schmidt [2003]). Let the level of altruism shown by DMj to DM$(3-j)$, be denoted by α_j. Hence, the utility obtained by DMj when he/she obtains a payoff of y and DM$(3-j)$ obtains a payoff of z is given by $u_j = y + \alpha_j z$. By assumption, $0 \leq \alpha_j \leq 1$, where $\alpha_j = 0$ corresponds to DMj being economically rational (i.e. DMj maximizes his/her own payoff) and $\alpha_j = 1$ corresponds to DMj placing the same weight on the payoff of DM$(3-j)$ as on his/her own payoff. Each DM maximizes their own utility.

A summary of the parameters in the model is given in Table 1. It should be noted that this game is symmetrical if and only if $\alpha_1 = \alpha_2$.

Table 1. Summary of the Functions and Parameters Used in the Game Theoretic Model

Parameter	Description
ρ_1	Correlation between the two signals of the value of an offer observed by a single DM
ρ_2	Correlation between the values of a single signal as seen by the two DMs (a measure of the coherence of preferences)
α_j	Level of altruism shown by DMj to the other DM
c_i	Functions describing search costs in the i-th round of inspection

The particular form of this model used to obtain numerical results is presented in Sect. 5.

4   Some Theoretical Results

In this section, we consider the form of solutions to problems of a similar form to the game defined in Sect. 3 when the DMs have independent assessments of the signals, i.e. $\rho_2 = 0$.

First, we consider the length of the short list given the numbers of offers initially selected by the two DMs. Let the random variable $L_n(k_1, k_2)$ denote the length of the short list formed when DMj selects k_j offers to be closely inspected on the basis of the initial signal, $j \in \{1, 2\}$, and a total of n offers are available. Let $\tilde{L}_n(k) = L_n(k, k)$. When $\rho_2 = 0$, the distribution of $L_n(k_1, k_2)$ is independent of the distribution of the signals and can be derived by induction based on the following rules, applied together with the law of total probability[1]. As noted previously, $0 \leq k_j \leq 0.5n$.

1. $L_n(k_1, 0)$ is equal to k_1 with probability 1, $\forall k_1$. Note that $L_n(k_1, 0)$ corresponds to DM1 selecting the short list on his/her own.
2. $L_n(k_1, k_2 + 1) = L_n(k_1, k_2) + 1$ with probability $\frac{n - L_n(k_1, k_2)}{n - k_2}$. This is due to the fact that when DM2 selects his/her $k_2 + 1$-th offer for the short list, one of the $n - k_2$ offers not previously chosen by him/her is selected. Of these offers, $n - L_n(k_1, k_2)$ have not yet been selected for the short list. Analogously, $L_n(k_1, k_2 + 1) = L_n(k_1, k_2)$ with probability $\frac{L_n(k_1, k_2) - k_2}{n - k_2}$.
3. Suppose that the distribution of $L_n(k_1, k_2)$, where $k_1 \geq k_2$, has been derived, i.e. we have derived $P[L_n(k_1, k_2) = m]$ for $m \in \{k_1, k_1 + 1, \ldots, k_1 + k_2\}$. Using the law of total probability, it follows that

$$P[L_n(k_1, k_2+1)=i+1] = \frac{n-i}{n-k_2} P[L_n(k_1, k_2)=i] + \frac{i+1-k_2}{n-k_2} P[L_n(k_1, k_2)=i+1]$$

(6)

for $i \in \{\tilde{k}, \tilde{k} + 1, \ldots, k_1 + k_2 + 1\}$, where $\tilde{k} = \max\{k_1, k_2 + 1\}$.
4. By symmetry, $L_n(k_1, k_2)$ and $L_n(k_2, k_1)$ have identical distributions.

In particular, using a similar approach we can derive the distribution of the length of the short list when the DMs are constrained to select the same number of offers in the initial stage. Suppose that we know the distribution of $\tilde{L}_n(k)$. The probabilities of changes in the length of the short list when both of the DMs select an additional offer is illustrated in Fig. 2. It follows that

---

[1] The distribution of such random variables can be derived using the properties of the hypergeometric distribution. However, the approach used here is useful when calculating the marginal increase in search costs from increasing the number of offers selected.

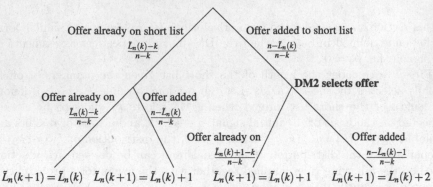

Fig. 2. Probabilities of various increases in the length of the short list when the DMs each select their $k + 1$-th offer

$$P[\tilde{L}_n(k + 1) = \tilde{L}_n(k)] = \left[\frac{\tilde{L}_n(k) - k}{n - k}\right]^2$$

$$P[\tilde{L}_n(k + 1) = \tilde{L}_n(k) + 1] = \frac{[n - \tilde{L}_n(k)][2\tilde{L}_n(k) + 1 - 2k]}{(n - k)^2}$$

$$P[\tilde{L}_n(k + 1) = \tilde{L}_n(k) + 2] = \frac{[n - \tilde{L}_n(k)][n - \tilde{L}_n(k) - 1]}{(n - k)^2}.$$

Applying the total law of probability, we obtain that for $k + 1 \leq i \leq 2k + 2$

$$P[\tilde{L}_n(k + 1) = i] = P[\tilde{L}_n(k) = i - 2]\frac{[n - i + 2][n - i + 1]}{(n - k)^2}$$

$$+ P[\tilde{L}_n(k) = i - 1]\frac{[n - i + 1][2i - 1 - 2k]}{(n - k)^2} + P[\tilde{L}_n(k) = i]\left[\frac{i - k}{n - k}\right]^2 \quad (7)$$

Equation (7) can be used to inductively define the distributions of the random variables $\tilde{L}_n(1), \tilde{L}_n(2), \tilde{L}_n(3), \ldots$ using the fact that $\tilde{L}_n(0) = 0$ with probability 1. Table 2 gives the distribution of the length of the short list formed when both of the DMs select k offers based on initial information for $n = 10$ and $k \leq 5$.

4.1   A Similar Optimization Problem

Here we consider an optimization problem which is derived from the game described in Sect. 3 with the following adaptations:

1. In the initial round, both DMs are constrained to select the same number of offers as each other (based on their individual rankings of the offers at this stage).

Table 2. Distribution of the length of the short list formed when both DMs select the same number of offers in the initial phase (the total number of offers $n = 10$)

	1	2	3	4	5	6	7	8	9	10
$\tilde{L}_{10}(1)$	0.1000	0.9000	0	0	0	0	0	0	0	0
$\tilde{L}_{10}(2)$	0	0.0222	0.3556	0.6222	0	0	0	0	0	0
$\tilde{L}_{10}(3)$	0	0	0.0083	0.1750	0.5250	0.2917	0	0	0	0
$\tilde{L}_{10}(4)$	0	0	0	0.0048	0.1143	0.4286	0.3810	0.0714	0	0
$\tilde{L}_{10}(5)$	0	0	0	0	0.0040	0.0992	0.3968	0.3968	0.0992	0.0040

2. It is assumed that $\rho_2 = 0$, i.e. the DMs have independent preferences.
3. The common goal of the DMs is to maximize the sum of their rewards from the search procedure (note that this is equivalent to $\alpha_1 = \alpha_2 = 1$).
4. In the second round of inspection, the DMs are able to precisely assess the value of an offer. It thus follows that the DMs should ultimately select the offer on the short list for which the sum of the values ascribed by them is maximized.

In order to derive the form of the solution to such a problem, we make the following definitions. Let $V(k)$ be the sum of the values of the ultimately selected offer to the DMs given that both DMs select k offers in the initial round. Let $\tilde{V}(k)$ be the sum of the values of the ultimately selected offer to the DMs given that DM1 chooses $k+1$ offers and DM2 chooses k offers in the initial round. Let $U_1(k)$ be the sum of the values to the DMs of the offer initially ranked $k + 1$ by DM1 given that this offer is not amongst the k best ranked offers in the initial round according to DM2. Let $U_2(k)$ be the sum of the values to the DMs of the offer initially ranked $k + 1$ by DM2 given that this offer is not amongst the $k + 1$ best ranked offers in the initial round according to DM1. It follows that

$$E[\tilde{V}(k)] = E[V(k)] + \frac{n - k}{n} E[\max\{0, U_1(k) - V(k)\}]. \tag{8}$$

The logic behind this equation is as follows. Suppose DM1 selects an additional offer in the initial round (his/her $k + 1$-th ranked). Since the preferences of the DMs are independent, the probability that DM2 has not previously selected this offer (i.e. this new offer is added to the short list) is $(n - k)/n$. Suppose that this offer is added to the list. This offer is the one finally accepted if and only if the sum of its values to the DMs, $U_1(k)$, is greater than the sum of the values of the ultimately accepted offer when both DMs choose k offers in the initial stage, $V(k)$. If this condition is not satisfied then $\tilde{V}(k) = V(k)$, otherwise $\tilde{V}(k) = U_1(k)$.

Arguing in a similar fashion, it follows that

$$E[V(k + 1)] = E[\tilde{V}(k)] + \frac{n - k - 1}{n} E[\max\{0, U_2(k) - \tilde{V}(k)\}]. \tag{9}$$

Combining Eqs. (8) and (9), we obtain $E[V(k + 1)] = E[V(k)] + M(k)$, where

$$M(k) = \frac{n-k}{n} E[\max\{0, U_1(k) - V(k)\}] + \frac{n-k-1}{n} E[\max\{0, U_2(k) - \tilde{V}(k)\}] \tag{10}$$

is the marginal increase in the expected sum of the values of the ultimately selected offer to the DMs when the number of offers they both choose in the initial round increases from k to $k+1$.

The corresponding marginal increase in the search costs is given by

$$C(k) = 2[c_1(k+1,n) - c_1(k,n)] + \frac{2c_{2,0}(2n-2k-1)}{n}, \qquad (11)$$

where c_1 is the function describing the search costs of a DM in the initial round according to the number of offers selected, $c_{2,0}$ is the cost of closely inspecting each additional offer in the second round. Here, the coefficient of $c_{2,0}$ is simply twice the marginal increase in the expected number of offers placed on the short list when both DMs select $k+1$ offers in the initial round rather than k (it is assumed that both players incur the costs of closely observing these offers).

Theorem 4.1. Let $R(k)$ be the expected sum of the rewards of the DMs when they both choose k offers in the initial round in this optimization problem. This function either i) has a unique maximum $R(k^*)$ or ii) two neighboring maxima such that $R(k^*) = R(k^* + 1)$. The optimal number of offers to select in the initial round, k^*, is the smallest natural number satisfying the condition $M(k) \leq C(k)$. □

Proof. Note that $R(k+1) \leq R(k)$ if and only if $M(k) \leq C(k)$.

From Eqs. (10) and (11), the inequality $M(k) \leq C(k)$ is equivalent to

$$(n-k)E[\max\{0, U_1(k) - V(k)\}]$$
$$+(n-k-1)E[\max\{0, U_2(k) - \tilde{V}(k)\}] \leq 2n[c_1(k+1,n) - c_1(k,n)] + 2c_{2,0}(2n-2k-1).$$

Subtracting $2c_{2,0}(2n-2k-1)$ from both sides leads to

$$(n-k)E[\max\{-2c_{2,0}, U_1(k) - V(k) - 2c_{2,0}\}]$$
$$+(n-k-1)E[\max\{-2c_{2,0}, U_2(k) - \tilde{V}(k) - 2c_{2,0}\}] \leq 2n[c_1(k+1,n) - c_1(k,n)]. \quad (12)$$

By assumption, the function c_1 is convex and increasing. Hence, the right hand side of this inequality is non-decreasing in k and positive. By definition both $V(k)$ and $\tilde{V}(k)$ are stochastically increasing in k, whereas both $U_1(k)$ and $U_2(k)$ are stochastically decreasing in k. Also, $\tilde{V}(k)$ stochastically dominates $V(k)$, but is stochastically dominated by $V(k+1)$, while $U_2(k)$ is stochastically dominated by $U_1(k)$, but stochastically dominates $U_1(k+1)$. It thus suffices to consider the following cases:

1. For all natural numbers k, both $E[\max\{-2c_{2,0}, U_1(k) - V(k) - 2c_{2,0}\}]$ and $E[\max\{-2c_{2,0}, U_2(k) - \tilde{V}(k) - 2c_{2,0}\}]$ are non-positive.
2. For some k_0, $E[\max\{-2c_{2,0}, U_1(k) - V(k) - 2c_{2,0}\}]$ and $E[\max\{-2c_{2,0}, U_2(k) - \tilde{V}(k) - 2c_{2,0}\}]$ are both positive for $k \leq k_0$ and both non-positive for $k > k_0$.
3. For some k_0, $E[\max\{-2c_{2,0}, U_1(k) - V(k) - 2c_{2,0}\}]$ and $E[\max\{-2c_{2,0}, U_2(k) - \tilde{V}(k) - 2c_{2,0}\}]$ are both positive for $k < k_0$ and both non-negative for $k > k_0$, while $E[\max\{-2c_{2,0}, U_1(k_0) - V(k_0) - 2c_{2,0}\}] > 0$ and $E[\max\{-2c_{2,0}, U_2(k_0) - \tilde{V}(k_0) - 2c_{2,0}\}] \leq 0$.

In the first case, the left hand side of Inequality (12) is always negative and $k^* = 1$. In either of the remaining cases, the left hand side of Inequality (12) is decreasing for $k \leq k_0$ and negative for $k > k_0$. Hence, either $M(k) \leq C(k)$ for all natural numbers k or there exists a unique k^* such that for $k < k^*$, $M(k) > C(k)$ and for $k \geq k^*$, $M(k) \leq C(k)$. In the first case, $k^* = 1$ and in the second case, $R(k)$ is maximized for $k = k^*$. In both of these cases, if $M(k^*) = C(k^*)$, then there exist two neighboring maxima of the function R such that $R(k^*) = R(k^* + 1)$. Otherwise, there exists a unique maximum, $R(k^*)$ where k^* is the smallest integer k satisfying $M(k) < C(k)$. $\square$

4.2   A Similar Game Where the DMs Have Independent Preferences

In this section we consider a game which is derived from the optimization problem considered in the previous subsection by removing the assumption that the DMs have to select the same number of offers as each other in the initial round. As before, it is assumed that the DMs can perfectly assess the value of an offer in the second round and both DMs wish to maximize the sum of their rewards from the search procedure. It follows that the game considered in this subsection is symmetric.

As before, the condition that both DMs wish to maximize the sum of the rewards from search is equivalent to the assumption that $\alpha_1 = \alpha_2 = 1$. Given this, the only difference from the game presented in Sect. 3 is that the players can precisely observe the values of the offers in the second round of inspection, rather than simply being able to rank the offers. This similarity will be used to predict what form an equilibrium of the original game will take (particularly when the DMs are highly altruistic towards each other) and assess the efficiency of such search procedures.

Let $R_2(k_1, k_2)$ be the expected sum of the rewards of the DMs from search and $W(k_1, k_2)$ be the sum of the values of the ultimately selected offer to the DMs when DMj chooses k_j offers in the initial round, $j \in \{1, 2\}$. Define $Y(k_1, k_2)$ to be the sum of the values of an offer that is ranked k_1 by DM1 in the initial round and is ranked below k_2 by DM2.

Arguing as in the derivation of Eq. (8), we obtain

$$W(k_1 + 1, k_2) = W(k_1, k_2) + \frac{n - k_2}{n} \max\{0, Y(k_1 + 1, k_2) - W(k_1, k_2)\}. \quad (13)$$

Define

$$M_2(k_1, k_2) = W(k_1 + 1, k_2) - W(k_1, k_2) = \frac{n - k_2}{n} \max\{0, Y(k_1 + 1, k_2) - W(k_1, k_2)\}$$

to be the marginal increase in the sum of the values of the ultimately selected offer when DM1 selects $k_1 + 1$ rather than k_1 offers in the initial round.

We now consider the optimal response of DM1 when k_2 is fixed, $B(k_2)$. The marginal increase in the search costs when DM1 selects $k_1 + 1$ offers in the initial round rather than k_1 is given by $C_2(k_1, k_2)$, where

$$C_2(k_1, k_2) = c_1(k_1 + 1) - c_1(k_1) + \frac{c_{2,0}(n - k_2)}{n}.$$

Theorem 4.2. **Unless there exists k_1 such that $M_2(k_1, k_2) = C_2(k_1, k_2)$, there exists a unique response $B(k_2)$. This best response is the smallest integer k_1 such that $M_2(k_1, k_2) < C_2(k_1, k_2)$. If $M_2(k_1, k_2) = C_2(k_1, k_2)$, then both k_1 and $k_1 + 1$ are best responses to k_2.** □

Proof. Note that $R_2(k_1 + 1, k_2) > R_2(k_1, k_2)$ if and only if $M_2(k_1, k_2) > C_2(k_1, k_2)$. This is equivalent to

$$\frac{n - k_2}{n} E[\max\{0, Y(k_1 + 1, k_2) - W(k_1, k_2)\}] > c_1(k_1 + 1) - c_1(k_1) + \frac{c_{2,0}(n - k_2)}{n}$$

$$E[\max\{0, Y(k_1 + 1, k_2) - W(k_1, k_2)\}] > \frac{n[c_1(k_1 + 1) - c_1(k_1)]}{n - k_2} + c_{2,0}. \quad (14)$$

Since c_1 is convex, the right hand side of this inequality is non-decreasing in k_1. From their definitions, $Y(k_1 + 1, k_2)$ is stochastically decreasing and $W(k_1, k_2)$ is stochastically increasing in k_1. Hence, the left hand side is decreasing in k_1. □

Theorem 4.3. **The best response $B(k_2)$ is non-increasing in k_2.** □

Proof. The right hand side of Inequality (14) is clearly increasing in k_2. From their definitions, $Y(k_1 + 1, k_2)$ is stochastically decreasing and $W(k_1, k_2)$ is stochastically increasing in k_2. It follows that if Inequality (14) is not satisfied for the pair (k_1, k_2), then it is not satisfied for the pair $(k_1, k_2 + i)$, where $i \geq 1$. The proof then follows directly from Theorem 4.2. □

Note that analogous statements can be made regarding the best response of DM2 to k_1 due to the symmetry of the game. We now consider the conditions that a Nash equilibrium of such a game must satisfy. Since the game under consideration is symmetric, we look for symmetric equilibria.

Theorem 4.4. **The only possible solution to the equation $B(k_2) = k_2$ is $k_2 = k^*$, where k^* is the optimal number of offers to accept in the initial round in the problem considered in Sect. 4.1. If k^* satisfies this condition, then it follows that the unique symmetric pure Nash equilibrium of this game is $(k_1, k_2) = (k^*, k^*)$.** □

Proof. Let $k < k^*$. It follows that $R_2(k, k) < R_2(k + 1, k + 1)$. Assume that $B(k) = k$, thus $R_2(k + 1, k) < R_2(k, k)$. However, if this condition is satisfied, then $R_2(k+1, k+1) > R_2(k+1, k) = R_2(k, k+1)$. It follows that $B(k+1) \geq k+1$. This is a contradiction and thus there is no solution of $B(k) = k$ where $k < k^*$.

Now let $k > k^*$. It follows that $R_2(k - 1, k - 1) \geq R_2(k, k)$. Assume that $B(k) = k$, thus $R_2(k, k) > R_2(k - 1, k)$. However, if this condition is satisfied, then $R_2(k-1, k-1) > R_2(k-1, k) = R_2(k, k-1)$. It follows that $B(k-1) \leq k-1$. This is a contradiction and thus there is no solution of $B(k) = k$ where $k > k^*$.

When $B(k^*) = k^*$, then (k^*, k^*) is a Nash equilibrium, since both DMs are using their best response to the strategy of the other player. □

It might be useful to interpret the game considered here in relation to the optimization problem considered in Sect. 4.1. Although this interpretation might be somewhat simplistic, it gives insight into how altruistic players should act in the game described in Sect. 3. In the initial round, the DMs take turns to select offers to be placed on the short list (without informing the other what offers have been chosen) until the optimal number of offers have been selected. Either the DMs select the same number of offers (i.e. the total number of offers chosen is even) or one DM selects one more offer than the other (i.e. the total number of offers chosen is odd). Assuming that the number of offers to be placed on the short list is very small compared to the total number of offers available, we may ignore the possibility that any of the selections of the two DMs coincide. Based on such an interpretation, when the total number of offers to be chosen in the initial round is even, say $2k^*$, then k^* satisfies $B(k^*) = k^*$. When this number is odd, then it seems reasonable to assume from the form of the best response function that either $B(k^*) = k^* - 1$ or $B(k^*) = k^* + 1$. If $B(k^*) = k^* - 1$, then it is expected that at a symmetric equilibrium of the game considered here the DMs would randomize between selecting $k^* - 1$ and k^* offers in the initial round. Analogously, if $B(k^*) = k^* + 1$, then it is expected that at a symmetric equilibrium of the game considered here the DMs would randomize between selecting k^* and $k^* + 1$ offers in the initial round. This conclusion is also supported by the results from simulations, which will be presented in Sect. 5. Although the author has not been able to prove that this is true, the following argument seems to indicate that in practical cases, this is likely to be the case. This argument relies on considering the possibility that the best response to k^* is at least $k^* + 2$. The case $\dot{B}(k^*) \leq k^* - 2$ is analogous and thus not considered.

Suppose that $B(k^*) > k^*$. Note that by definition $R(k^*, k^*) > R(k^* + 1, k^* + 1)$. Since by assumption and symmetry $R(k^* + 1, k^*) = R(k^*, k^* + 1) > R(k^*, k^*) > R(k^* + 1, k^* + 1)$, it follows that $B(k^* + 1) \leq k^*$.

Suppose DM2 selects k^* offers in the initial stage. The expected gain in the sum of the values of the ultimately selected offer when DM1 selects $k^* + 2$ offers rather than $k^* + 1$ in the first round is given by

$$M_2(k^* + 1, k^*) = \frac{n - k^*}{n} E[\max\{0, Y(k^* + 2, k^*) - W(k^* + 1, k^*)\}]. \quad (15)$$

Suppose DM2 selects $k^* + 1$ offers in the initial stage. The expected gain in the sum of the values of the ultimately selected offer when DM1 selects $k^* + 1$ offers rather than k^* in the first round is given by

$$M_2(k^*, k^* + 1) = \frac{n - k^* - 1}{n} E[\max\{0, Y(k^* + 1, k^* + 1) - W(k^* + 1, k^*)\}] \quad (16)$$

Comparing these two marginal gains, when n is large we have $(n - k^*)/n$ is marginally greater than $(n - k^* - 1)/n$. In practical cases, it is likely that this is outweighed by the comparative values of $Y(k^* + 1, k^* + 1)$ and $Y(k^* + 2, k^*)$. The first term is the sum of the values of the offer given that DM1 initially ascribes a rank of $k^* + 1$ to this offer and DM2 initially ascribes a rank of $> k^* + 1$.

The second term is the sum of the values of the offer given that DM1 initially ascribes a rank of $k^* + 2$ to this offer and DM2 initially ascribes a rank of $> k^*$. Assuming k^* is small compared to n, the positive effect in the first term due the higher rank ascribed by DM1 is likely to outweigh the negative effect due to averaging over the possible ranks ascribed by DM2. Hence, it likely that $M_2(k^*, k^* + 1) > M_2(k^* + 1, k^*)$.

Now we compare the corresponding marginal increase in the search costs.

$$C_2(k^* + 1, k^*) = c_1(k^* + 2) - c_1(k^* + 1) + \frac{c_{2,0}(n - k^*)}{n} \tag{17}$$

$$C_2(k^*, k^* + 1) = c_1(k^* + 1) - c_1(k^*) + \frac{c_{2,0}(n - k^* - 1)}{n}. \tag{18}$$

From the convexity of the function c_1, it is clear that $C_2(k^* + 1, k^*) > C_2(k^*, k^* + 1)$. Since $B(k^* + 1) \leq k^*$, it follows that $M_2(k^*, k^* + 1) < C_2(k^*, k^* + 1)$. Based on the comparisons of these marginal gains and costs, it thus seems reasonable to conclude that for this scenario $M_2(k^* + 1, k^*) < C_2(k^* + 1, k^*)$ and hence $B(k^*) < k^* + 2$.

Hence, it is expected that at the symmetric equilibria of such games altruistic DMs will either use a pure strategy (choose a fixed number of offers in the initial round) or randomize between choosing k and $k + 1$ offers in the initial round for some k. How the DMs are expected to act when they are less altruistic and/or show differing levels of altruism will be considered in Sect. 6.

5   A Procedure for Estimating the Nash Equilibrium and Value of the Original Game

Note that in this section the term payoff is used for the expected "individual reward" of a DM from search, i.e. the value of the ultimately selected offer to him/her minus the search costs incurred. These payoffs are used to define the expected utility of both players based on their level of altruism.

The payoff matrices for games of the form presented in Sect. 3 are estimated using 100 000 simulations (written in R) of the search process for each of the pure strategy pairs considered (see below). In each simulation, a total of 100 offers are available. Here, we consider an additive model of the attractiveness of an offer to a DM based on the two signals observed, i.e. the value of an offer to DMj is $V_j = X_{1,j} + X_{2,j}$, The signals describing the value of an offer to the two DMs are assumed to come from a four-dimensional joint normal distribution $(X_{1,1}, X_{2,1}, X_{1,2}, X_{2,2})$, where the mean is standardized to be equal to $(0, 0, 0, 0)$ and the correlation matrix is given by Eq. (5). The variance of the first signal describing an offer and the residual variance of the second signal given the first are both assumed to be equal to one (regardless of the DM).

In general, DMs may ascribe a relative importance to each signal. The effect of the relative importance of the second signal has been investigated in Ramsey [2019] and [2020b]. Intuitively, as the importance of the second signal increases, the number of offers placed on the short list increases. For the purposes of this article, we wish to investigate the role of the coherence of the preferences of the players and the level of altruism. Hence, the relative importance of the signals is fixed (under this model, the signals are equally important).

The overall variance of the second signal is given by

$$\text{Var}(X_{2,j}) = \frac{1}{1 - \rho_1^2}, \quad j \in \{1, 2\}.$$

Hence, the overall variance of the value of an offer to a DM is given by

$$\text{Var}(V_j) = 1 + \frac{1}{1 - \rho_1^2} + \frac{2\rho_1}{\sqrt{1 - \rho_1^2}}, \quad j \in \{1, 2\}. \tag{19}$$

To simulate the values of the signals observed by the DMs, the following procedure is used: First, a vector of four signals, $\mathbf{Y} = (Y_{1,1}, Y_{2,1}, Y_{1,2}, Y_{2,2})$, whose covariance matrix is given by ρ, is generated using the Cholesky decomposition (see Horn and Johnson [1985]). Using this approach, the correlation matrix ρ may be written as $\rho = \mathbf{L}\mathbf{L}^T$, where T denotes transposition and

$$\mathbf{L} = \begin{pmatrix} 1 & 0 & 0 & 0 \\ \rho_1 & \sqrt{1 - \rho_1^2} & 0 & 0 \\ \rho_2 & 0 & \sqrt{1 - \rho_2^2} & 0 \\ \rho_1\rho_2 & \rho_2\sqrt{1 - \rho_1^2} & \rho_1\sqrt{1 - \rho_2^2} & \sqrt{1 - \rho_1^2 - \rho_2^2 + \rho_1^2\rho_2^2} \end{pmatrix} \tag{20}$$

Let $\mathbf{Z}^T = (Z_1, Z_2, Z_3, Z_4)$ be a vector of independent realizations from the standard normal distribution, i.e. with mean and standard deviation equal to 0 and 1, respectively. Setting $\mathbf{Y} = \mathbf{L}\mathbf{Z}$, we obtain a set of realizations from the standard normal distribution whose correlation matrix is ρ.

As the standard deviation of each component of this vector is equal to one, it is necessary to multiply each of them by the appropriate standard deviations to obtain the vector of signals corresponding to the assessment of an offer by the two DMs, $(X_{1,1}, X_{2,1}, X_{1,2}, X_{2,2})$. Since the standard deviations of the signals are equal to 1 and $1/\sqrt{1 - \rho_1^2}$, respectively, it follows that

$$X_{1,i} = Y_{1,i}; \quad X_{2,i} = \frac{1}{\sqrt{1 - \rho_1^2}}, \quad i \in \{1, 2\}. \tag{21}$$

Assume that the costs incurred in the first round of search by DMj are given by

$$c_1(k_j, n) = c_{1,0}(n + k_j + k_j^2), \tag{22}$$

where $c_{1,0}$ is a constant. The costs incurred by each DM in the second round of search are given by $c_2(K) = Kc_{2,0}$, where K is the number of items placed on the short list and $c_{2,0}$ is a constant. Note that the search costs incurred by a DM in the initial round are independent of the strategy of the other DM (the number of items selected for the short list). On the other hand, the search costs incurred by a DM in the second round depend on the total number of items placed on the short list, i.e. are dependent on the strategy of the other DM. The function $c_1(k, n)$ is convex in k.

The parameters $c_{1,0}$ and $c_{2,0}$ are chosen to satisfy the following conditions: a) as long as k_j is not large, the search costs incurred in the initial round are small compared to those incurred in the second round, b) the search costs incurred in the second round are of an order such that it is optimal to place a moderate number of offers on the short list. For example, when the value of an offer is based entirely on the second signal, $c_{2,0} = 0.1$ and the value of an offer comes from the exponential distribution, then the optimal strategy based on selecting the number of offers to view is to observe 10 offers and then select the best (see Ramsey [2019]). It should be noted that the tail of the exponential distribution is heavier than the tail of the normal distribution and the intensity of search is generally positively associated with the heaviness of a distribution's tail.

It is assumed that in the first round, each of the DMs select between 1 and 12 offers. The 12×12-dimensional payoff matrix representing a game is estimated using 100 000 simulations of the search process for each pair of pure strategies. From the form of the cost functions, it is expected that this matrix is sufficient to derive any Nash equilibrium of the game. In addition to deriving the payoff matrix of the game, the optimal solution to the problem described in Sect. 4.1 was derived.

The parameter sets used were combinations of the following sets

1. $\alpha_j \in \{0, 1/2, 1\}$, $j = 1, 2$.
2. $\rho_i \in \{0, 1/3, 2/3\}$, $i = 1, 2$.

It follows that $3^4 = 81$ sets of simulations were carried out. Once the payoff matrix has been estimated, the utility matrix is estimated using the appropriate linear transformations. This is considered in Sect. 6.1.

The best response of DM1 to k_2, $B_1(k_2)$, corresponds to the largest utility obtained by DM1 in the column representing k_2. Analogously, the best response of DM2 to k_1, $B_2(k_1)$, corresponds to the largest utility obtained by DM2 in the row representing k_1. Any pair (k_1, k_2) satisfying the pair of equations $B_1(k_2) = k_1$, $B_2(k_1) = k_2$ is a pure Nash equilibrium of the game.

Due the symmetry between the DMs, some of these games are essentially the same, i.e. switching the values of α_1 and α_2 simply switches the roles of the DMs. Hence, there are only 6 essentially different combinations of α_1 and α_2, which gives a total of 54 different games. The utility matrix of the games in which $\alpha_1 \neq \alpha_2$ were thus estimated twice. In addition, when $\alpha_1 = \alpha_2$, at a symmetric equilibrium the DMs obtain the same expected reward. This enables us to assess the accuracy to which the expected payoffs are estimated. This is considered in Sect. 6.2.

6   Numerical Results

Before presenting the results, it will be useful to consider how the equilibrium of a game is likely to be affected by the DMs' levels of altruism. In Sect. 4, it was shown that when DMs show a high level of altruism (i.e. $\alpha_1 = \alpha_2 = 1$), then the Nash equilibrium will be very similar (if not identical) to the socially optimal solution.

Now suppose that the DMs exhibit equal levels of altruism, but place a higher weight on their own payoff than on the other's payoff. The marginal benefit resulting from DM1 selecting an additional offer in the initial round mostly accrues to DM1. This is due to the fact that if the additional offer selected is the one finally chosen, it will almost definitely be highly valued by DM1, but not necessarily by DM2. On the other hand, the marginal costs of closely inspecting another offer are shared between the players. This is similar to the situation in the tragedy of the commons (see Hardin [2009]) and leads to both players selecting more offers in the initial round than is socially optimal. Increasing ρ_2 (the parameter describing the coherence of the DMs preferences) is expected to move the equilibrium towards the social optimal. This is due to the fact that the marginal gains from DM1 selecting an additional offer in the first round are more equally split between the DMs.

Arguing similarly, it is expected that when one DM shows a lower level of altruism than the other, then the DM showing a lower level of altruism will select a higher number of offers in the initial round than is socially optimal. It is possible that this effect is counteracted (to some degree) by the more altruistic DM selecting fewer offers in the initial round and this will be investigated by the simulations.

Of the 54 games simulated in which $\alpha_1 \leq \alpha_2$, there were 48 games which had a unique pure Nash equilibrium. In two of the 27 symmetric games, there existed k such that $B_j(k) = k + 1, B_j(k + 1) = k$, $j \in \{1, 2\}$. Hence, in these games there were 2 asymmetric pure equilibria $(k, k + 1)$ and $(k + 1, k)$, as well as a mixed equilibrium where both players randomized between selecting k or $k + 1$ offers in the initial round. In 4 of the 27 asymmetric games with $\alpha_1 < \alpha_2$, there existed a pair (k_1, k_2) such that $k_1 > k_2$ and

$$B_1(k_2) = k_1, B_1(k_2 + 1) = k_1 + 1, B_2(k_1) = k_2 + 1, B_2(k_1 + 1) = k_2.$$

In these 4 games, there was a unique (mixed) Nash equilibrium at which DM1 selected either k_1 or $k_1 + 1$ offers in the initial round and DM2 selected either k_2 and $k_2 + 1$ offers. In these games, either ρ_1 or ρ_2 was reasonably large.

Section 6.1 considers the estimation of these mixed equilibria. Section 6.2 considers the accuracy of the estimation procedure. Section 6.3 considers the effect of the parameters of the game on the equilibrium strategies and the relative efficiency of search under the game theoretic procedure.

6.1 Mixed Equilibria

Consider the game with $\alpha_1 = \alpha_2 = \rho_1 = 0, \rho_2 = 2/3$. Since the DMs do not exhibit altruism, the utility of each player is simply equal to their expected reward from search (the value of the selected offer to a DM minus the search costs that he/she incurs). Investigation of the utility matrix indicates that

$B_1(3) = 4, B_1(4) = 3, B_2(3) = 4$ and $B_2(4) = 3$. Hence, there are two asymmetric equilibria of this game, $(4, 3)$ and $(3, 4)$. At the symmetric mixed equilibrium of this game, both DMs randomize between choosing 3 or 4 offers in the initial stage. The estimated utility matrix in the reduced game where the DMs only use these two pure strategies is given by

$$\begin{pmatrix} \mathbf{U}(3,3) & \mathbf{U}(3,4) \\ \mathbf{U}(4,3) & \mathbf{U}(4,4) \end{pmatrix} = \begin{pmatrix} (2.355613, 2.359013) & (2.275695, 2.360040) \\ (2.355867, 2.277765) & (2.272134, 2.275109) \end{pmatrix}, \quad (23)$$

where $\mathbf{U}(k_1, k_2) = [U_1(k_1, k_2), U_2(k_1, k_2)]$ is the vector of expected utilities when DM1 selects k_1 offers in the initial round and DM2 selects k_2 offers.

Note that deviations from symmetry in the payoff matrix result from statistical errors resulting from the simulations. In order to symmetrize this game, define

$$\overline{U}(k_1, k_2) = \frac{U_1(k_1, k_2) + U_2(k_2, k_1)}{2}$$

to be the payoff of DM1 in the corresponding symmetrized game. This is defined by the matrix

$$\begin{pmatrix} \overline{U}(3,3) & \overline{U}(3,4) \\ \overline{U}(4,3) & \overline{U}(4,4) \end{pmatrix} = \begin{pmatrix} 2.3573130 & 2.2767300 \\ 2.3579535 & 2.2736215 \end{pmatrix}. \quad (24)$$

In order to derive the mixed equilibrium for this symmetric game, we can use the Bishop-Cannings theorem (BCT, see Bishop and Cannings [1978]). This states that when one DM plays according to the mixed equilibrium, the other DM is indifferent between the two choices available. Assume that at the mixed equilibrium both DMs choose 3 offers with probability p (and thus 4 offers with probability $1 - p$). It follows that this probability and the value of the game to both DMs, v, satisfy

$$2.3573130p + 2.2767300(1 - p) = 2.3579535p + 2.2736215(1 - p) = v. \quad (25)$$

It follows from this that at the estimated Nash equilibrium of this game both DMs select three offers in the initial round with probability $p \approx 0.8292$ and the expected utility (also the expected individual reward) from the game is $v \approx 2.3435$.

The other mixed equilibria in a symmetric game existed when $\alpha_1 = \alpha_2 = 0.5, \rho_1 = 0, \rho_2 = 2/3$. In this case there were two asymmetric equilibria $(3, 2)$ and $(2, 3)$. The estimated probability of choosing 2 offers in the initial round at the symmetric equilibrium is $p \approx 0.0980$ (otherwise 3 offers are selected). The expected individual reward of both DMs at this equilibrium is ≈ 2.3649. As expected, due to the higher level of altruism exhibited, the DMs select on average fewer offers in the first round and the expected individual rewards from search are higher.

Now consider the asymmetric game where $\alpha_1 = 0.5, \alpha_2 = 1, \rho_1 = 1/3$ and $\rho_2 = 0$. Analysis of the utility matrix indicates that there is a mixed equilibrium where DM1 selects either 3 or 4 offers in the initial round and DM2 selects either

1 or 2 offers. Since the players exhibit altruism, the matrix of individual rewards should be transformed to obtain the utility matrix. The estimated matrix of individual rewards given that the DMs use a pure strategy from the appropriate support is

$$\begin{pmatrix} \mathbf{R}(3,1) & \mathbf{R}(3,2) \\ \mathbf{R}(4,1) & \mathbf{R}(4,2) \end{pmatrix} = \begin{pmatrix} (2.66238, 1.28046) & (2.32608, 1.65704) \\ (2.69105, 1.20325) & (2.44828, 1.44174) \end{pmatrix}, \quad (26)$$

where $\mathbf{R}(k_1, k_2) = [R_1(k_1, k_2), R_2(k_1, k_2)]$ is the vector of expected individual rewards when DM1 selects k_1 offers in the initial round and DM2 selects k_2 offers. Since the expected utilities are given by

$$U_1(k_1, k_2) = R_1(k_1, k_2) + 0.5R_2(k_1, k_2); \quad U_2(k_1, k_2) = R_1(k_1, k_2) + R_2(k_1, k_2),$$

the estimated utility matrix is given by

$$\begin{pmatrix} \mathbf{U}(3,1) & \mathbf{U}(3,1) \\ \mathbf{U}(4,2) & \mathbf{U}(4,2) \end{pmatrix} = \begin{pmatrix} (3.30261, 3.94284) & (3.15460, 3.98312) \\ (3.29267, 3.89430) & (3.16916, 3.89003) \end{pmatrix}. \quad (27)$$

Applying BCT twice, the Nash equilibrium of this game is

1. DM1 selects 3 offers in the initial round with probability 0.5943 (otherwise DM1 selects 4 offers).
2. DM2 selects 1 offer in the initial round with probability 0.09584 (otherwise DM2 selects 2 offers).

The expected utilities of the DMs at this equilibrium are (3.2426, 3.8990). In order to derive the expected individual rewards, (v_1, v_2) at this equilibrium, it is necessary to solve the pair of linear equations

$$v_1 + \alpha_1 v_2 = 3.2426; \quad v_1 + \alpha_2 v_2 = 3.8990.$$

From this, the expected individual rewards of the DMs are $v_1 = 2.5862$ and $v_2 = 1.3128$. As expected, since DM1 is less altruistic, he/she selects a larger number of offers in the initial round and has a greater expected individual reward.

One might ask what are the factors that lead to such an equilibrium. Since DM2 is "fully" altruistic, he/she wishes to maximize the sum of the individual rewards. In such a case, selecting an appropriate number of offers overall (here 5) for the short list is a very important factor. Hence, $B_2(3) = 2$ and $B_2(4) = 1$. On the other hand, DM1 is not fully altruistic and thus, to some degree, competes against DM2. When DM2 selects only 1 offer in the initial round, it seems sufficient that DM1 selects 3 offers in the initial round in order to almost ensure that the ultimately selected offer is very attractive to him/her. This is due to the fact that the offer selected by DM2 is very likely to be ranked lowly by DM1 after close inspection of the offers on the short list. When DM2 selects two offers in the initial round, DM1 should select a higher number of offers in order to ensure that the ultimately selected offer is very attractive to him/her. Hence, $B_1(3) = 1$ and $B_1(4) = 2$.

6.2   Accuracy in Estimating the Individual Payoffs

The estimates of the individual rewards of the searchers at the symmetric pure equilibria of the symmetric games (25 cases) were used to assess the statistical errors made in the simulation. Let (v_1, v_2) be the estimates of these rewards. Since we are considering symmetric equilibria of a symmetric game, the expected values of v_1 and v_2 are equal. Table 3 gives results regarding the absolute differences $|v_1 - v_2|$, and the relative differences [defined to be $100 \left(\frac{\max\{v_1, v_2\}}{\min\{v_1, v_2\}} - 1 \right)$]. It should be noted that the relative error was significantly negatively correlated with ρ_2. This is probably due to the fact that as ρ_2 increases the preferences of the DMs become more similar and so the variance in the difference between their payoffs decreases.

Table 3. Statistical errors in the estimation of the individual payoffs: Based on the pure symmetric equilibria of symmetric games (25 cases)

	Mean	Std. dev	Max.
Absolute	0.00561	0.00392	0.01661
Percentage	0.24689	0.17705	0.65970

These differences are generally small, but can have an effect on the inferred Nash equilibrium when the second best response to an action that constitutes an element of a pure equilibrium is only very slightly worse than the best response. This effect was investigated by comparing the inferred equilibria for the 27 pairs of games in which the values of α_1 and α_2 are reversed (this corresponds to reversing the roles of the DMs). When the inferred Nash equilibria for such a pair of games were pure, they were said to be in accord when the Nash equilibrium strategies were mirror images of each other, i.e. if (k_1, k_2) was inferred to be the Nash equilibrium in one game, then (k_2, k_1) was the inferred Nash equilibrium in the other game. When the inferred Nash equilibria for such a pair of games were both mixed, they were said to be in accord when the support of DM1's equilibrium strategy in one game was the support of DM2's equilibrium strategy in the other game and vice versa. Based on this definition, 23 of the 27 pairs of equilibria were found to be in accord. The four pairs of equilibria found not to be in accord are described in Table 4. In each of these cases, the value of ρ_2 is relatively high, i.e. the preferences of the DMs are coherent. In such cases, the expected utility of both DMs, particularly the more altruistic DM, is more dependent on the total number of offers that are selected in the initial round than on who selects them. Analysis of the estimated utility matrices indicates that the utility of the DMs is almost constant close to the equilibrium. In the case of the discordant pair where both equilibria are pure, the total number of offers selected in the initial round was always six. In the remaining cases, one of the equilbria was mixed and one pure, such that the actions taken at the pure equilibrium were in the supports of the strategies used at the mixed equilibrium.

Table 4. Pairs of Nash equilibria not in accord (at Equilibrium 2 the roles of the players are reversed, e.g. DM1's level of altruism is given by α_2).

ρ_1	ρ_2	α_1	α_2	Equilibrium 1	Equilibrium 2
0	2/3	0	0.5	Pure: (4, 2)	Pure: (3, 3)
0	2/3	0	1	Mixed: DM1 chooses 3 or 4 DM2 chooses 1 or 2	Pure: (2, 3)
1/3	1/3	0	1	Pure: (4, 1)	Mixed: DM1 chooses 1 or 2, DM2 chooses 3 or 4
2/3	2/3	0	1	Pure: (3, 2)	Mixed: DM1 chooses 1 or 2, DM2 chooses 3 or 4

6.3   Effect of the Parameters of the Game

Let (v_1, v_2) be the vector of the expected rewards of the DMs (i.e. not taking the reward of the other DM into account) at a Nash equilibrium and r be the estimated optimal sum of these rewards for the optimization problem in which i) $\alpha_1 = \alpha_2 = 1$, ii) the players must select the same number of offers in the first round and iii) are able to perfectly assess the value of an offer in the second round. Note that this optimization problem is the one considered in Sect. 4.1 without the assumption that the preferences of the DMs are independent (unless ρ_2 is defined to be zero). This optimal value is estimated via the simulations. The efficiency of the game theoretic solution is defined to be $\epsilon = (v_1 + v_2)/r$.

Table 5 illustrates the effect of the level of altruism shown by the DMs when $\rho_1 = \rho_2 = 0$. It should be noted that the imperfect effectiveness of search results mainly from two factors: i) in the second round of search the DMs can only rank offers, rather than observe their values, ii) incoherence of the DMs' preferences. When neither of the DMs show altruism, the "tragedy of the commons" effect leads to both DMs selecting significantly more offers in the initial round than is socially optimal. As the level of altruism of both DMs increases, the number of offers selected in the initial round falls towards the social optimum and effectiveness increases. One noticeable effect is that search is relatively effective even when only one of the DMs exhibits altruism. Suppose $\alpha_1 = 0$ and let α_2 vary. As α_2 increases, DM2 selects significantly fewer offers in the first round than at the non-altruistic equilibrium. This results in the non-altruistic DM1 also selecting slightly fewer offers, due to the form of the best response function. In accordance with intuition, DM1 "takes advantage" of the good nature of the altruistic DM2. However, the overall search costs are significantly lowered. Hence, the individual payoff of DM2 is almost independent of α_2, while the individual payoff of DM1 is clearly increasing in α_2. Taking into account DM2's altruism, the relative levels of utility of both DMs are thus increasing in α_2. Note, however, that it is difficult to compare overall levels of utility for different combinations of α_1 and α_2. This is due to the fact that when calculating the mean utility, the higher expected payoff in a pair will obtain a high weighting.

Table 5. Effect of the level of altruism on the Nash equilibrium when $\rho_1 = \rho_2 = 0$. The solution to the corresponding optimization problem is $k^* = 3$ and $r = 3.7696$. All the Nash equilibria are pure.

		$\alpha_2 = 0$	$\alpha_2 = 0.5$	$\alpha_2 = 1$
$\alpha_1 = 0$	Equilibrium	(6, 6)	(5, 3)	(4, 1)
	Rewards (v_1, v_2)	(1.08001, 1.0771)	(1.5848, 1.1003)	(1.9613, 0.9486)
	ϵ	0.5723	0.7123	0.7719
$\alpha_1 = 0.5$	Equilibrium	(3, 5)	(3, 3)	(3, 2)
	Rewards (v_1, v_2)	(1.1049, 1.5801)	(1.4525, 1.4578)	(1.6913, 1.2706)
	ϵ	0.7123	0.7720	0.7857
$\alpha_1 = 1$	Equilibrium	(1, 4)	(2, 3)	(2, 2)
	Rewards (v_1, v_2)	(0.9448, 1.9592)	(1.2733, 1.6906)	(1.4899, 1.4973)
	ϵ	0.7704	0.7863	0.7924

For medium or higher levels of altruism, the Nash equilibrium is very similar to the socially optimal solution, regardless of the values of ρ_1 and ρ_2. Hence, the effect of the correlation structure on the equilibrium search procedures is most visible when the DMs do not show altruism towards each other. This is illustrated in Table 6. The efficiency of the equilibrium search procedure is clearly increasing in ρ_2 (the coherence of the DMs' preferences) and the number of offers selected in the initial round is decreasing in ρ_2 (particularly when ρ_1, the coefficient of correlation between the two signals is large). Since neither of the DMs are altruistic, the ultimately selected offer should be attractive to both DMs. Hence, the negative relation between ρ_2 and the number of offers selected into the initial round is likely to result from the following reasoning. When their preferences are independent it is necessary to closely inspect a relatively large number of offers in order to be likely to find such an offer. However, when the DMs have similar preferences, $\rho_2 = 2/3$, it is likely that an offer which is attractive to both DMs can be found from a smaller set of offers. The reduced level of competition between the two searchers in this case means that the Nash equilibrium is much closer to the socially optimal solution.

On the other hand, the efficiency of the search procedure is virtually independent of ρ_1 and the number of offers selected in the initial round is increasing in ρ_1, particularly when the preferences of the DMs are independent ($\rho_2 = 0$). For ρ_2 fixed, as ρ_1 increases, the first signal becomes a more reliable indicator of the overall value of an offer to an individual player, while not giving any additional information about the value of the offer to the other player. Also, by selecting a larger number of offers than the other player, a player increases the probability that the offer finally selected was one that he/she selected for the short list (i.e. attractive to him/her, which is not necessarily the case when the other player selected the offer). Hence, when the players do not show altruism towards each other, as ρ_1 increases the marginal gain to a player from selecting an additional offer is likely to also increase. In this case, a situation similar to the tragedy of commons arises and when ρ_1 is large the players select significantly more offers than according to the social optimum.

Table 6. Effect of the correlation structure on the Nash equilibrium when $\alpha_1 = \alpha_2 = 0$. The solution of the corresponding optimization problem is given, k^* and $R(k^*)$. Details of the mixed equilibrium are given in Sect. 6.1.

		$\rho_2 = 0$	$\rho_2 = 1/3$	$\rho_2 = 2/3$
$\rho_1 = 0$	k^*, $R(k^*)$	3, 3.1696	3, 4.6207	3, 5.3639
	Equilibrium	(6, 6)	(5, 5)	Mixed: Support $\{3, 4\}$
	Rewards (v_1, v_2)	(1.08001, 1.0771)	(1.7007, 1.6952)	(2.3435, 2.3435)
	ϵ	0.5723	0.7349	0.8738
$\rho_1 = 1/3$	k^*, $R(k^*)$	3, 4.8293	3, 5.8917	3, 6.8106
	Equilibrium	(8, 8)	(5, 5)	(4, 4)
	Rewards (v_1, v_2)	(1.2639, 1.2640)	(2.3077, 2.2977)	(2.9712, 2.9708)
	ϵ	0.5235	0.7817	0.8725
$\rho_1 = 2/3$	k^*, $R(k^*)$	3, 6.5452	3, 7.9036	2, 9.0724
	Equilibrium	(10, 10)	(7, 7)	(4, 4)
	Rewards (v_1, v_2)	(1.7471, 1.7356)	(2.9654, 2.9565)	(4.0684, 4.0709)
	ϵ	0.5321	0.7490	0.8971

7   Conclusion

This paper has presented a model of two DMs searching for a unique valuable resource (e.g. a flat) using both online and offline information. The DMs have symmetrical roles, the only possible difference being that one DM might show a higher level of altruism. Based on initial (online) information, the DMs individually select a number of offers that are potentially attractive to them. Each of the offers selected at this stage are placed on a short list and then inspected more closely (offline). After the round of close inspection, the DMs each make a ranking of the offers on the short list and the offer associated with the smallest sum of ranks is selected.

A major goal of this article was to investigate how the relation between the DMs (their level of altruism and the coherence of their preferences) affects their behavior at equilibrium and the efficiency of the search procedure. When the DMs neither show altruism to each other nor have coherent preferences, then the search costs incurred at equilibrium are high, since both DMs wish to find an offer that is particularly attractive to them. This is difficult due to the lack of coherence in their preferences. Suppose at least one of the DMs is altruistic (say DM1). It is much easier to find an acceptable offer, since one that is very highly attractive to DM2 will almost certainly be acceptable to both DMs. When the preferences of the DMs are coherent, then it is much easier to find an offer that is attractive to both DMs. Hence, as either the level of altruism exhibited or the coherence of preferences grows, the search costs incurred fall and the efficiency of joint search increases. This is particularly visible in the case of coherent preferences. In economic terms, altruism between the DMs and coherence of preferences are factors that lower the transaction costs involved in consumer decisions (see Platje [2004]).

In the model presented here, the DMs play a symmetric role. The only possible difference between the DMs lies in the level of altruism one might show to the other. Future research should investigate the role that other asymmetries play in such decision procedures. For example, the DMs might place different weights on the relative importance of the signals obtained at each stage. Another form of asymmetry might lie in the fact that one DM might (at least partially) dominate the other. In such a case, the dominant DM is expected to act similarly to one who shows a lower level of altruism to the other in the model considered here. However, if the subordinate DM does not feel altruism to the dominant DM, then this will affect the level of satisfaction that the subordinate DM feels from the result of the search process.

acknowledgements. This research was funded by Polish National Science Centre grant number 2018/29/B/HS4/02857, "Logistics, Trade and Consumer Decisions in the Age of the Internet".

References

Analytis, P.P., Kothiyal, A., Katsikopoulos, K.: Multi-attribute utility models as cognitive search engines. Judgm. Decis. Mak. **95**, 403–419 (2014)

Armouti-Hansen, J., Kops, C.: This or that? Sequential rationalization of indecisive choice behavior. Theor. Decis. **84**(4), 507–524 (2017). https://doi.org/10.1007/s11238-017-9634-8

Bishop, D.T., Cannings, C.: A generalized war of attrition. J. Theor. Biol. **70**(1), 85–124 (1978)

Bobadilla-Suarez, S., Love, B.C.: Fast or frugal, but not both: decision heuristics under time pressure. J. Exp. Psychol. Learn. Mem. Cogn. **44**(1), 24 (2018)

Borah, A., Kops, C.: Rational choices: an ecological approach. Theor. Decis. **86**(3–4), 401–420 (2019)

Fehr, E., Schmidt, K.M.: The economics of fairness, reciprocity and altruism? Experimental evidence and new theories. In: Kolm, S.C., Ythier, J.M. (eds.) Handbook of the Economics of Giving, Altruism and Reciprocity, vol. 1, pp. 615–691 (2006)

Hardin, G.: The tragedy of the commons. J. Nat. Resour. Policy Res. **1**(3), 243–253 (2009)

Horn, R.A., Johnson, C.R.: Matrix Analysis. Cambridge University Press, Cambridge (1985)

Lleras, J.S., Masatlioglu, Y., Nakajima, D., Ozbay, E.Y.: When more is less: limited consideration. J. Econ. Theory **170**, 70–85 (2017)

Mandler, M., Manzini, P., Mariotti, M.: A million answers to twenty questions: choosing by checklist. J. Econ. Theory **147**(1), 71–92 (2012)

Masatlioglu, Y., Nakajima, D., Ozbay, E.Y.: Revealed attention. Am. Econ. Rev. **102**(5), 2183–2205 (2012)

Maschler, M., Solan, E., Zamir, S.: Game Theory, 2nd edn. Cambridge University Press, Cambridge (2020)

Platje, J.: Institutional change and Poland's economic performance since the 1970's. Rijksuniversiteit te Groningen (2004). https://www.researchgate.net/profile/Joo st_Platje/publication/40266753_Institutional_Change_and_Poland's_Economic_Perfo rmance_since_the_1970s_incentives_and_transaction_costs/links/5ab0c466aca2721710 fe4cd6/Institutional-Change-and-Polands-Economic-Performance-since-the-1970s-in centives-and-transaction-costs.pdf

Ramsey, D.M.: Optimal Selection from a set of offers using a short list. Multiple Criteria Decis. Making **14**, 75–92 (2019)

Ramsey, D.M.: Group decision making based on constructing a short list. In: Nguyen, N.T., Kowalczyk, R., Mercik, J., Motylska-Kuźma, A. (eds.) Transactions on Computational Collective Intelligence XXXV. LNCS, vol. 12330, pp. 52–75. Springer, Heidelberg (2020). https://doi.org/10.1007/978-3-662-62245-2_4

Ramsey, D.M.: A game theoretic model of choosing a valuable good via a short list heuristic. Mathematics **8**(2), 199 (2020)

Simon, H.A.: A behavioral model of rational choice. Q. J. Econ. **69**(1), 99–118 (1955)

Simon, H.A.: Rational choice and the structure of the environment. Psychol. Rev. **63**(2), 129 (1956)

Todd, P.M., Gigerenzer, G.: Précis of simple heuristics that make us smart. Behav. Brain Sci. **23**(5), 727–741 (2000)

Operation Comfort of Multistate System vs. The Importance of Its Components

Krzysztof J. Szajowski[1]([⊠]) [iD] and Małgorzata Średnicka[2] [iD]

[1] Faculty of Pure and Applied Mathematics, Wrocław University of Science and Technology, Wybrzeże Wyspiańskiego 27, 50-370 Wrocław, Poland
Krzysztof.Szajowski@pwr.edu.pl
http://szajowski.wordpress.com/
[2] Wrocław University of Science and Technology, Wrocław, Poland

Abstract. A milestone in the mathematical modeling of complex systems is the analysis of the significance of the system components. When examining the reliability, Birnbaum (1968) proposed measures of element significance. This direction of research into mathematical models of systems has led to many alternative analyzes. The aim of the article is to further expand the diagnostic capabilities of systems through a specialized analysis of their mathematical models. We propose, using the methods of game theory and stochastic processes, functionals that measure the structural reliability of the system and the operational performance related to maintenance. This allows for the construction of a new measure of significance, using knowledge of system design, reliability, and wear to optimize repair and maintenance. The considerations of this work are aimed at showing the ways of applying this approach to multi-state systems.

Keywords: Birnbaum importance · Barlow-Proschan importance · Binary system · Components importance · Coherent system · Cost-based importance · Multistate system · Natvig measure · Risk-based importance · Structural function · Universal generating function

Subject Classifications: MSC 90B25 · 91B12 (62G10 62N05 90B25)

1 Introduction

1.1 Preliminaries

A system[1], i.e. a complex structure with specific functionality is under investigation. The mathematical model of the system is based on the set theory as the family of subsets of a given set (set of elements) $C = \{c_1, \ldots, c_n\}$ having

---

[1] System (in Ancient Greek: σύστημα – romanized: systema – a complex thing) – a set of interrelated elements realizing the assumed goals as a whole.

© Springer-Verlag GmbH Germany, part of Springer Nature 2021
N. T. Nguyen et al. (Eds.): TCCI XXXVI, LNCS 13010, pp. 44–72, 2021.
https://doi.org/10.1007/978-3-662-64563-5_3

some properties. An example is technical devices whose design is dictated by the need to perform specific functions. The constructed system should function in a planned and predictable manner. This property is a requirement that should also be considered in the design and construction (fabrication) process. The goal is therefore to reduce the risk (v. B.1) of a break in the planned operation of the system. So we have to model randomness[2]. For this purpose, we establish that all random phenomena are modeled using the probabilistic space $(\Omega, \mathcal{F}, \mathbf{P})$ (v. A).

Contemporary systems are characterized by their structural complexity. Its design is purposeful, which means that its purpose is to ensure the implementation of specific tasks. Due to the complexity of tasks and their multi-threading, the evaluation of functionality should be carried out on many levels. In short, the working complex system is able to be in many states. The first mathematical models of systems focused on component and structure reliability. This allowed a limitation to two-level assessments, the system (element) is operational or damaged (working or not working)[3]. Already such an approach made it possible to methodologically support a designer with mathematical models, the analysis of which resulted in guidelines allowing for rational solutions in terms of the complexity of the structure and effective selection of elements so as to guarantee the reliability of the structure (system readiness) at the appropriate level for a sufficient time. Graph theory and the structures constructed in this theory are an excellent tool for modeling binary systems. The random graph is a good model of the binary system[4]. To put it simply, a coherent graph is a standby system model, and lack of consistency means no readiness. Turning off nodes and arcs in a connected graph leads to its decomposition, and thus destruction. Each operation of the system, the model of which is a random graph, leads to the moment in which the next disabled element of the structure leads to failure (lack of readiness). By analyzing the lifetime of the elements, it is possible to determine the order in which the elements are switched off and determine how often the failure of the tested element is the cause of the failure of the entire system. The more often an element is crucial, the greater its importance for the system. This line of reasoning led to the definition of Birnbaum's [8] importance measure. There are known alternative results on the evaluation of the weight of components on the reliability of the system. The introduced measures of significance of elements on reliability will be the basis for the introduction of diagnostic algorithms about the possibility of which they wrote at the end of his seminal paper (cf. Birnbaum [8,9] (v. Barlow et al. [7]). The indication of these algorithms is the subject of the authors' study (v. Szajowski and Srednicka [37]).

---

[2] The foundation of stochastic methods in the reliability theory can be found in the monograph by Barlow and Proschan [5].

[3] The definition of state "working" is defined as *ready to perform some list of tasks*.

[4] The idea of random graphs has started by Erdős and Rényi [14] and Gilbert [18]. Its application to modeling of complex systems, also to analyze their reliability, is well known.

The concept of significance measures (v. B.2) is essentially based on establishing a criterion against which we measure the significance of an element. [8] investigated the importance of the position of an element in a structure, valuing the elements whose failure less frequently decomposes the system. In order to determine the importance of the reliability (failure rate) of individual system components for the reliability of the entire system, measures sensitive to changes in the system and changes in component reliability are constructed. It also allows for the rationalization of the design and maintenance planning. The issues are complex due to the need to take into account both the effective reliability of the constructed system and the costs of maintaining it in readiness for a given period. Profitability analysis is of great importance. It is natural to formulate the problem by defining the overarching goal of minimizing costs while guaranteeing the expected level of reliability. In the whole process of analysis, the point of reference are two states (of the system and elements): functional or damaged. There are measures that are sensitive to a change of state, measure the importance of an element in relation to other elements, and the susceptibility of a system to a change of state from operation to failure. Thanks to this approach, it is possible to define weights for the cost of individual elements in a given time horizon, while ensuring a specific level of security or readiness. This approach can be found in the article by Wu and Coolen [39]. At the same time, other key goals and parameters of system analysis should not be forgotten. Their inclusion in the balanced model is possible with the use of natural methods of analysis when formulating many criteria based on elements of game theory.

We try to present the issue comprehensively, although there is currently no consistent approach to the method of determining the importance of elements in the system (v. B.3). This is one of the reasons why the loss of functionality of an element often does not significantly affect the system's ability to perform most tasks. This aspect is emphasized by numerous examples presented in the literature, which show the significant impact of the state of the environment in which the systems are operated (time of day, weather conditions, environmental pollution). We write more about these issues in an earlier work (v. Szajowski and Średnicka [37]). From the analytical point of view, by introducing well-defined states of the system, referring, for example, to its function, one can investigate the meaning of structure elements in connection with the adopted description of its states.

As in binary systems, the rank of an element is determined by the availability of the system to scheduled tasks, so when evaluating elements of multi-state systems, the rank of an element in terms of state is determined by the availability of the system in this state.

The presented aspects relate to being in a fixed state, excluding the need for maintenance and repairs, including the costs of these activities (cost of parts, repair and maintenance time, penalties for unavailability). In system maintenance tasks, issues such as detecting failed components while the system is in that state are important in determining the importance of components to the steady state of the system. The element that should be checked first (because it is most suspected of a failure) can be treated as important for the efficient conduct of maintenance or repair (v. e.g. Ping [28]).

1.2 Investigation of Element Role in a Given State

If the system cannot be in the tested state, it is often important to determine the sequence of actions to restore the system to that state. To facilitate such analyzes, the weights (measures of significance regarding repair) of the elements should be determined. Otherwise, in these considerations, the measure of the importance of a component (group of components) in a given system is based on the quantification of the "role" of that component (group of components) and of the unavailability of the examined state of the system. Examples of such analyzes can be found in Fussell and Vesely [17], Barlow and Proschan [4], El-Neweihi et al. [13], El-Neweihi and Sethuraman [12] and Abouammoh et al. [1]. Defined measures (indicators) with significance allow to identify components (groups) that are probably responsible for "causing" the inability to use the analyzed state. In turn, the determination of these indicators leads to an effective control and maintenance principle, as well as to the optimization of spare parts storage and the optimal allocation of repairs to appropriate maintenance technicians of the relevant system components.

When examining the significance of the elements of binary systems, a few years after the publication of the results of Birnbaum and Proschan, it was noticed that similar solutions in the form of significance measures are used in parallel in the analysis of multi-person project management, voting analysis and other issues related to cooperative games (v. Ramamurthy [30]). As in the theory of cooperative games, the purpose of such research is to propose new importance measures for degrading components (v. Cao et al. [10]). The motivation is based on Shapley values, which can provide answers about how important players are to the whole cooperative game and what payoff each player can reasonably expect. The proposed importance measure characterizes how a specific degrading component contributes to the degradation of system reliability by using Shapley value. Degradation models are also introduced to assess the reliability of degrading components. The reliability of the system consisting independent degrading components is obtained by using structure functions, while the reliability of system comprising correlated degrading components is evaluated with a multivariate distribution. The ranking of degrading components according to this importance measure depends on the degradation parameters of components, system structure, and parameters characterizing the association of components. A reliability degradation of engineering systems and equipment are often attributed to the degradation of a particular component or set of components that are characterized by degrading features. This approach reflects the responsibility of each degrading component for the deterioration of system reliability. The results are also able to give timely feedback of the expected contribution of each degrading component to system reliability degradation.

1.3 Organization of the Paper

The rest of the paper is structured as follows. Section 2 provides the details of analysis of multistate systems. We start out, in Sect. 2.1, by showing how the coherency of multi-state systems is modeled. The remaining considerations are carried out on the assumption that the system is coherent. In the Sect. 2.3, we show what guidelines are to be provided by the constructed measures in the case of non-repairable systems (modules), and for whom these indicators are of interest. Other issues are interesting in the case of repairable systems and this is what the next Sect. 2.4 is about. The Sect. 3 describes the main problem of the paper, namely, the construction of a significance (importance) measure for an element or module of a system in the face of maintaining system consistency and activity. We recognize that the difficulty in maintaining the system is equal to the difficulty in maintaining its individual modules. These in turn are all the more important the more difficult it is to reconstruct them at the time of failure. The final Sect. 4 contains conclusions and suggestions for further research on diagnostics and maintenance of complex, multi-state systems. At the end of the work, and before the extensive bibliography, we have included a list of symbols, terms, and abbreviations. We chose them based on the belief that they may differ from those to which the reader is used to. In the next part, we have included end-notes to which we refer the reader when the main narrative requires them.

2 Multistate Systems

2.1 Coherent Multistate Systems

In the Sect. B.3 we mentioned coherent structures for binary system, while in this section we adapt the concept of coherence to the multistate systems. Many assumptions with given formulas regarding binary systems have natural continuation and analogous behavior in a multistate system, however are more complex Barlow and Wu [6].

Suppose we have specified the following objects (cf. [23, 26]):

a) the **set** C consisting of n ordered elements $C = \{1, 2, ..., n\}$ (elements collection, elements space)–it will be the space of elements;

b) for every element $i \in C$ there is defined set of states $\mathbb{C}_i$ which is a completely ordered and finite[5], i.e., $\{(\mathbb{C}_i, \prec_i)\}_{i \in C}$ and $|\mathbb{C}_i| = w_i \in \mathbb{N}$;

c) let $\overrightarrow{x}^A$ be an element of the set $\mathbb{C}_A = \times_{i \in A} \mathbb{C}_i$;

d) if a subset $A \subset C$, then $C \backslash A \equiv A' \equiv \{j \in C | j \notin A\}$;

e) if $B \subset A \subset C$, then P_B is a surjection $P_B : \mathbb{C}_A \to \mathbb{C}_B$[6];

f) if $\Gamma \subset \mathbb{C}_A$ and $B \subset A \subset C$, then $P_{\mathbb{C}_B}\Gamma = \{P_B \overrightarrow{x} \in \mathbb{C}_B | \overrightarrow{x} \in \Gamma\}$, i.e., it is a subset of states indexed by B

g) the partition of $A \subset C$ expressed as a family $\mathcal{B} = \{B_j\}_{j=1}^m$, such that

---

[5] An ordered set for which any two elements(i.e. states) can be compared–in this context every two states should be compared.

[6] The operator P_B is sometimes denoted $P_{\mathbb{C}_B}$.

1. $A = \bigcup\limits_{j}^{m} B_j \subset C$, $B_i \cap B_j = \emptyset$, for $1 \leq i,j \leq m$, $i \neq j$;

2. for every $\overrightarrow{x}_j \in \times_{i \in B_j} \mathfrak{C}_i$, $1 \leq j \leq m$, we have $\overrightarrow{x} = (\overrightarrow{x}_1, \ldots, \overrightarrow{x}_m) \in \mathfrak{C}_A$ is such that $P_{B_j} \overrightarrow{x} = \overrightarrow{x}_j$;

3. for every $\overrightarrow{x} \in A \subset C$, $\overrightarrow{x} = (\overrightarrow{x}^{B_1}, \ldots, \overrightarrow{x}^{B_m})$, where $\overrightarrow{x}^{B_j} = P_{B_j}(\overrightarrow{x}) = \overrightarrow{x}_j$, $j = 1, \ldots, m$

h) for $A \subset C$, $i \in A$, the state vector $(k_i, \overrightarrow{x}_{-i}) \in \mathfrak{C}_A$ is such that $k_i \in \mathfrak{C}_i$ and $\overrightarrow{x}_{-i} \in \times_{j \in A \setminus \{i\}} \mathfrak{C}_j$.

Let there be a fixed space of elements $C = \{1, 2, \ldots, n\}$, the spaces of their states with an order established in them $\mathfrak{C}_C = \times_{i \in C} \mathfrak{C}_i$, and the set of possible states of the system $\mathfrak{S}$.

Definition 1. *The general system of n components is a triplet $(\mathfrak{C}_C, \mathfrak{S}, \phi)$ where*

1. *the mapping $\phi : \mathfrak{C}_C \to \mathfrak{S}$ is surjection;*
2. *an inverse image of state set $\mathfrak{S}$ has following property. If $\mathfrak{s} \neq \mathfrak{t}$, $\mathfrak{t}, \mathfrak{s} \in \mathfrak{S}$, then*

$$V_\mathfrak{s}(\phi) \cap V_\mathfrak{t}(\phi) = \emptyset,$$

where for any $\mathfrak{L} \subset \mathfrak{S}$, $V_\mathfrak{L}(\phi)$ is given by

$$V_\mathfrak{L}(\phi) = \{\overrightarrow{x} \in \mathfrak{C}_C : \phi(\overrightarrow{x}) = \mathfrak{l}, \quad for \; \mathfrak{l} \in \mathfrak{L}\}.$$

For subset $\mathfrak{L} = \{\mathfrak{l}\}$ we write $V_\mathfrak{l}(\phi)$.

We define the natural classes of system by specifying the ϕ mapping properties. We also specify the unique properties of the system.

α A system $(\mathfrak{C}_C, \mathfrak{S}, \phi)$ is increasing if and only if for every $\overrightarrow{x}, \overrightarrow{y} \in \mathfrak{C}_C$, $\overrightarrow{x} \preccurlyeq_{\mathfrak{C}_C} \overrightarrow{y}$ we have $\phi(\overrightarrow{x}) \preccurlyeq_\mathfrak{S} \phi(\overrightarrow{y})$.

β Component i is essential (*relevant*) for a system ϕ if and only if

$$\bigwedge_{\substack{\rho, \mathfrak{s} \in \mathfrak{S} \\ \rho \neq \mathfrak{s}}} \bigvee_{k, l \in \mathfrak{C}_i} \overrightarrow{x}_{C \setminus \{i\}} \in \times_{j \neq i} \mathfrak{C}_j, \; (k, \overrightarrow{x}_{-i}) \in V_\rho, \; (l, \overrightarrow{x}_{-i}) \in V_\mathfrak{s}$$

i.e., any changing the system state is possible by changing the state of the i-th element.

γ The system is called *relevant* if and only if every element is relevant to the system.

Definition 2. *The system is called a* coherent *if and only if the mapping ϕ is* increasing *and* relevant.

Example 1. Various description of there same structure. Consider the layout of the elements connected according to the scheme in the Fig. 1. The set of all items is $C = \{c_1 \ldots, c_5\}$. The set of $A = \{c_1, c_2\}$ elements is a series system with model $(\{0,1\}_A, \mathfrak{A}, \varphi_A)$, where $\varphi_A(x_1, x_2) = \prod_{j \in A} x_j \in \mathfrak{A} = \{\mathfrak{t}_0, \mathfrak{t}_1\}$. The

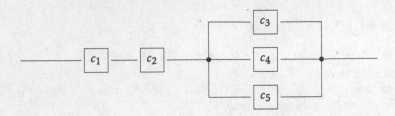

Fig. 1. Series and parallel structure – as binary and multistate system.

rest of the elements– $B = \{c_3, c_4, c_5\}$, forms another subsytem – which can take four states: $\mathcal{B} = \{\mathfrak{s}_0, \mathfrak{s}_1, \mathfrak{s}_2, \mathfrak{s}_3\}$. For example, a combined car lamp with frosted glass gives different light intensity in different states. The user does not know which elements are functional and which are damaged – so the original model

$$\varphi_B(x_3, x_4, x_5) = x_3 \vee x_4 \vee x_5 \in \mathcal{A}$$

is useless in this case because the system has more than two states. We can propose for part B the model: $(\{0,1\}_B, \mathcal{B}, \psi_B)$, where

$$\psi_B(x_3, x_4, x_5) = \sum_{j=3}^{5} x_j \in \mathcal{B}$$

and the model of hole system $(\{0,1\}_C, \mathcal{B}, \phi)$ with the structure function

$$\phi(\overrightarrow{x}) = \varphi_A(x_1, x_2) * \psi_B(x_3, x_4, x_5) \in \mathcal{B}.$$

2.2   Introductory Characteristic for the Importance Measure

There are at least two major reasons why we should investigate a measure of importance of components in a system. First of them is a need to specify the elements of the system that contribute to its destruction to a greater extent and directly lower system reliability, which is why they should be subjected to more attentive observation, so one can focus on development while saving costs. The second reason is the ability to choose the most effective way to recognize system damage by creating a repair checklist helpful in further analysis. However, it must be emphasized that there is no universal measure that can be used anytime regardless of the circumstances. Such measures for the binary system based on the binary elements are presented in [37] (v. [30, Chap. 3]). In this chapter, following [24, Chap. 6] and paper cited therein, some extension of importance analysis of the elements based on the idea of multistate system is considered. The research aims attention on components' importance measures that could be versatile, focusing on items that can be repaired at the specific period of time.

In practice, we can deal with systems in which the possible sets of the states of individual elements can be different and the states of the system are not of the same type as the states we assign to the elements of the system. However, in this analysis we can disregard the meaning of individual states. The important thing is that the number of states of individual elements is finite and there is an established order in the set of states. Where there may be ambiguities, we will label the states of the system with German Fracture letters with indexes and states of the elements by the Latin letters. To comply with the notations adopted in the former studies (v. [23]), the states are indexed from 0 to M, so if $|\mathfrak{S}| = s$ (i.e. $\mathfrak{S} = \{\mathfrak{s}_0, ..., \mathfrak{s}_{s-1}\}$), then $M = s$. We assume that low indices correspond to worse states, and higher ones to better ones. When switching from a multistate to a binary system, we can assume that the number of states has been reduced: $\{\mathfrak{s}_0, \mathfrak{s}_s\} \subset \mathfrak{S}$. For given states $\overrightarrow{x} \in \mathfrak{C}_C$ we have the state of the system $\mathfrak{s} = \phi(\overrightarrow{x})$. A reduction to the binary system is determined by indication of the critical state $\mathfrak{s}^*$ which by the order structure of $\mathfrak{S}$ define maximal index of *worse states* j^* is such that $\mathfrak{s}_{j^*} = \mathfrak{s}^*$. Let $\mathfrak{s}_j^* \in \mathfrak{S}$ be such state. This choice of critical element reduce the state space as follows: $\mathfrak{s}' = \mathfrak{s}_0 \mathbb{I}_{\{\mathfrak{s}_0,...,\mathfrak{s}_{j-1}\}}(\mathfrak{s}) + \mathfrak{s}_M \mathbb{I}_{\{\mathfrak{s}_j,...,\mathfrak{s}_M\}}(\mathfrak{s})$.

Following Natvig [23, p. 525], let us introduce notations: $\mathfrak{S}_{i\cdot} = \mathfrak{C}_i \times \mathfrak{S}$, $\mathfrak{S}_{i\,A} = \mathfrak{C}_i \times \mathfrak{S}_A$, where $\mathfrak{S}_A = \{\mathfrak{s}_j : j \in A\}$. Define $\mathsf{F} = \{\mathfrak{s}_j : \mathfrak{s}_j \preceq \mathfrak{s}_j^*\}$ and $A_\mathsf{F} = \{j < j^*\}$.

Definition 3. *A multistate monotone system with the space of elements C is called*

a) *the multistate serial system if* $\phi_{MSs}(\overrightarrow{x}) = \min\limits_{1 \leq i \leq n} x_i$;

b) *the multistate parallel system* $\phi_{MPs}(\overrightarrow{x}) = \max\limits_{1 \leq i \leq n} x_i$.

Definition 4. *A multistate monotone system with the space of elements C and the structure function ϕ is called strongly coherent if*

$$\phi_{MSs}(\overrightarrow{x}) \preceq \phi(\overrightarrow{x}) \preceq \phi_{MPs}(\overrightarrow{x})$$

and for every $j \in \mathfrak{M} \setminus \{0\}$, $i \in N$ *we have*

$$\mathfrak{s}_j \preceq \phi(k, \vec{x}_{-i}) \qquad \text{for every } (k, \vec{x}_{-i}) \in \mathfrak{S}_{i,j}^1$$

$$\mathfrak{s}_j \succ \phi(l, \vec{x}_{-i}) \qquad \text{for every } (l, \vec{x}_{-i}) \in \mathfrak{S}_{i,j}^0$$

where $\mathfrak{S}_{i,j}^0 = \mathfrak{S}_{iA_\mathsf{F}}$ *and* $\mathfrak{S}_{i,j}^1 = \mathfrak{S}_{iA_\mathsf{F}'}$.

Remark 1. Furthermore, let us assume that for $i \in C$, $|C| = n$ the i-th component has the random state $X_i(t) \in \mathfrak{C}_i$ at time t. With the corresponding vector of independent random processes $\overrightarrow{X}(t) = (X_1(t), ..., X_n(t)) \in \mathfrak{C}_C$ we have description of the states of all elements of the system, and the corresponding state of the system is given by $\phi(\overrightarrow{X}(t)) \in \mathfrak{S}$. Without losing generality, we can use indexes of system components and state indexes, both for elements and for the entire system, instead of state names. In the following part we will denote the set of elements as N (instead of C, $|N| = n$, and the sets of states $\mathfrak{C}$. and $\mathfrak{M}$. If this does not lead to an ambiguity, it will be $\mathfrak{C}_i = \mathfrak{M} = \{0, ..., M\}$. To emphasize the different sizes of state sets, where it is important, we will mark it by indexing state sets (e.g. $\mathfrak{M}_r$).

2.3 Nonrepairable Coherent Multistate Systems

First, we will focus on multistate systems, where repair of the components is not permitted. Let assume that

a) $\mathfrak{C}_i = \mathfrak{C}$, where $i \in N$
b) $X_i(t)$, for $t \geq 0$ and $i \in N$, is a Markov process on the probability space $(\Omega, \mathcal{F}, \mathbf{P})$ with continuous time and the state space $\mathfrak{M}_i$.
c) $X_i(0) = M_i$, which means that all components are in the properly functioning state M_i, $i \in N$, at time $t = 0$.

Furthermore, let present some notation

$$\overrightarrow{\mathbf{r}}(t) = (r_1^1(t), ..., r_1^M(t), r_2^1(t), ..., r_2^M(t), ..., r_n^1(t), ..., r_n^M(t))$$

$$P(X_i(t) \geq j) = p_i^j(t) = \sum_{k=j}^{M} r_i^s(t), \qquad\qquad j \in \mathfrak{M}$$

$$P(X_i(t) = j) = r_i^j(t), \qquad\qquad j \in \mathfrak{M}$$

$$p_i^{(k,l)}(t, t+u) = P[X_i(t+u) = l | X_i(t) = k], \qquad 0 \leq l < k \leq M$$

$$P[\phi(\overrightarrow{X}(t)) \succeq \mathfrak{s}_j] = P[\mathbb{1}(\phi(\overrightarrow{X}(t)) \succeq \mathfrak{s}_j) = 1] = p_\phi^j(\overrightarrow{\mathbf{r}}(t))$$

$$\lambda_i^{(k,l)}(t) = \lim_{h \to 0} \frac{p_i^{(k,l)}(t, t+h)}{h}, \qquad\qquad 0 \leq l < k \leq M$$

where at time t: reliability of the i-th component to the level j is given by $p_i^j(t)$ while $p_\phi^j(r(t))$ is the reliability of the i-th component to the system [23]. To simplify, let us accept that for $0 \leq l < k \leq M$ we have $\lambda_i^{(k,l)}(t) = 0$. Moreover, let us assume that for each component i, time spent in state k before change to state $k - 1$, has a continuous distribution $F_i^k(t)$ with density $f_i^k(t)$. It is assumed that the times spent in particular states are independent random variables. Besides that, let us introduce row vector with dimension $M + 1$, such as

$$\begin{cases} e^k = (1_k, 0) & \text{for } k = 1, ..., n \\ e^0 = 0 \end{cases}$$

2.3.1 The Birnbaum's Importance Measure

In [37] we discussed Birnbaum's importance measure for the binary system, while in this Sect. 2.3.1 we propose a measure for a non-repairable and multistate system - generalized weighted and not weighted Birnbaum's measure. These measures help in judgment which components of the system are the most valuable and important for the faultless functioning and higher reliability of the system. Nevertheless, they measure importance only at fixed points of the time. Furthermore, they are not dependent on the i-th component, what means that the importance of the system is dependent on the operation of all components. Generalized Birnabaum's measure $I_B^{(i,k,j)}(t)$ is the probability at time t that the system is in such state, in which its functioning of i-th component in state k is decisive for the system to be in $\{j, ..., M\}$ states [23]. It is formulated as

$$I_B^{(i,k,j)}(t) = P\Big[I\big(\phi(k, X(t)) \geq j\big) - I\big(\phi(k-1, X(t)) \geq j\big) = 1\Big]$$
$$= p_\phi^j((e^k)_i, r(t)) - p_\phi^j((e^{k-1})_i, r(t)),$$

where $i \in \mathbf{N}$, and $j, k \in \mathfrak{M} \setminus \{0\}$. Since $\sum_{k=0}^M r_i^k(t) = 1$ for $i = 1, ..., n$, $p_i^k(t) = 1$, for $k < 1$, and $p_i^k(t) = 0$, for $k > M$, then

$$p_\phi^j(r(t)) = \sum_{k=0}^M r_i^k(t) p_\phi^j((e^k)_i, r(t))$$
$$= \sum_{k=1}^M p_i^k(t) \Big[p_\phi^j((e^k)_i, r(t)) - p_\phi^j((e^{k-1})_i, r(t))\Big] + p_\phi^j((e^0)_i, r(t)).$$

When $i \in \mathbf{N}$ and $j, k \in \mathfrak{M} \setminus \{0\}$, we obtain

$$\frac{\partial p_\phi^j(r(t))}{\partial r_i^k(t)} = p_\phi^j((e^k)_i, r(t)) - p_\phi^j((e^0)_i, r(t))$$
$$\frac{\partial p_\phi^j(r(t))}{\partial p_i^k(t)} = p_\phi^j((e^k)_i, r(t)) - p_\phi^j((e^{k-1})_i, r(t)) = I_B^{(i,k,j)}(t).$$

For case of $M = 1$ we have a corresponding Birnbaum's importance measure (v. [37]).

In some cases, it is better to use the weighted Birnbaum's measure for the multistate system. Hence, for critical state $j \in \mathfrak{M} \setminus \{0\}$ an utility w' of being in particular states is assigned in such a way that $w'(\mathfrak{s}) = w_j \mathbb{I}_{\{\mathfrak{s} \succeq \mathfrak{s}_j\}}(\mathfrak{s}) + w_j^c \mathbb{I}_{\mathfrak{s} \prec \mathfrak{s}_j}(\mathfrak{s})$ where $w_j \geq w_j^c$, $\{w_j\}_{j=1}^M$ and $\{w_j^c\}_{j=1}^M$ are nonincreasing. We have for the system leaving the set of states $\{j, ..., M\}$ a utility loss $c_j = w_j - w_j^c \geq 0$. Without losing generality, we can additionally impose a condition $\sum_{j=1}^M c_j = 1$ on these losses.

The generalized weighted Birnbaum's measure takes the form

$$\hat{I}_B^{(i)}(t) = \sum_{j=1}^M c_j \cdot I_B^{(i,j)}(t), \quad \text{where } 0 \leq \hat{I}_B^{(i)}(t) \leq 1, \tag{1}$$

while generalized Birnbaum measure is expressed by

$$I_B^{(i,j)}(t) = \frac{\sum_{k=1}^M I_B^{(i,k,j)}(t)}{\sum_{r=1}^n \sum_{k=1}^M I_B^{(r,k,j)}(t)} \quad \text{where } 0 \leq I_B^{(i,j)}(t) \leq 1. \tag{2}$$

We have $\sum_{i=1}^n \hat{I}_B^{(i)}(t) = \sum_{i=1}^n I_B^{(i,j)}(t) = 1$.

2.3.2   The Barlow-Proschan Importance Measure

The Barlow-Proschan measure also helps in deciding, which components of the system are the most valuable for the proper functioning of the system and achieving its greater reliability. Moreover, the system failure reason can be identified via repair checklist generation. The Barlow and Proschan importance measure $I_{B-P}^{(i)}$ of the i-th component is the probability that leaving the states $\{1, ..., M\}$ by the system converges in time with the jump down of the i-th component and is denoted as

$$I_{B-P}^{(i,j)} = \int_0^\infty \sum_{k=1}^M I_B^{(i,k,j)}(t) \cdot r_i^k(t) \cdot \lambda_i^{(k,k-1)}(t) dt$$

$$= \int_0^\infty \sum_{k=1}^M \lambda_i^{(k,k-1)}(t) \cdot r_i^k(t) \cdot \left[p_\phi^j((e^k)_i, r(t)) - p_\phi^j((e^{k-1})_i, r(t)) \right] dt,$$

where $j \in \{0, ..., M\}$, $i = 1, ..., n$ and $\sum_{i=1}^n I_{B-P}^{(i,j)} = 1$. For a binary case when $M = 1$, there is a following relationship

$$I_{B-P}^{(i,1)} = I_{B-P}^{(i)}$$

The Barlow-Proschan measure also occurs in generalized weighted form $\hat{I}_{B-P}^i$ and the importance of the i-th component is denoted as

$$\hat{I}_{B-P}^i = \sum_{j=1}^M c_j \cdot I_{B-P}^{(i,j)}, \quad \text{where } 0 \le \hat{I}_{B-P}^{(i)} \le 1 \text{ and } \sum_{i=1}^n \hat{I}_{B-P}^{(i)} = 1.$$

Weighted and nonweighted generalized Barlow-Proschan measure are in fact generalized Birnbaum measure's weighted averages. These measures indicates that when component's importance increases, the chance of this component to be the direct reason of the system worsening also increases.

2.3.3   The Natvig Importance Measure

The Natvig measure concentrates on how component's transition between states influence performance of the system regarding the given system state.

For $k \in \{0, ..., M-1\}$ and $i = 1, ..., n$ let introduce $T_{i,k}$ which stands for the i-th component's time of the jump into state k and $T'_{i,k}$ is an assumed time of the i-th component's jump into state k after it was believed to undergo a minimal repair at $T_{i,k}$. Next, for $j \in \{1, ..., m\}$, $k \in \{1, ..., M\}$, $i = 1, ..., n$ and interval $[T_{i,k-1}, T'_{i,k-1}]$ we have $Y_{i,k,j}^1$ which is the system time in $\{j, ..., M\}$ states right away the i-th component changed it state from k to $k-1$ and then instantly is a subject of the fictive minimal repair. Furthermore, $Y_{i,k,j}^0$ has the same definition as $Y_{i,k,j}^1$, however, at the end the i-th component does not undergo repair immediately, it stays in the state $k-1$ for the whole interval $[T_{i,k-1}, T'_{i,k-1}]$, such that

$$Z_{i,k,j} = Y^1_{i,k,j} - Y^0_{i,k,j}$$

$$\bar{Z}_{i,k,j} = \frac{Z_{i,k,j}}{\sum_{r=1}^{n} \sum_{k=1}^{M} \mathbf{E} Z_{r,k,j}}. \tag{3}$$

Hence, for $j \in \{1, ..., M\}$, $k \in \{1, ..., M\}$, $i = 1, ..., n$ and applying the expectation with assumption $\mathbf{E} Z_{i,k,j} < \infty$, we obtain from (3), the generalized Natvig importance measure of the i-th component $I_N^{(i,j)}$ and its weighted version $\hat{I}_N^{(i,j)}$, given by

$$I_N^{(i,j)} = \sum_{k=1}^{M} \mathbf{E} \bar{Z}_{i,k,j}$$

$$= \frac{\sum_{k=1}^{M} \mathbf{E} Z_{i,k,j}}{\sum_{r=1}^{n} \sum_{k=1}^{M} \mathbf{E} Z_{r,k,j}}, \qquad \text{where } 0 \le I_N^{(i,j)} \le 1 \text{ and } \sum_{i=1}^{n} I_N^{(i,j)} = 1,$$

$$\hat{I}_N^{(i,j)} = \sum_{j=1}^{M} c_j \cdot I_N^{(i,j)}, \qquad \text{where } 0 \le \hat{I}_N^{(i)} \le 1 \text{ and } \sum_{i=1}^{n} \hat{I}_N^{(i)} = 1.$$

Thus, the weighted Natvig measure may be interpreted as the extended, more sophisticated Barlow-Proschan's weighted measure.

2.4   Repairable Coherent Multistate Systems

In this section we analyze importance measures of multistate systems, where components can be repaired after their failure. We assume that components are in state M at time $t = 0$, that is all of them are functioning properly. To simplify, we set the assumption of complete degradation from fully functioning state to the absolute failure state. Furthermore, in the repairable system for each component i, time spent in the state k before its transition to the state $k - 1$, has a fully continuous distribution $F_i^k(t)$ with density $f_i^k(t)$ and mean μ_i^k. Moreover, we accept that repair time of the i-th element has a density $g_i(t)$, fully continuous distribution $G_i(t)$ and mean μ_i^0 with independent times spent in particular states.

Let present the notation for such system

$$P\big[X_i(t) = j\big] = a_i^i(t), \qquad j = 0, ..., M$$

$$a(t) = \big(a_1^1(t), ..., a_1^M(t), a_2^1(t), ..., a_2^M(t), ..., a_n^1(t), ..., a_n^M(t)\big)$$

$$p_\phi^j(a(t)) = P\Big[I\big(\phi(X(t) \ge j) = 1\big] = P\Big[\phi(X(t) \ge j)\Big],$$

where $a_i^j(t)$ at time t is the i-th component availability at level j and $p_\phi^j(a(t))$ at time t is the system availability to level j. For $j \in \mathfrak{M}$ and $i \in N$ there are corresponding availabilities

$$a_i^j = \lim_{t \to \infty} a_i^j(t) = \frac{\mu_i^j}{\sum_{l=0}^{M} \mu_i^l} = \bar{\mu}_i^j.$$

To simplify, let denote $a(t) \equiv a$.

2.4.1   The Birnbaum Importance Measure

The generalized Birnbaum importance measure in the multistate repairable system is given by

$$I_B^{(i,k,j)}(t) = p_\phi^j((e^k)_i, a(t)) - p_\phi^j((e^{k-1})_i, a(t)), \tag{4}$$

where $i = 1, ..., n$, $j, k \in \{1, ..., M\}$. From (1), (2) and (4) we may propose stationary measures for the same i, j, k, expressed as

$$I_B^{(i,k,j)} = \lim_{t \to \infty} I_B^{(i,k,j)}(t) = p_\phi^j((e^k)_i, a) - p_\phi^j((e^{k-1})_i, a)$$

$$I_B^{(i,j)} = \frac{\sum_{k=1}^M I_B^{(i,k,j)}}{\sum_{r=1}^n \sum_{k=1}^M I_B^{(r,k,j)}}, \qquad \text{where } 0 \le I_B^{(i,j)} \le 1 \text{ and } \sum_{i=1}^n I_B^{(i,j)} = 1$$

$$\hat{I}_B^{(i)} = \sum_{j=1}^M c_j \cdot I_B^{(i,j)}, \qquad \text{where } 0 \le \hat{I}_B^{(i)} \le 1 \text{ and } \sum_{i=1}^n \hat{I}_B^{(i)} = 1. \tag{5}$$

2.4.2   Universal Generating Function

Let us consider a multistate system in steady state with a constant demand w, (v. [20]), then we are able to extend the Birnbaum measure of the component importance

$$I_A^{(ij)}(w) = \frac{\partial A(w)}{\partial p_{ij}},$$

where p_{ij} stands for the probability of i-th component being in the specific state j with a rate of performance g_{ij} and $A(w)$ is a multistate system's steady-state availability with a constant demand w, given by

$$A(w) = \sum_{i=1}^M p_i \mathbb{1}(F(g_i, w) \ge 0),$$

where $j \in \mathfrak{M} \setminus \{0\}$, p_i is a steady-state probability that the system's performance is equal g_i and $F(g_i, w)$ is a function of acceptability.

Let introduce a universal generating function (UGF) $u(z)$, for the i-th component with m_i number of states g_{ij} and corresponding probabilities p_{ij}, Lisnianski [20], Qin et al. [29], we have

$$u_i(z) = \sum_{j=1}^{m_i} p_{ij} \cdot z^{g_{ij}}.$$

Therefrom, we have a u-function $U(z)$, expressed by

$$U(z) = \mathfrak{C}_f(u_1(z), u_2(z), ..., u_n(z)) \equiv \otimes(u_1(z), u_2(z), ..., u_n(z))$$

Demand can be a variable and then it may be described with two vectors: $w = \{w_1, ..., w_M\}$, where w_i is a possible level of demand, and $q = \{q_1, ..., q_M\}$, where q_i is a matching steady-state probability. Then, the extended Birnbaum's importance for any j-th component is given by

$$I_A^{(ij)}(w,q) = \sum_{m=1}^{M} q_m \cdot I_A^{(ij)}(w_m)$$

These importance measures depend on the i-th component's system position, its performance level and system demand. The UGF method, due to the simpler calculations and not necesarlly using Markov approach, is an excellent choice of computing importance.

2.4.3   The Barlow-Proschan Importance Measure

For $j,k \in \{1,...,M\}$ and $i = 1,...,n$ let introduce the number of jumps $N_i^{(k)}(t)$ from state k to $k-1$ of the i-th component in the time interval $[0,t]$, $\tilde{N}_i^{(k,j)}(t)$ which is the number of times in $[0,t]$, when system leaves states $\{j,...,M\}$ as a result of the i-th component jump from state k to $k-1$ and $\mathbf{E}N_i^{(k)}(t) \equiv M_i^{(k)}(t)$. From [4] for $j,k \in \{1,...,M\}$ and $i = 1,...,n$, we have

$$\mathbf{E}\tilde{N}_i^{(k,j)}(t) = \int_0^t I_B^{(i,k,j)}(s)dM_i^{(k)}(s)$$

with $I_B^{(i,k,j)}(t)$ defined as (4). Thus, time dependent generalized Barlow and Proschan importance measure $I_{B-P}^{(i,j)}(t)$ of the i-th component in the interval $[0,t]$ in the multistate repairable system and the corresponding weighted importance measure $\hat{I}_{B-P}^{(i)}(t)$ is given by

$$I_{B-P}^{(i,j)}(t) = \frac{\sum_{k=1}^{M} \mathbf{E}\tilde{N}_i^{(k,j)}(t)}{\sum_{r=1}^{n} \sum_{k=1}^{M} \mathbf{E}\tilde{N}_r^{(k,j)}(t)},$$

where $0 \le I_{B-P}^{(i,j)}(t) \le 1$ and $\sum_{i=1}^{n} I_{B-P}^{(i,j)}(t) = 1$,

$$\hat{I}_{B-P}^{(i)}(t) = \sum_{j=1}^{M} c_j \cdot I_{B-P}^{(i,j)}(t),$$

where $0 \le \hat{I}_{B-P}^{(i)}(t) \le 1$ and $\sum_{i=1}^{n} \hat{I}_{B-P}^{(i)}(t) = 1$.

Denote $\mu_i = \sum_{l=0}^{M} \mu_i^l$ and $\bar{I}_B^{(i,j)} = \sum_{k=1}^{M} I_B^{(i,k,j)} \cdot \mu_i^{-1}$. From Barlow and Proschan [4] we introduce analogous stationary measures

$$I_{B-P}^{(i,j)} = \lim_{t\to\infty} I_{B-P}^{(i,j)}(t) = \frac{\bar{I}_B^{(i,j)}}{\sum_{i=1}^{n} \bar{I}_B^{(i,j)}}, \tag{6}$$

$$\hat{I}_{B-P}^{(i)} = \sum_{j=1}^{M} c_j \cdot I_{B-P}^{(i,j)}, \tag{7}$$

where $\hat{I}_{B-P}^{(i,j)}$ is the weighted average of $I_{B-P}^{(i,j)}$, which is exactly the probability of component i downward jump being the reason that the system leaves $\{j, ..., M\}$ states.

Theorem 1. *For the multistate repairable system in series, where* $\phi(x) = \min\limits_{1 \leq i \leq n} x_i$, $i = 1, ..., n$ *and* $j \in \{1, ..., M\}$, *we have*

$$I_{B-P}^{(i,j)} = \frac{\frac{1}{\sum_{k=j}^{M} \mu_i^k}}{\sum_{r=1}^{n} \frac{1}{\sum_{k=j}^{M} \mu_r^k}}.$$

Proof. From (6) and (5) we have

$$I_{B-P}^{(i,j)} = \left(\frac{I_B^{(i,j,j)}}{\sum_{l=0}^{M} u_i^l} \right) \left(\sum_{r=1}^{n} \frac{I_B^{(r,j,j)}}{\sum_{l=0}^{M} u_r^l} \right)^{-1}$$

$$= \left(\frac{\prod\limits_{m \neq i} \frac{\sum_{k=j}^{M} \mu_m^k}{\sum_{l=0}^{M} \mu_m^l}}{\sum_{l=0}^{M} \mu_i^l} \right) \left(\sum_{r=1}^{n} \frac{\prod\limits_{m \neq r} \frac{\sum_{k=j}^{M} \mu_m^k}{\sum_{l=0}^{M} \mu_m^l}}{\sum_{l=0}^{M} \mu_r^l} \right)^{-1}$$

$$= \frac{\prod_{m \neq i} \sum_{k=j}^{M} \mu_m^k}{\sum_{r=1}^{n} \prod_{m \neq r} \sum_{k=j}^{M} \mu_m^k} = \frac{\frac{1}{\sum_{k=j}^{M} \mu_i^k}}{\sum_{r=1}^{n} \frac{1}{\sum_{k=j}^{M} \mu_r^k}}.$$

Theorem 2. *For the multistate repairable parallel system, where* $\phi(x) = \max\limits_{1 \leq i \leq n} x_i$, $i = 1, ..., n$ *and* $j \in \{1, ..., M\}$, *we obtain*

$$I_{B-P}^{(i,j)} = \frac{\frac{1}{\sum_{k=0}^{j-1} \mu_i^k}}{\sum_{r=1}^{n} \frac{1}{\sum_{k=0}^{j-1} \mu_r^k}}.$$

For the multistate system in series the stationary Barlow and Proschan importance measure of the component i decreases in μ_i^k for $k = j, ..., M$, the weaker the more important, and unsatisfactory is not dependent on component's mean time to repair.

Proof. The proof for the parallel system is analogous to the proof of the theorem 1

$$I_{B-P}^{(i,j)} = \frac{\frac{I_B^{(i,j,j)}}{\sum_{l=0}^{M} u_i^l}}{\sum_{r=1}^{n} \frac{I_B^{(r,j,j)}}{\sum_{l=0}^{M} u_r^l}} = \left(\frac{\prod\limits_{m \neq i} \frac{\sum_{k=0}^{j-1} \mu_m^k}{\sum_{l=0}^{M} \mu_m^l}}{\sum_{l=0}^{M} \mu_i^l} \right) \left(\sum_{r=1}^{n} \frac{\prod\limits_{m \neq r} \frac{\sum_{k=0}^{j-1} \mu_m^k}{\sum_{l=0}^{M} \mu_m^l}}{\sum_{l=0}^{M} \mu_r^l} \right)^{-1}$$

$$= \frac{\prod_{m \neq i} \sum_{k=0}^{j-1} \mu_m^k}{\sum_{r=1}^{n} \prod_{m \neq r} \sum_{k=0}^{j-1} \mu_m^k} = \frac{\frac{1}{\sum_{k=0}^{j-1} \mu_i^k}}{\sum_{r=1}^{n} \frac{1}{\sum_{k=0}^{j-1} \mu_r^k}}.$$

For the multistate system in parallel the stationary Barlow and Proschan importance measure of the component i also decreases in μ_i^k for $k = 1, ..., j - 1$ and in the μ_i^0, hence the better the more significant. Nonetheless, in this case the measure depends on mean times to repair of the component and also on mean times to jumps downward.

Theorem 3. *Let the component i be serial $(\phi(x) = min(x_i, \phi(M_i, x)))$ or parallel $(\phi(x) = max(x_i, \phi(0_i, x)))$ to the system. For $j \in \{1, ..., M\}$ and $k \neq i$ let $\sum_{l=j}^{M} \mu_i^l \leq \mu_k^M$ in series case and $\sum_{l=0}^{j-1} \mu_i^l \leq \mu_k^0$ in the parallel case, then $I_{B-P}^{(i,j)} \geq I_{B-P}^{(k,j)}$. In addition, the numerator has corresponding properties. Hence,*

$$\frac{\sum_{r=1}^{M} I_B^{(i,r,j)}}{\sum_{l=0}^{M} \mu_i^l} \geq \frac{\sum_{r=1}^{M} I_B^{(k,r,j)}}{\sum_{l=0}^{M} \mu_k^l} + \frac{p_\phi^j((e^0)_k, a)}{\sum_{l=j}^{M} \mu_i^l}$$

$$= \frac{\sum_{r=1}^{M} I_B^{(k,r,j)}}{\sum_{l=0}^{M} \mu_k^l} + \frac{1 - p_\phi^j((e^M)_k, a)}{\sum_{l=0}^{j-1} \mu_i^l}.$$

2.4.4 The Natvig Importance Measure

The Natvig measure for the multistate repairable systems is a natural extension of the one for nonrepairable system 2.3.3. For $m = 1, 2, ..., k \in \{0, ..., M\}$ and $i = 1, ..., n$ we introduce the i-th component's time of the m-th jump into state k given by $T_{i,k,m}$ and the i-th component's length of the m-th time of repair $D_{i,m}$, such that

$$T_{i,M,m} = T_{i,0,m} + D_{i,m}, \qquad \text{where } T_{i,M,0} = 0.$$

For the same i and m and $k \in \{0, ..., M - 1\}$ we introduce a $T'_{i,k,m}$, which is a fictive time of the i-th component's m-th jump into state k after it was believed to undergo a fictive minimal repair at $T_{i,k,m}$. Now, for the same i, m and $j, k \in \{1, ..., M\}$ we define $Y_{i,k,j,m}^1$ as the time of the system in $\{j, ..., M\}$ states in the period $[min(T_{i,k-1,m,t}, t), min(T'_{i,k-1,m,t}, t)]$ immediately after the i-th component changes the state from k to $k - 1$ and then its prompt fictive minimal repair. $Y_{i,k,j,m}^0$ is defined the same as $Y_{i,k,j,m}^1$, however it is assumed that the i-th component stays in its state and does not undergo any repair. Hence, we have

$$Z_{i,k,j,m} = Y_{i,k,j,m}^1 - Y_{i,k,j,m}^0.$$

To examine the effect of the fictitious minimal repairs, we need to sum up their contribution. Thus, for $j \in \{1, ..., M\}$, $k \in \{1, ..., M - 1\}$, $i = 1, ..., n$, and applying the expectation we obtain

$$\mathbf{E}\Big[\sum_{m=1}^{\infty} Z_{i,k,j,m} \cdot I\big(T_{i,k,m} \leq t\big) \Big] \overset{d}{=} \mathbf{E}Y_{i,k,j}(t)$$

$$\mathbf{E}\Big[\sum_{m=1}^{\infty} Z_{i,M,j,m} \cdot I\big(T_{i,M,m-1} \leq t\big) \Big] \overset{d}{=} \mathbf{E}Y_{i,M,j}(t).$$

Hence, for $j, k \in \mathfrak{M} \setminus \{0\}$, $i \in \mathbf{N}$ and assumption $\mathbf{E}Y_{i,k,j}(t) < \infty$, we obtain the generalized Natvig importance measure of the i-th component in the period of time $[0, t]$ expressed by $I_N^{(i,j)}(t)$ and its weighted version $\hat{I}_N^{(i,j)}(t)$, given by

$$I_N^{(i,j)}(t) = \frac{\sum_{k=1}^M \mathbf{E}Y_{i,k,j}(t)}{\sum_{r=1}^n \sum_{k=1}^M \mathbf{E}Y_{r,k,j}(t)},$$

where $0 \leq I_N^{(i,j)}(t) \leq 1$ and $\sum_{i=1}^n I_N^{(i,j)}(t) = 1$,

$$\hat{I}_N^{(i)}(t) = \sum_{j=1}^M c_j \cdot I_N^{(i,j)}(t),$$

where $0 \leq \hat{I}_N^{(i)}(t) \leq 1$ and $\sum_{i=1}^n \hat{I}_N^{(i)}(t) = 1$.

Theorem 4. *For* $k \in \{1, ..., M-1\}$

$$\mathbf{E}Y_{i,k,j}(t) = \int_0^t \int_u^t I_B^{(i,k,j)}(w) \cdot \bar{F}_i^k(w - u) \cdot \left(-\ln \hat{F}_i^k(w - u) \right) dw dM_i^{(k+1)}(u)$$

$$\mathbf{E}Y_{i,M,j}(t) = \int_0^t I_B^{(i,M,j)}(w) \cdot \bar{F}_i^M(w) \cdot \left(-\ln \hat{F}_i^M(w) \right) dw$$

$$+ \int_0^t \int_u^t I_B^{(i,M,j)}(w) \cdot \bar{F}_i^M(w - u) \cdot \left(-\ln \hat{F}_i^M(w - u) \right) dw dR_i(u)$$

The proof of the theorem can be found in Natvig [23]. Expressions in theorem 4 can be transformed into corresponding stationary importance measures by dividing by t and applying limit with respect to $t \to \infty$ and renewal theory argument presented by Barlow and Proschan [4]:

$$I_N^{(i,j)} = \lim_{t \to \infty} I_N^{(i,j)}(t) = \frac{\mu_i^{k(p)} \cdot \frac{\sum_{k=1}^M I_B^{(i,k,j)}}{\sum_{l=0}^M \mu_i^l}}{\sum_{r=1}^n \left(\mu_r^{k(p)} \cdot \frac{\sum_{k=1}^M I_B^{(r,k,j)}}{\sum_{l=0}^M \mu_r^l} \right)}$$

$$\hat{I}_N^{(i)} = \sum_{j=1}^M c_j \cdot I_N^{(i,j)}, \tag{8}$$

where

$$\mu_i^{k(p)} \overset{d}{=} \mathbf{E}[T'_{i,k-1,m} - T_{i,k-1,m}] = \int_0^\infty \bar{F}_i^k(t) \cdot (-\ln \bar{F}_i^k(t)) dt$$

Theorem 5. *For the multistate repairable series system, where* $j \in \{1, ..., M\}$ *and* $i = 1, ..., n$, *we have*

$$I_N^{(i,j)} = \frac{\mu_i^{j(p)}}{\sum_{k=j}^M \mu_i^k} \left(\sum_{r=1}^n \frac{\mu_r^{j(p)}}{\sum_{k=j}^M \mu_r^k} \right)^{-1}$$

and for parallel case we obtain

$$I_N^{(i,j)} = \frac{\mu_i^{j(p)}}{\sum_{k=0}^{j-1} \mu_i^k} \left(\sum_{r=1}^{n} \frac{\mu_r^{j(p)}}{\sum_{k=0}^{j-1} \mu_r^k} \right)^{-1}$$

Thus, the stationary measures (8) for the multistate system in series give unsatisfactory results due to not being dependent on components' mean time to repair. Unlike the series case, the stationary measure for the parallel system depend on mean time to repair as well as on the distribution of the downward transitions of components' states.

2.4.5 The Natvig Measure - Dual Extension

Since the Natvig measure does not give satisfactory results for all multistate systems, we introduce its dual extension. Now, for $m = 1, 2, \ldots$ and $i = 1, \ldots, n$, $T'_{i,M,m}$ is a fictive time of the i-th component's m-th jump into state M following a fictive minimal total failure at $T_{i,M,m}$. For the same i, m and $j \in \{1, \ldots, M\}$ we define $Y_{i,0,j,m}^1$ as the time of the system in $\{0, \ldots, j-1\}$ states in the period $[min(T_{i,M,m,t}, t), min(T'_{i,M,m,t}, t)]$ immediately after the i-th component state transition from 0 to M and its prompt fictive minimal total failure. $Y_{i,0,j,m}^0$ is defined the same as $Y_{i,k,j,m}^1$, however it is assumed that the i-th component stays in its state for the whole period. Hence, we have

$$Z_{i,0,j,m} = Y_{i,0,j,m}^1 - Y_{i,0,j,m}^0$$

$$Y_{i,0,j}(t) \stackrel{d}{=} \Big[\sum_{m=1}^{\infty} Z_{i,0,j,m} \cdot I(T_{i,0,m} \leq t) \Big]. \tag{9}$$

To examine the effect, we need to sum up repair contributions at $T_{i,M,m}$. Thus, for $i = 1, \ldots, n$, $j \in \{1, \ldots, M\}$, $m = 1, 2, \ldots$, and applying the expectation, we obtain

Theorem 6. *For $j \in \{1, \ldots, M\}$ and $i = 1, \ldots, n$*

$$\mathbf{E}Y_{i,0,j}(t) = \int_0^t \int_u^t \sum_{k=1}^M I_B^{(i,k,j)}(w) \cdot \bar{F}_i(w-u) \cdot (-\ln \bar{F}_i(w-u)) dw dM_i^1(u).$$

Hence, from (9) and Theorem 6, for $j \in \{1, \ldots, M\}$, $i = 1, \ldots, n$, $k \in \{0, \ldots, M\}$, and assumption of $\mathbf{E}Y_{i,k,j}(t) < \infty$, we obtain the dual generalized non-weighted and weighted Natvig measure, $I_{D,N}^{(i,j)}(t)$ and $\hat{I}_{D,N}^{(i)}(t)$ respectively, given by

$$I_{D,N}^{(i,j)}(t) = \frac{\mathbf{E}Y_{i,0,j}(t)}{\sum_{r=1}^n \mathbf{E}Y_{r,0,j}(t)}, \tag{10a}$$

where $0 \leq I_{D,N}^{(i,j)}(t) \leq 1$ and $\sum_{i=1}^n I_{D,N}^{(i,j)}(t) = 1$

$$\hat{I}_{D,N}^{(i)}(t) = \sum_{j=1}^M c_j \cdot I_{D,N}^{(i)}(t), \tag{10b}$$

where $0 \leq \hat{I}_{D,N}^{(i)}(t) \leq 1$ and $\sum_{i=1}^{n} \hat{I}_{D,N}^{(i)}(t) = 1$. Moreover, for the same i, k, j, and assumption of $\mathbf{E}Y_{i,k,j}(t) < \infty$, we may introduce extended versions of (10a) - $I_N^{*(i,j)}(t)$ and (10b) - $\hat{I}_N^{*(i)}(t)$, denoted as

$$I_N^{*(i,j)}(t) = \mathbf{E}Y_{i,0,j}(t) \left(\sum_{r=1}^{n} \mathbf{E}Y_{r,0,j}(t) \right)^{-1},$$

where $0 \leq I_N^{*(i,j)}(t) \leq 1$, $\sum_{i=1}^{n} I_N^{*(i,j)}(t) = 1$. We have $\hat{I}_N^{*(i)}(t) = \sum_{j=1}^{M} c_j \cdot I_N^{*(i,j)}(t)$, where $0 \leq \hat{I}_N^{*(i)}(t) \leq 1$ and $\sum_{i=1}^{n} \hat{I}_N^{*(i)}(t) = 1$. Furthermore, corresponding stationary measures for (10) are

$$I_{D,N}^{(i,j)} = \lim_{t \to \infty} I_{D,N}^{(i,j)}(t) = \frac{\mu_i^{0(p)} \cdot \frac{\sum_{k=1}^{M} I_B^{(i,k,j)}}{\sum_{l=0}^{M} \mu_i^l}}{\sum_{r=1}^{n} \left(\mu_r^{0(p)} \cdot \frac{\sum_{k=1}^{M} I_B^{(r,k,j)}}{\sum_{l=0}^{M} \mu_r^l} \right)}$$

$$I_N^{*(i,j)} = \lim_{t \to \infty} I_N^{*(i,j)}(t) = \frac{(\mu_i^{k(p)} + \mu_i^{0(p)}) \cdot \frac{\sum_{k=1}^{M} I_B^{(i,k,j)}}{\sum_{l=0}^{M} \mu_i^l}}{\sum_{r=1}^{n} \left((\mu_r^{k(p)} + \mu_r^{0(p)}) \cdot \frac{\sum_{k=1}^{M} I_B^{(r,k,j)}}{\sum_{l=0}^{M} \mu_r^l} \right)}$$

$$\hat{I}_{D,N}^{(i)} = \sum_{j=1}^{M} c_j \cdot I_{D,N}^{(i,j)}, \qquad \text{and} \qquad \hat{I}_N^{*(i)} = \sum_{j=1}^{M} c_j \cdot I_N^{*(i,j)},$$

where

$$\mu_i^{0(p)} \overset{d}{=} \mathbf{E}[T_{i,M,m}' - T_{i,M,m}] = \int_0^\infty \bar{G}_i(t) \cdot (-\ln \bar{G}_i(t)) dt$$

Theorem 7. *For the multistate repairable series system, where $j \in \{1, ..., M\}$ and $i = 1, ..., n$, we have*

$$I_N^{*(i,j)} = \frac{\mu_i^{j(p)} + \mu_i^{0(p)}}{\sum_{k=j}^{M} \mu_i^k} \left(\sum_{r=1}^{n} \frac{\mu_r^{j(p)} + \mu_r^{0(p)}}{\sum_{k=j}^{M} \mu_r^k} \right)^{-1}$$

and for parallel case we obtain

$$I_N^{*(i,j)} = \frac{\mu_i^{j(p)} + \mu_i^{0(p)}}{\sum_{k=0}^{j-1} \mu_i^k} \left(\sum_{r=1}^{n} \frac{\mu_r^{j(p)} + \mu_r^{0(p)}}{\sum_{k=0}^{j-1} \mu_r^k} \right)^{-1}$$

Thus, for both parallel and series repairable multistate system, the extended generalized Natvig measures depend on the repair times distribution and on the component's distribution of time to downward jumps, what gives a desirable results.

3   State Dependent Importance Measure

As in the case of binary systems and semi-coherent structures (v. [37]), also in multistate systems, we ask about the role (importance) of the structure element in maintaining it in the analyzed state. We focus on the element and its state c_{ij}. The responsibility for that is the place of the element in the structure and an inner properties of it emanated by its state. These are the basis for assessing its meaning. The set of elements of the system should be described their states: $\mathcal{C} = \mathcal{E} \times \mathcal{S} = \{(\vec{\mathbf{C}}_1, \vec{\mathbf{C}}_2, \ldots, \vec{\mathbf{C}}_s) : c_{ij} \in E \times S\}$, where vector components are the elements state. Let us imagine that each element has its administrator. If we treat the administrator of element in the system a player in a cooperative game, then in multi-state systems the tendency to remain in the examined state requires identifying the sets of elements (coalitions) responsible for that: the element and its state. The system may be in one of the numbered states $j \in S = \{1, 2, \ldots, K\}$. Let $\mathcal{P}_{ij}$ be a family of sets of states such that if $\mathcal{A} \in \mathcal{P}_i$, $c_{ij} \in \mathcal{A}$, then $\mathcal{A} \backslash \{c_{ij}\} \notin \mathcal{P}_{ij}$. Let $\bar{\mathcal{P}}_{ij}$ be a family of sets created from sets of the $\mathcal{P}_{ij}$ family by removing critical elements. We will take such a family as the basis for the aggregation of structure elements and, similarly to the multiplayer model with stopping moments as strategies (v. Szajowski and Yasuda [35]), the signal to stop will be the agreement of the elements from the set belonging to this family $\bar{\mathcal{P}}_{ij}$ (the coalitions between elements are formed taking into account thier states).

Multi-player decision problems assume that each game participant has a preference function based on a scalar function defined on the states of a certain process. If the elements of the structure are assigned to conservators (hypothetical players) who take care of the condition of these elements so that they fulfill their functions properly, the mentioned function can estimate profits and losses resulting from the state of the element. In principle, this condition should be form the set S. However, in reality, it is the diagnostician who decides when to perform maintenance or replacement (and bear the cost of it). An element in a system usually lowers its efficiency (e.g., mating components in a driveline may need lubrication to reduce friction, which results in increased energy expenditure and lower system efficiency), but the maintenance downtime is wasted and cannot always be managed. The operating conditions of the system make it possible to determine the correct payment function (cost) for each maintenance technician. Each of the n (which are less or equal the number of the elements in the structure) conservators, observing the states on which its payment depends, decides whether to order a maintenance break or to carry out uninterrupted operation. For safety reasons and the structure of the system, it is clear whether such a decision of a single observer is effective - it can start work when the system is stopped, and the stoppage requires the consensus of conservators from some critical path.

To analyze the effects of action, we will use the model of the following antagonistic game with elements of cooperation defined by the $\mathcal{P}_{ij}$, which are defined by the functionality of the structure and the state of the element i. Further consideration in this section assume that the conditionality structure is determined by $\mathcal{P}_{ij}$.

Following the results of the author and Yasuda [35] the multilateral stopping of a Markov chain problem can be described in the terms of the notation used in the non-cooperative game theory (see [21, 22, 27]). To this end the process and utilities of its states should be specified.

Definition 5. (ISS-Individual Stopping Strategies). *Let* $(\overrightarrow{X}_n, \mathcal{F}_n, \boldsymbol{P}_x)$, $n = 0, 1, 2, \ldots, N$, *be a homogeneous Markov chain with the state space* $(\mathbb{E}, \mathcal{B})$.

- *The players are able to observe the Markov chain sequentially. The horizon can be finite or infinite:* $N \in \mathbb{N} \cup \{\infty\}$.
- *Each player has their utility function* $f_i : \mathbb{E} \to \mathcal{R}\varepsilon$, $i = 1, 2, \ldots, p$, *such that* $\mathbb{E}_x |f_i(\overrightarrow{X}_1)| < \infty$ *and the cost function* $c_i : \mathbb{E} \to \mathcal{R}\varepsilon$, $i = 1, 2, \ldots, p$.
- *If the process is not stopped at moment* n, *then each player, based on* $\mathcal{F}_n$, *can declare independently their willingness to stop the observation of the process.*

Definition 6. (see [40]). *An individual stopping strategy of the player* i *(ISS) is the sequence of random variables* $\{\sigma_n^i\}_{n=1}^N$, *where* $\sigma_n^i : \Omega \to \{0, 1\}$, *such that* σ_n^i *is* $\mathcal{F}_n$*-measurable.*

The interpretation of the strategy is following. If $\sigma_n^i = 1$, then player i declares that they would like to stop the process and accept the realization of X_n.

Definition 7. (SS–Stopping Strategy (the aggregate function).). *Denote*

$$\sigma^i = (\sigma_1^i, \sigma_2^i, \ldots, \sigma_N^i)$$

and let $\mathscr{S}^i$ *be the set of ISSs of player* i, $i = 1, 2, \ldots, p$. *Define* $\mathscr{S} = \mathscr{S}^1 \times \mathscr{S}^2 \times \ldots \times \mathscr{S}^p$. *The element* $\sigma = (\sigma^1, \sigma^2, \ldots, \sigma^p)^T \in \mathscr{S}$ *will be called the stopping strategy (SS).*

The stopping strategy $\sigma \in \mathscr{S}$ is a random matrix. The rows of the matrix are the ISSs. The columns are the decisions of the players at successive moments. The factual stopping of the observation process, and the players realization of the payoffs is defined by the stopping strategy exploiting p-variate logical function.

Let $\delta : \{0, 1\}^p \to \{0, 1\}$ be the aggregation function. In this stopping game model the stopping strategy is the list of declarations of the individual players. The aggregate function δ converts the declarations to an effective stopping time.

Definition 8. (An aggregated SS). *A stopping time* $\tau_\delta(\sigma)$ *generated by the SS* $\sigma \in \mathscr{S}$ *and the aggregate function* δ *is defined by*

$$\tau_\delta(\sigma) = \inf\{1 \le n \le N : \delta(\sigma_n^1, \sigma_n^2, \ldots, \sigma_n^p) = 1\}$$

$(\inf(\emptyset) = \infty)$. *Since* δ *is fixed during the analysis we skip index* δ *and write* $\tau(\sigma) = \tau_\delta(\sigma)$.

Definition 9. (Process and utilities of its states).

- $\{\omega \in \Omega : \tau_\delta(\sigma) = n\} = \bigcap_{k=1}^{n-1}\{\omega \in \Omega : \delta(\sigma_k^1, \sigma_k^2, \ldots, \sigma_k^p) = 0\} \cap \{\omega \in \Omega : \delta(\sigma_n^1, \sigma_n^2, \ldots, \sigma_n^p) = 1\} \in \mathcal{F}_n;$
- $\tau_\delta(\sigma)$ *is a stopping time with respect to* $\{\mathcal{F}_n\}_{n=1}^N.$
- *For any stopping time* $\tau_\delta(\sigma)$ *and* $i \in \{1, 2, \ldots, p\}$ *the payoff of player* i *is defined as follows (cf. [33]):*

$$f_i(X_{\tau_\delta(\sigma)}) = f_i(X_n)\mathbb{I}_{\{\tau_\delta(\sigma)=n\}} + \limsup_{n \to \infty} f_i(X_n)\mathbb{I}_{\{\tau_\delta(\sigma)=\infty\}}.$$

Definition 10. (An equilibrium strategy (cf. [35])**).** *Let the aggregate rule* δ *be fixed. The strategy* $^*\sigma = (^*\sigma^1, ^*\sigma^2, \ldots, ^*\sigma^p)^T \in \mathscr{S}$ *is an equilibrium strategy with respect to* δ *if for each* $i \in \{1, 2, \ldots, p\}$ *and any* $\sigma^i \in \mathscr{S}^i$ *we have*

$$v_i(\overrightarrow{x}) = \mathbf{E}_x[f_i(\overrightarrow{X}_{\tau_\delta(^*\sigma)}) + \sum_{k=1}^{\tau_\delta(^*\sigma)} c_i(\overrightarrow{X}_{k-1})] \le \mathbf{E}_x[f_i(\overrightarrow{X}_{\tau_\delta(^*\sigma(i))}) + \sum_{k=1}^{\tau_\delta(^*\sigma(i))} c_i(\overrightarrow{X}_{k-1})].$$

Definition 11. (Voting Game Importance). *Let the aggregate rule* $\delta = h$ *be fixed and the strategy* $^*\sigma = (^*\sigma^1, ^*\sigma^2, \ldots, ^*\sigma^p)^T \in \mathscr{S}$ *be an equilibrium strategy with respect to* δ. *The voting game importance of the elements is the component of*

$$VGI = \frac{\mathbf{E}_{\overrightarrow{Q}^0}\,\overrightarrow{v}(\overrightarrow{X})}{\mathbf{E} < \overrightarrow{v}(\overrightarrow{X}), \overrightarrow{Q}^0 >}.$$

The measure of significance of a structure element introduced in this way takes into account its role in the structure by the aggregation function h, it is normalized in the sense that the measures of all elements sum up to 1. It takes into account the external loads of elements, the cost of maintenance and repairs. Its use requires in-depth knowledge of the system and its components, which is a significant obstacle in its introduction into diagnostic practice. The hardest part is figuring out the payout functions (cost, risk, profit). The simplified version of the method may include in the payout functions only the operating risk with components in a condition requiring maintenance or repair, which is usually associated with less safety.

4   Concluding Remarks

4.1   Summary

Ensuring the reliability and secure performance of the simple as well as complex systems has an indisputable significance in system analysis. Therefore, the aim of the research was to answer the question how to recognize the most influential elements of the system to improve its reliability. This paper has demonstrated several approaches to the concept of importance measure depending on the parameters and assumptions characterizing the system.

This analysis showed that the importance measures first introduced by Birnbaum in 1968 became the foundation for further search of more convenient and versatile definitions of the importance of components in system reliability and the stable exploration of the multistate systems. Since then, the research has expanded in different directions but until nowadays the importance evaluation of highly complex structures such as networks may cause many computational problems. Besides, restrictions regarding coherence may exclude examination of certain systems. Therefore, this subject is under constant exploration.

4.2   Important Direction of Further Investigations

Wu and Coolen [39], when interpreting component importance, concluded that the importance of a component should depend on the following factors:

1. The location of the component in the system.
2. The reliability of the component.
3. The uncertainty in the estimate of the component reliability and related cost.
4. The costs of maintaining this component in a given time interval $(0, t)$ and the state.

(v. also Rausand et al. [31]). The factor (3) highly depends on the statistical method implemented in the analyzes of exploratory data analyzes. Due to source of the data, the role of structure of the system to the reliability of it, the importance measure should take these elements into accounts. We are not observing the hidden state of the system directly and the information taken from the sensors should by interpreted and evaluated to infer on the hidden state of the elements and the system. The details of the construction needed, based on the results by Szajowski [36], are subject of a paper under editorial process. The works known to us show that betweenness centrality measure (v. Freeman [16]) is closely related to the Shapley value and Banzhaf value (v. Grofman and Owen [19]), and thus to importance measure in the reliability theory. While authors find it more convenient to use the terminology of reliability theory, the reader may as well transition to the terminology introduced by Freedman in community science. It would be at least potentially usable to discuss the various discoveries in general classification of the network elements by the game theory methods (v. e.g. Skibski et al. [34]).

Author contributions. Both authors equally contributed to the conceptualization, methodology, formal analysis, investigation and writing–original draft preparation. Małgorzata Średnicka is responsible for the description of the importance measure concepts, examples, visualisation (v. [32]) and Krzysztof J. Szajowski is responsible for the project conceptualization and its administration.

Funding Information. This research received no external funding. Springer remains neutral with regard to jurisdictional claims in published maps and institutional affiliations.

A   List of Symbols

Abbreviations

The following abbreviations are used in this manuscript:

$\emptyset$-An empty set(p. 68) $A, B, C-$ The sets of elements and its subsets (p. 48)

$\Omega_i, \mathcal{S}-$ the sets of states (p. 48) $|A|-$ the number of elements in A (p. 48)

$\times_{i \in A} \Omega_i = \Omega_1 \times \ldots \times \Omega_{|A|}$-the Cartesian $A' = C \setminus A$-A' is the complement product of sets (p. 48)   of A to the space of elements C (p. 48)

$\vec{x} = (x_1, x_2, \ldots, x_n)$

$\vec{x}_{-j} = (x_1, \ldots, x_{j-1}, x_{j+1}, \ldots, x_n)$ $(a, \vec{x}_{-j}) = (x_1, \ldots, x_{j-1}, a, x_{j+1}, \ldots, x_n)$

$\vec{1} = (1, 1, \ldots, 1)$ $\vec{0} = (0, 0, \ldots, 0)$

$B^{|J|} = \times_{j \in J} B_j$, where $B_j = B, J \subset \mathbf{N}$ $\vec{x}^J = (x_{i_1}, x_{i_2}, \ldots, x_{i_{|J|}}) \in B^{|J|}, J \subset \mathbf{N}$

$\vec{x}^J = \vec{x}_{-(\mathbf{N} \setminus J)} \in B^{|J|}$, where $J \subset \mathbf{N}$ $\langle \vec{x}, \vec{y} \rangle-$ the inner product in $\mathfrak{Re}^n$

$(a, \vec{x}_{-j}) = (\vec{x}_{-j}, a) = (x_1, \ldots, x_{j-1}, a, x_{j+1}, \ldots, x_n)$

$\vec{F}(t) = (F_1(t), F_2(t), \ldots, F_n(t))$ $\prod_{i=1}^{n} p_i = p_1 \cdot p_2 \cdot \ldots \cdot p_n$ (p. 58)

$\preceq$ The partial ordering (p. 69)

BS   Binary system (p. 67)   **MSS**   Multi-state system (p. 67)

PRAs   Probabilistic Risk Assessments

B   Endnotes

B.1   Risk

It is difficult to define *risk* in general. In short, when we think about risk, we mean the possibility of an unexpected loss caused by an unpredictable event or harmful behavior (human, machine, animal, nature). One can think about the possibility of loss or injury. From the other side, the risk is the chance or probability that a person (a system) will be harmed or experience an adverse health (functioning) effect if exposed to a hazard. It may also apply to situations with property or equipment loss, or harmful effects on the environment. Therefore, we are talking about reducing ownership and loss as a result of a random event. Risk reduction means minimizing the chance of a loss occurring or limiting its size. To better understand the risk and the possibilities of risk management, the task of measuring risk has been set. The task is not formulated so that its solution is universal. This allowed to determine the desired properties of such measures [3].

B.2   General Idea of Importance Measure

The systems can be split into two categories: (i) binary systems (BS) and (ii) multistate systems (MSS).

     There are four main classes of importance measures (v. Birnbaum [9], Amrutkar and Kamalja [2])

  (I) Reliability importance measure
 (II) Structural importance measure
(III) Lifetime importance measure
(IV) Failure and its recovery costs importance measure

The cost of failure (leaving the given state) and its recovery importance measure (IV) depends on the lifetime distribution of the component, its position in the system, and the loss related to the nonavailability of the system in the given state, diagnosis and repair. It is a new look at the importance of the components of a complex system. The analysis and significance measure proposed in this paper is based on the possibility of observing the components and a rational system maintenance policy, which consists in stopping the system for maintenance and repair at a time when it pays off to a sufficient number of components. The details are based on a cooperative analysis of costs and losses in the operation of such a system (v. Sect. 3, Szajowski and Yasuda [35]).

B.3   Review of Importance Measure Concepts

Since Birnbaum [8, 9] the importance measures were investigated and extended in various directions (v. Amrutkar and Kamalja [2]). The basis for the construction of significance measures is the observation that the binary system is well modeled by random graphs. The basis is the concept of structure.

Definition 12 (The structure). *For a non-empty and finite set N^7, we denote by $\mathcal{P}$ the family of subsets N having the following properties*

(1) $\emptyset \in \mathcal{P}$
(2) $N \in \mathcal{P}$;
(3) $S \subseteq T \subseteq N$ and $S \in \mathcal{P}$ imply $T \in \mathcal{P}$.

The family $\mathcal{P}$ is called structure.

This basic structure has been studied in many areas under a variety of names. Monograph by Ramamurthy [30] unified the definitions and concepts in two main fields of application, that is cooperative game theory (simple games) (v. Tijs [38, Chapt. 10]) and reliability theory (semi-coherent and coherent structures, v. Esary and Proschan [15], Barlow and Wu [6], Ohi [26]).

    The relationships with cooperative games can be helpful in determining the importance of elements for the reliability of the system and at the same time a role in the possibility of efficient diagnosis in the event of a failure, as well as in determining the rules of the procedure for removing a failure. Removing the failure causes that the features of the element and the repaired module are restored. However, it should be remembered that the method of repair and the quality of the elements used reproduce the original features to varying degrees (v. e.g.

---

[7] The list of symbols and abbreviations used in the work has been collected in the section abbreviation on page 25.

Navarro et al. [25]). This has an impact on further operation, diagnosis and main-tenance (uplift). Rules are easier to set when they are associated with objective measures of the features of components, modules, and the system. Analysis of significance measures in the context of repair helps to understand such relation-ships. Let us therefore establish these relationships (v. Do and Bérenguer [11]).

In game theory, consider the set $C = \{1, 2, \ldots, n\}$ of players and the power set 2^C of coalitions. A function $\lambda : 2^C \to \{0, 1\}$ is called a simple game on C in characteristic function form if

(1) $\lambda(\emptyset) = 0$;
(2) $\lambda(C) = 1$;
(3) $S \subseteq T \subseteq C$ implies $\lambda(S) \leq \lambda(T)$.

A coalition $S \subset C$ is called winning if $\lambda(S) = 1$ and it is called blocking if $\lambda(C \backslash S) = 0$. Indeed, the collection of winning (or blocking) coalitions in a simple game satisfies the three properties of the basic structure mentioned at the beginning.

In reliability theory, consider the set $C = \{1, 2, \ldots, n\}$ of components with which a system g has been built. The state of the system as well as any compo-nent can either be 0 (a failed state) or 1 (a functioning state). The knowledge of the system is represented by the knowledge of the structure function of the system, which is defined as a switching function (Boolean) $g : \{0, 1\}^n \to \{0, 1\}$ of n variables (or n dimensional vector $\vec{x}$)[8]. The structure function g (simply the structure g) is called semicoherent if (1) g is monotone, i.e. $\vec{x} \preceq \vec{y}$ implies $g(\vec{x}) \leq g(\vec{y})$, and (2) $g(\vec{0}) = 0$ and $g(\vec{1}) = 1$.

The semicoherent structure can be called coherent when all its elements are significant. A subset $A \subset C$ is called a path set of g, if $g(\vec{1}^A, \vec{0}^{C \backslash A}) = 1$, i.e. the system is working if the items forming the set A [resp. $C \backslash A$] are working [resp. failed]. Similarly, $A \subset C$ is called a cut set of g, if $g(\vec{0}^A, \vec{1}^{C \backslash A}) = 0$. Clearly, the assemblage of path [cut] sets of a semicoherent structure g satisfies the three properties of the basic structure mentioned at the beginning.

B.4   Cooperative Games vs. Semicoherent Systems

[30, Sect. 2] indicates the correspondence between the terminology of cooperative game theory and reliability by means of a list of equivalent notions: players or components; simple game or semicoherent structure; characteristic function or structure function; winning [blocking] coalition or path [cut] set; minimal winning [blocking] coalition or minimal path [cut] set. The review of the various types of simple games and semicoherent structures encountered in the literature are mentioned there. The most interesting is [30, Chap. 3], where a detailed study of the problem of assessing the importance [power] of components [players] comprising the system [game] is described. The emphasis is on the probabilistic approach to the quantification of relative importance.

---

[8] With the same symbol, we denote the system and the analytical description of the system using the structure function wherever it does not lead to misunderstandings.

References

1. Abouammoh, A.M., El-Neweihi, E., Sethuraman, J.: The role of a group of modules in the failure of systems. Prob. Eng. Inf. Sci. **8**(1), 89–101 (1994). https://doi.org/10.1017/S0269964800003223

2. Amrutkar, K.P., Kamalja, K.K.: An overview of various importance measures of reliability system. Int. J. Math. Eng. Manag. Sci. **2**(3), 150–171 (2017)

3. Artzner, P., Delbaen, F., Eber, J.-M., Heath, D.: Coherent measures of risk. Math. Financ. **9**(3), 203–228 (1999). https://doi.org/10.1111/1467-9965.00068. ISSN 0960-1627; 1467–9965/e

4. Barlow, R.E., Proschan, F.: Importance of system components and fault tree events. Stoch. Proc. Their Appl. **3**(2), 153–173 (1975). https://doi.org/10.1016/0304-4149(75)90013-7. ISSN 0304-4149

5. Barlow, R.E., Proschan, F.: Mathematical Theory of Reliability. Classics in Applied Mathematics, vol. 17. SIAM, Philadelphia (1996). ISBN 0-89871-369-2. With contributions by Larry C. Hunter, Reprint of the 1965 original. https://doi.org/10.1137/1.9781611971194. MR 1392947

6. Barlow, R.E., Wu, A.S.: Coherent systems with multi-state components. Math. Oper. Res. **3**(4), 275–281 (1978). https://doi.org/10.1287/moor.3.4.275. ISSN 0364-765X

7. Barlow, R.E., Fussell, J.B., Singpurwalla, N.D. (eds.) Reliability and Fault Tree Analysis. SIAM, Philadelphia (1975). Theoretical and applied aspects of system reliability and safety assessment, Conference held at the University of California, Berkeley, California, 3–7 September 1974, Dedicated to Professor Z. W. Birnbaum

8. Birnbaum, Z.W.: On the importance of components in a system. In: European Meeting 1968, Selected Statistical Paper, vol. 2, pp. 83–95 (1968)

9. Birnbaum, Z.W.: On the importance of different components in a multicomponent system. In: Krishnaiah, P. (ed.) Multivariate Analysis, II (Proceedings of Second International Symposium, Dayton, Ohio, 1968), pp. 581–592. Academic Press, New York (1969)

10. Cao, Y., Liu, S., Fang, Z.: Importance measures for degrading components based on cooperative game theory. Int. J. Qual. Reliabil. Manag. **37**(2), 189–206 (2019). https://doi.org/10.1108/IJQRM-10-2018-0278

11. Do, P., Bérenguer, C.: Conditional reliability-based importance measures. Reliabil. Eng. Syst. Saf. **193**, 106633 (2020). https://doi.org/10.1016/j.ress.2019.106633. ISSN 0951-8320

12. El-Neweihi, E., Sethuraman, J.: A study of the role of modules in the failure of systems. Probab. Eng. Inf. Sci. **5**(2), 215–227 (1991). ISSN 0269-9648; 1469–8951/e

13. El-Neweihi, E., Proschan, F., Sethuraman, J.: A simple model with applications in structural reliability, extinction of species, inventory depletion and urn sampling. Adv. Appl. Probab. **10**, 232–254 (1978). ISSN 0001-8678

14. Erdős, P., Rényi, A.: On random graphs. I. Publ. Math. Debrecen **6**, 290–297 (1959). ISSN 0033-3883. MR 120167

15. Esary, J.D., Proschan, F.: Coherent structures of non-identical components. Technometrics **5**, 191–209 (1963). ISSN 0040-1706; 1537–2723/e

16. Freeman, L.C.: A set of measures of centrality based on betweenness. Sociometry **40**(1), 35–41 (1977). https://doi.org/10.2307/3033543. ISSN 00380431

17. Fussell, J., Vesely, W.: New methodology for obtaining cut sets for fault trees. Trans. Am. Nucl. Soc. **15**(1), 262–263 (1972). 18. Annual American Nuclear Society Conference, Las Vegas, Nevada, 18 June 1972

18. Gilbert, E.N.: Random graphs. Ann. Math. Statist. **30**, 1141–1144 (1959). https://doi.org/10.1214/aoms/1177706098. ISSN 0003-4851
19. Grofman, B., Owen, G.: A game theoretic approach to measuring degree of centrality in social networks. Soc. Netw. **4**(3), 213–224 (1982/83). ISSN 0378-8733. https://doi.org/10.1016/0378-8733(82)90022-3
20. Lisnianski, A.: Multi-state System Reliability Analysis and Optimization for Engineers and Industrial Managers. Springer, London (2010). https://doi.org/10.1007/978-1-84996-320-6
21. Moulin, H.: Game theory for the Social Sciences. Studies in Game Theory and Mathematical Econofnic, New York University Press, New York (1982). ISBN 0- 8147-5386-8/hbk; 0-8147-5387-6/pbk. Transl. from the French by the author. Zbl 0626.90095
22. Nash, J.: Non-cooperative games. Ann. Math. **2**(54), 286–295 (1951). https://doi.org/10.2307/1969529. ISSN 0003-486X. MR 43432
23. Natvig, B.: Measures of component importance in nonrepairable and repairable multistate strongly coherent systems. Methodol. Comput. Appl. Probab. **13**(3), 523–547 (2011). https://doi.org/10.1007/s11009-010-9170-2. ISSN 1387-5841
24. Natvig, B.: Multistate systems reliability theory with applications. Wiley Series in Probability and Statistics, Wiley, Chichester (2011). https://doi.org/10.1002/9780470977088. ISBN 978-0-470-69750-4
25. Navarro, J., Arriaza, A., Suárez-Llorens, A.: Minimal repair of failed components in coherent systems. Eur. J. Oper. Res. **279**(3), 951–964 (2019). ISSN 0377-2217. Zbl 1430.90217
26. Ohi, F.: Multistate coherent systems. In: Stochastic Reliability Modeling, Optimization And Applications, pp. 3–34. World Scientific Publishing, Co., Pte. Ltd. (2010). ISBN 9789814277440
27. Owen, G.: Game Theory, 4th edn. Emerald Group Publication, Limited, Bingley (2013). ISBN 987-1-7819-0507-4. MR 3443071
28. Ping, Z.: Measures of importance with applications to inspection policies. ProQuest LLC, Ann Arbor, MI (2004). ISBN 978-0496-73752-9. https://www.proquest.com/docview/305074799. Thesis (Ph.D.)–Univ. of Illinois at Chicago. MR 2705807
29. J. Qin, Y. Niu, and Z. Li. A combined method for reliability analysis of multistate system of minor-repairable components. Eksploatacja niezawodnoŚć - Maint. Reliabil. **20**(1) (2016). https://doi.org/10.17531/ein.2016.1.11
30. Ramamurthy, K.G.: Coherent Structures and Simple Games. Theory and Decision Library. Series C: Game Theory, Mathematical Programming and Operations Research, vol. 6. Kluwer Acadamic Publication Group, Dordrecht (1990). ISBN 0-7923-0869-7. https://doi.org/10.1007/978-94-009-2099-6
31. Rausand, M., Barros, A., Høyland, A.: System Reliability Theory. Models, Statistical Methods, and Applications. Wiley, Hoboken (2021). ISBN 978-1-119-37352-0. 2nd ed.: ISBN 0-471-47133-X. xix, 636 p. (2004)
32. Średnicka, M.: Importance measure in multi-state systems reliability. Master's thesis, Wrocław Univ. of Sci. & Tech., Poland (2019). 40 p
33. Shiryayev, A.N.: Optimal Stopping Rules. Springer, New York (1978). English translation of Статистический последователный анализ by A. B. Aries
34. Skibski, O., Rahwan, T., Michalak, T. P., Wooldridge, M.: Enumerating connected subgraphs and computing the Myerson and Shapley values in graph-restricted games. ACM Trans. Intell. Syst. Technol. **10**(2) (2019). https://doi.org/10.1145/3235026. ISSN 2157-6904

35. Szajowski, K., Yasuda, M.: Voting procedure on stopping games of Markov chain. In: Christer, A.H., Osaki, S., Thomas, L.C. (eds.) Stochastic Modelling in Innovative Manufacturing. Lecture Notes in Economics and Mathematical Systems, vol. 445, pp. 68–80. Springer, Heidelberg (1997). https://doi.org/10.1007/978-3-642-59105-1_6

36. Szajowski, K.J.: Rationalization of detection of the multiple disorders. Stat. Pap. **61**(4), 1545-1563 (2020). ISSN 0932-5026; 1613-9798/e. https://doi.org/10.1007/s00362-020-01168-2. Zbl 1448.91017

37. Szajowski, K.J., Średnicka, M.: Operation comfort vs. the importance measure of system components. Math. Appl. **48**(2), 191–226 (2020). ISSN 1730-2668. https://doi.org/10.14708/ma.v48i2.7058. MR 4243105

38. Tijs, S.: Introduction to Game Theory. Texts and Readings in Mathematics, vol. 23. Hindustan Book Agency, New Delhi (2003). ISBN 81-85931-37-2

39. Wu, S., Coolen, F.P.: A cost-based importance measure for system components: An extension of the Birnbaum importance. European J. Oper. Res. **225**(1), 189–195 (2013). https://doi.org/10.1016/j.ejor.2012.09.034. ISSN 0377-2217

40. Yasuda, M., Nakagami, J., Kurano, M.: Multivariate stopping problems with a monotone rule. J. Oper. Res. Soc. Jpn. **25**(4), 334–350 (1982). ISSN 0453-4514. https://doi.org/10.15807/jorsj.25.334. MR 692543

Implicit Power Indices for Measuring Indirect Control in Corporate Structures

Jochen Staudacher[1]([✉]) [iD], Linus Olsson[1], and Izabella Stach[2] [iD]

[1] Fakultät Informatik, Hochschule Kempten,
Bahnhofstr. 61, 87435 Kempten, Germany
jochen.staudacher@hs-kempten.de, linus.m.olsson@stud.hs-kempten.de
[2] AGH University of Science and Technology,
Al. Mickiewicza 30, 30-059 Kraków, Poland
istach@zarz.agh.edu.pl

Abstract. This article deals with measuring indirect control in complex corporate shareholding networks using the concept of power indices from cooperative game theory. We focus on the approaches by Mercik-Łobos and Stach-Mercik which measure the control power of all firms involved in shareholding networks with algorithms based on the raw Johnston index. We point out how these approaches can be generalized replacing the raw Johnston index by various other power indices in a modular fashion. We further extend the algorithmic framework by investigating more than one regression and present requirements for software and modelling. Finally, we test the new framework of generalized implicit power indices for a network with 21 players and discuss how properties of the underlying power index like efficiency or null player removability influence the measurements of indirect control.

Keywords: Cooperative game theory · Power indices · Corporate shareholding structures · Direct and indirect control

1 Introduction

Measuring the power of firms in complex corporate shareholding networks can be difficult and challenging. Such networks can be large and may contain cycles of cross-ownership as well as pyramidal constructions and several layers of ownership [18,19,37]. Frequently, it is far from obvious if a firm is in control of other companies or how much power a firm possesses in the whole network.

In this paper we employ the concept of power indices from the theory of cooperative games as it provides a rigorous approach for estimating indirect control. The idea of power indices for measuring voting power goes back as far as Luther Martin, a Maryland delegate who participated in drafting the constitution of the United States in 1787 [48], but it was not formalized before Penrose (1946) [47] and Shapley and Shubik (1954) [50]. However, it was only the pioneering work by Gambarelli and Owen (1994) [23] that started the usage of power indices

© Springer-Verlag GmbH Germany, part of Springer Nature 2021
N. T. Nguyen et al. (Eds.): TCCI XXXVI, LNCS 13010, pp. 73–93, 2021.
https://doi.org/10.1007/978-3-662-64563-5_4

for corporate networks. Their approach was restricted to computing the voting power of investors, i.e. firms without shareholdings, in networks without loops. However, we wish to refrain from giving a comprehensive overview of the historic developments or the literature in this field and refer to [10, 11, 18, 19, 46, 52] instead.

This article concentrates on power index based approaches estimating the direct and indirect control power of all firms (meaning both the investors and the stock companies they control) in a corporate shareholding structure. To our knowledge, there exists only a small number of such methods, namely the approaches by Karos and Peters [32, 33], by Levy and Szafarz [39] as well as the algorithm by Mercik and Łobos [44] and its modification by Mercik and Stach [46]. The purpose of this article is to generalize the Mercik-Łobos and Stach-Mercik implicit indices by employing a number of different power indices in place of the raw Johnston index [31] originally used in [44, 46]. The new framework of generalized implicit power indices appeals due to its straightforward and modular structure. It can be regarded as an extension and generalization of a 2020 article [55] in this series where the raw Johnston index [31] was replaced by the absolute Banzhaf index [6, 12] within the Stach-Mercik method. We implemented our algorithms using the R programming environment and point out how we structured our software for indirect control making use of R packages for graph theory and the computation of power indices. In this sense, our paper also answers a demand for efficient software for game-theoretic methods in indirect control made at the very end of a previous paper by Mercik and Stach (2018) [46] in this series.

The article is structured as follows: Sect. 2 introduces the concepts and definitions from cooperative game theory as well as all the power indices used later in the paper. Section 3 forms the heart of methodological innovation of this work. It first motivates the problem of indirect control in shareholding networks with an example with 21 players. Then we generalize the Mercik-Łobos and Stach-Mercik [46] frameworks by replacing the raw Johnston index with other power indices. Section 4 discusses computational and software aspects (thereby presenting both possibilities and limitations of the implementation) and argues why we decided to use the R environment. Section 5 discusses results for our network with 21 players pointing out favourable and unfavourable properties of power indices employed within our framework. In Sect. 6 we present our conclusions and an outlook to further research directions.

2   Preliminaries on Power Indices and Cooperative Game Theory

2.1   Cooperative Game Theory and Simple Games

Cooperative game theory [17, 24] studies the outcomes and benefits which players can achieve by entering into coalitions.

Let us briefly review the terminology for the definition of a TU cooperative game, i.e. a cooperative game with transferable utility. Let $N = \{1, ..., n\}$ be a finite set of n players. A group of players $S \subseteq N$ is called a coalition, whereas 2^N denotes the set of all subsets of N. The *empty coalition* is denoted by $\emptyset$ and the *grand coalition* is denoted by N. By $|S|$ we denote the cardinality of a coalition S, i.e. the number of its members, hence $|N| = n$. An n-person TU cooperative game can now be described as a pair (N, v) where $v : 2^N \to \mathbb{R}$ is the so-called *characteristic function* which assigns a real value to all coalitions $S \in 2^N$ whereby $v(\emptyset) = 0$. A cooperative game is called *monotone* if for all coalitions $S, T \in 2^N$ the relation $S \subseteq T$ implies $v(S) \leq v(T)$.

Furthermore, we call a cooperative game *simple* if it is monotone and $v(S) = 0$ or $v(S) = 1$ for each coalition $S \subseteq N$. Coalitions for which $v(S) = 1$ are referred to as *winning coalitions* in simple games, whereas coalitions for which $v(S) = 0$ are called *losing coalitions*. A player i is called a *critical player* (also known as a decisive player or swing player) in a winning coalition S if $v(S \backslash \{i\}) = 0$, i.e. the winning coalition S turns into a losing one if player i is missing. In return, a player i who is never critical for any coalition $S \in 2^N$, i.e. $v(S \cup i) - v(S) = 0$, is referred to as a *null player*. The set of coalitions for which player $i \in N$ is critical is denoted by $C_i = \{S \subseteq N : i \in S \wedge v(S) = 1 \wedge v(S \backslash \{i\}) = 0\}$ and $Cr(S)$ stands for the set of critical players for each coalition $S \in 2^N$. A coalition S with a least one critical player, i.e. $|Cr(S)| > 0$, is called a *vulnerable* coalition and by VC we denote the set of all vulnerable coalitions in our simple game. We call a coalition S a *minimal winning coalition* if every player $i \in S$ is a critical player.

Weighted voting games (also known as weighted majority games) are a very important subclass of simple games with plenty of practical applications. Weighted voting games are specified by n non-negative real weights $w_i, i = 1, \ldots, n$, and a non-negative real quota q, normally $q > \frac{1}{2} \sum_{i=1}^{n} w_i$. The corresponding characteristic function $v : 2^N \to \{0, 1\}$ takes the value $v(S) = 1$ if coalition S is winning, i.e. $w(S) = \sum_{i \in S} w_i \geq q$, and $v(S) = 0$ otherwise, meaning that coalition S is losing. We will later use weighted voting games to define voting situations in stock companies and hence they are the foundation for the game-theoretical approaches for estimating indirect control in corporate networks.

2.2 Power Indices

In general, a *power index* f is a function mapping a unique vector $f(v) = (f_1(v), \ldots, f_n(v))$ to a given simple n-person cooperative game specified by its player set N and its characteristic function v. In the following we present five properties of power indices and afterwards we define those power indices investigated in the rest of the article. For a deeper discussion of the subject we refer to the overview article by Bertini, Freixas, Gambarelli and Stach (2013) [9].

A power index f satisfies the *efficiency property* if for all simple games (N, v) (which are not the null game) there holds $\sum_{i=1}^{n} f_i(v) = v(N) = 1$. It possesses the *null player property* if $f_i(v) = 0$ for each null player $i \in N$ and all simple games (N, v). The *symmetry property* (also known as equal treatment property and different from the anonymity property, see Algaba, Fragnelli and Sánchez-Soriano (2020b) [4] and Malawski (2020) [41]) is fulfilled if, for all simple games (N, v) and each pair of players $i, j \in N$ satisfying $v(S \cup \{i\}) = v(S \cup \{j\})$ for all coalitions $S \in 2^{N \setminus \{i,j\}}$, the equality $f_i(v) = f_j(v)$ holds. The *non-negativity property* requires $f_i(v) \geq 0$ for all players $i \in N$ and all simple games (N, v). Finally, a power index f is said to have the *null-player removable property* if, after the removal of any null players from any simple game (N, v), the power measures for all non-null players are unchanged.

In the following, we define several well-established power indices, i.e. the Banzhaf, Deegan-Packel, Johnston, Public Good and Shapley-Shubik index and their variants. Let v be a simple n-player game, let W and W^m denote the sets of winning coalitions and minimal winning coalitions, respectively, and W_i and W_i^m the corresponding subsets containing player i. Further, we remind the reader that VC stands for the set of vulnerable coalitions and let $\eta_i(v) = |C_i|$ denote the number of coalitions for which i is a critical player and $\eta_i(v, c)$ the number of coalitions of cardinality c for which i is a critical player.

a) The *(absolute) Banzhaf index* [6,12] of player i is defined as

$$B_i = \frac{\eta_i(v)}{2^{n-1}}.$$

The *relative Banzhaf index* [12]

$$b_i = \frac{\eta_i(v)}{\sum_{k=1}^{n} \eta_k(v)}$$

is frequently used as an efficient counterpart, i.e. $\sum_{i=1}^{n} b_i = v(N) = 1$. Sometimes the number of swings $\mathcal{B}_i = \eta_i(v)$ itself is referred to as the *raw Banzhaf index* of player i, see e.g. [17], p. 118.

b) The *Deegan-Packel index* [21] of player i is defined as

$$d_i = \frac{1}{|W^m|} \sum_{S \in W_i^m} \frac{1}{|S|}.$$

If we forgo the scaling by $|W^m|$, we lose the efficiency property and receive the *raw Deegan-Packel index* of player i

$$D_i = \sum_{S \in W_i^m} \frac{1}{|S|}.$$

c) The *Johnston index* [31] of player i is defined as

$$j_i = \frac{\sum_{S \in VC, i \in Cr(S)} \frac{1}{|Cr(S)|}}{\sum_{k=1}^{n} \sum_{S \in VC, k \in Cr(S)} \frac{1}{|Cr(S)|}}$$

if i is not a null player and $j_i = 0$ otherwise. Correspondingly, the *raw Johnston index* of player i is given as

$$J_i = \sum_{S \in VC, i \in Cr(S)} \frac{1}{|Cr(S)|}$$

if i is not a null player and $J_i = 0$ otherwise. It loses the efficiency property of the Johnston index.

d) The *relative Public Good index* (also known as relative Holler index) [26,27, 30] of player i is defined as

$$h_i = \frac{|W_i^m|}{\sum_{k=1}^n |W_k^m|}.$$

In analogy to the absolute Banzhaf index, we can call

$$H_i = \frac{|W_i^m|}{|W^m|}.$$

the *absolute Public Good index* (or absolute Holler index) of player i, see [8,15]. Holler and Li (1995) [28] generalize the relative Public Good index from simple games to cooperative games and look at the quantity $|W_i^m|$ itself. The expression $\mathcal{H}_i = |W_i^m|$ is sometimes also referred to as a power index, see e.g. [13], and we henceforth call it the *raw Public Good index* (or raw Holler index) of player i.

e) The *Shapley-Shubik index* [50,51] of player i is defined as

$$\sigma_i = \sum_{c=1}^n \frac{\eta_i(v, c)}{c \binom{n}{c}}.$$

The Shapley-Shubik index is derived from the Shapley value, which was originally defined by Shapley (1953) [49] and is one of the most prominent solution concepts in cooperative game theory. For new theoretical and applied results on the Shapley value we refer to Algaba, Fragnelli and Sánchez-Soriano (2020a) [3].

We finally note that all the power indices defined above from a) to c) possess the null player, symmetry, non-negativity properties, see e.g. [9]. It is straightforward to show that only the raw Johnston and raw Banzhaf indices lack the null player removable property and that the "absolute" and "raw" indices are the ones which are not efficient.

3 A General Framework of Implicit Indices for Indirect Control

3.1 Modelling of Corporate Shareholding Networks

Corporate networks can be modelled as weighted directed graphs [18]. Therefore we briefly introduce some graph-theoretic concepts according to the textbook by

Bang-Jensen and Gutin (2008) [5] and the article by Crama and Leruth (2007) [18]. The firms of the corporate network correspond to the set of vertices V, while the arc set $A \subseteq V \times V$ describes the linkages between the firms. For each arc $(i,j) \in A$ the weight $w_{i,j}$ is the fraction of share ownership of firm i in firm j. For $(i,j) \in A$, i denotes a predecessor of j, while j is a successor of i. A path is a sequence of vertices $(i_1, ..., i_k)$ such that $(i_p, i_{p+1}) \in A$ for $p = 1, ..., k-1$, while no vertex is repeated. A path is called a cycle if $i_1 = i_k$. This means that cross-shareholdings become apparent through cycles in the directed graph.

For each $j \in V$, V_j denotes the set of predecessors of firm j. When $V_j = \emptyset$, firm j is called an *investor*, i.e. firm j is modelled as an uncontrolled entity. In any other case, i.e. $V_j \neq \emptyset$, firm j is called a *company* meaning that it is owned by shareholders and modelled as a controlled entity [55]. Following the notation of an article by Stach, Mercik and Bertini (2020) [55] in this series, N^C denotes the set of companies whereas N^I denotes the set of investors in a corporate network.

3.2 Motivation and Illustration: A Corporate Network with 21 Players

In the following we are studying a theoretical shareholding network with 10 companies (numbered from 1 to 10) and 11 investors (numbered from 11 to 21). It is displayed as a directed graph in Fig. 1 with the weights on the arcs representing the voting rights of a firm in a company. For clarity, Table 1 also presents direct ownership relations for our example. We can associate a weighted majority game with each company $c \in N^C$ in a network. Each shareholder $s \in V_c$, i.e. each individual predecessor of company c, is treated as a player with the weight $w_{s,c}$ corresponding to the arc $(s,c) \in A$. These weighted voting games model direct control, because only immediate shareholders are considered.

Our theoretical 21-player example network comprises a number of important features. Investor 12 holds more than 50% of the voting rights in company 9 and hence the other shareholders have no control in that company. Investors 11 and 17 are evidently null players exerting neither direct nor indirect control in any company within the network. We observe pyramidal structures, e.g. for companies 7, 6 and 2, as well as loops, e.g. for companies 4, 9 and 10. Companies 1 and 10 do not have any control in other firms in the network although company 10 has some voting rights in company 9. From a graph-theoretical perspective, we could describe company 1 as a sink in the network. Our network structure is complete in the sense that 100% of each company is controlled by other firms in the network. From now on, we will consider this example with a simple majority, i.e. the quota is 50% plus one share.

3.3 The Approaches by Karos-Peters, Mercik-Lobos and Stach-Mercik

To the authors' knowledge, Karos and Peters (2015) [33] proposed the first approach measuring the control power of all firms in a shareholding network. Karos

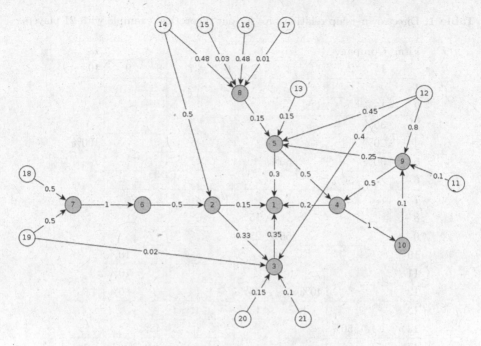

Fig. 1. A theoretical shareholding network with 21 players.

and Peters model relations of indirect control in a shareholding network by so-called invariant mutual control structures. In [33] they point out that any mutual control structure is associated with a vector of simple games, i.e. they define a simple game v_i for each firm $i \in N$ where each simple game indicates who controls firm i. For each coalition $S \in 2^N$, Karos and Peters define

$$v_i(S) = \begin{cases} 1, & \text{if firm } i \text{ is controlled by coalition } S, \\ 0, & \text{otherwise.} \end{cases}$$

We note that for an investor $i \in N^I$ the simple game v_i is the null game. In practice, one needs to find minimal winning coalitions considering both direct and indirect control in order to define the above simple game structure. Let us look at company 2 in our 21-player network. The minimal winning coalitions considering both direct and indirect control are $\{6, 14\}$, $\{7, 14\}$ and $\{14, 18, 19\}$. For any superset S of these three minimal winning coalitions there also holds $v_2(S) = 1$. We refer to [32] for a procedure of applying a sequence of elementary substitutions in order to create the simple game structure.

Based on their model of invariant mutual control and associated simple game structures Karos and Peters (2015) [33] propose the index Φ for measuring the indirect control power of firms in a corporate network. The index Φ is shown to satisfy five axioms, see [33] for details and plausible interpretations of these properties. The index Φ is computed for each firm $i \in N$ by applying the Shapley-

Table 1. Direct ownership relationships for our theoretical example with 21 players.

Firm	Company									
	1	2	3	4	5	6	7	8	9	10
1										
2	15%		33%							
3	35%									
4	20%										100%
5	30%			50%						
6		50%								
7						100%				
8					15%					
9				50%	25%					
10									10%	
11									10%	
12			40%		45%				80%	
13					15%					
14		50%						48%		
15								3%		
16								48%		
17								1%		
18							50%			
19			2%				50%			
20			15%							
21			10%							

Shubik index σ [50] (which we defined in Subsect. 2.2) to our vector of simple games $(v_1, \ldots, v_n)$ via

$$\Phi_i = \sum_{k \in N} \sigma_i(v_k) - v_i(N).$$

If i is a company, i.e. $i \in N^C$, then $v_i(N) = 1$ is subtracted from the sum of Shapley-Shubik indices in the above expression, because there must be at least one coalition controlling a company. Hence the index Φ takes real values in the range greater or equal -1 and is non-negative for all investors as $v_i(N) = 0$ for each shareholder $i \in N^I$.

Despite its desirable axiomatic properties the approach by Karos and Peters has a drawback in terms of practical applicability. In general, the simple games in the vector $(v_1, \ldots, v_n)$ are not weighted voting games. There are significantly more algorithms for computing power indices for weighted voting games than there are for more general simple games. Power indices for weighted voting games have been computed using generating functions, see e.g. [1,2,14], via a recent approach based on relational algebra called quasi-ordered binary decision diagrams [7,8,15,16] as well as based on the technique of dynamic programming [35,42,57,59]. Even though computing all of the power indices from Subsect. 2.2 for weighted voting games can be shown to be NP-hard [43], these algorithmic approaches make it possible to handle larger problems as they avoid the need to store the complete characteristic function of the simple game.

Mercik and Łobos (2016) [44] proposed a measure of reciprocal ownership and called the result of their algorithm an index of implicit power. Their approach is based on computing the raw Johnston index for the weighted majority games associated with direct control of individual companies. Major goals of the implicit power index were to estimate the powers of both investors and companies in a network and to address cyclic structures in a straightforward manner.

Each company $c \in N^C$ has a number of shareholders which may include investors and other companies. The set of investors of company c is denoted by N_c^I, while the companies that are shareholders of company c are denoted by N_c^C. The implicit power index π by Mercik and Łobos is computed by the following three-step algorithm.

Step 1. For each company c the raw Johnston index J_i is calculated for the associated weighted majority game v_c for each shareholder i of c. In this step only the direct ownership of the immediate shareholders is considered.

Step 2. For each non-individual shareholder, i.e. each shareholding-company, $\tilde{c} \in N_c^C$ the corresponding raw Johnston index calculated in Step 1 is divided equally among all investors of $\tilde{c}$. This is referred to as the regression of the first degree in [44].

Step 3. For each investor and each company the absolute implicit index Π is calculated by summing up the values assigned in Step 1 and 2. Finally, an appropriate standardization gives the implicit power index π of each entity in the network.

The three steps for calculating the implicit index π can be formalized in the following way [55]. For each investor $i \in N^I$ the implicit power index π is defined by

$$\pi_i = \frac{\Pi_i}{\sum\limits_{r \in N^I} \Pi_r}$$

where the absolute implicit index Π_i is given by

$$\Pi_i = \sum_{c \in N^C} \left(J_i(v_c) + \sum_{\substack{k \in N_c^C \\ i \in N_k^I}} \frac{J_k(v_c)}{|N_k|} \right).$$

For each company $c \in N^C$ the implicit power index π is defined by

$$\pi_c = \frac{\Pi_c}{\sum\limits_{r \in N^C} \Pi_r}$$

where the absolute implicit index Π_c is given by

$$\Pi_c = \sum_{i \in N_c^I} J_i(v_c) + \sum_{k \in N_c^C} \sum_{i \in N_k^I} \frac{J_k(v_c)}{|N_k|}.$$

Mercik and Łobos (2016) [44] argue that it was not necessary to calculate multiple regressions as they would not enhance the results of the implicit power index. Still, we open the possibility of a specified number of regressions in our implementation of the algorithm and will report our results and observations in Sect. 5. We argue that for networks where certain shareholder-companies of a company only have controlled entities, i.e. companies, as their shareholders additional regressions should be calculated for that particular company until an individual shareholder, i.e. an investor, has been found. In our 21-player network example such an additional regression appears to be warranted in the case of the weighted voting game for company 2. Investors 18 and 19 exert control in company 2 via company 7 which owns company 6 completely. Without an additional regression and a proportionate distribution of $J_6(v_2)$ to companies 18 and 19 this aspect of indirect control would not be reflected.

The equal division in Step 2 of the Mercik-Łobos algorithm is problematic. In general, the implicit index loses the null player property even though the raw Johnston index employed in Step 1 satisfies the null player property. For example, in our theoretical 21-player network investors 11 and 17 are null players. Still, both investors enjoy nonzero implicit indices π.

The implicit power index by Stach and Mercik [46,54] changes Step 2 in the three-step algorithm for the computation of the Mercik-Łobos implicit index such that the null player property is satisfied, i.e. it distributes the raw Johnston value assigned to company c in Step 1 proportionally to the raw Johnston index distribution given for the weighted majority game v_c of company c in Step 1. This modified implicit power index π' (also known as Stach-Mercik implicit index) satisfies the null-player property and can be formalized as follows. For each investor $i \in N^I$ the implicit power index π' is defined by

$$\pi_i' = \frac{\Pi_i'}{\sum\limits_{r \in N^I} \Pi_r'}$$

where the absolute implicit index Π_i' is given by

$$\Pi_i' = \sum_{c \in N^C} (J_i(v_c) + \sum_{\substack{k \in N_l^C \\ i \in N_k^I}} (J_k(v_c) * \frac{J_i(v_k)}{\sum\limits_{l \in N_k} J_l(v_k)})).$$

For each company $c \in N^C$ the implicit power index π' is defined by

$$\pi_c' = \frac{\Pi_c'}{\sum\limits_{r \in N^C} \Pi_r'}$$

where the absolute implicit index Π'_c is given by

$$\Pi'_c = \sum_{i \in N^I_c} J_i(v_c) + \sum_{k \in N^C_c} \sum_{i \in N^I_k} \left(J_k(v_c) * \frac{J_i(v_k)}{\sum_{l \in N_k} J_l(v_k)} \right).$$

As already stated, the first and third steps of the calculations of the Mercik-Łobos and Stach-Mercik implicit indices are identical.

3.4 Generalizing the Stach-Mercik and Mercik-Łobos Implicit Indices

In the previous subsection we already provided generalizations of the Stach-Mercik and Mercik-Łobos implicit indices by allowing for more than one regression within the second steps of the algorithms. Furthermore, both implicit indices can be generalized by substituting the underlying power index used in the first and second step. This was already demonstrated in the recent paper [55] where the raw Johnston index was replaced by the absolute Banzhaf index within the Stach-Mercik framework. For the motivations and arguments for employing the absolute Banzhaf index we refer to [55] and note that the corresponding implicit index is called π^β in that article.

We view the existing implicit indices as a modular framework, because the raw Johnston index can easily be replaced by another power index, ideally a power index satisfying the null player property. We are proposing and investigating a family of generalized implicit indices in this paper. By the term generalized implicit indices we mean that any of the power indices defined in Subsect. 2.2 can take the place of the raw Johnston index within the Stach-Mercik and Mercik-Łobos frameworks. In order to satisfy the null player property, we focus on the Stach-Mercik framework in the rest of the paper. The generalized implicit indices will be referred to as π^B, π^b, $\pi^{\mathcal{B}}$, π^D, π^d, π^J, π^j, π^H, π^h, $\pi^{\mathcal{H}}$ and π^σ when the absolute Banzhaf, relative Banzhaf, raw Banzhaf, raw Deegan-Packel, Deegan-Packel, raw Johnston, Johnston, absolute Public Good, relative Public Good, raw Public Good and Shapley-Shubik indices are employed within the Stach-Mercik framework. Note that with this terminology the Stach-Mercik index π' from [46,54,55] based on the raw Johnston index will be referred to as π^J and the implicit index π^β from [55] based on the absolute Banzhaf index will be called π^B. We present results and observations on all generalized implicit indices in Sect. 5.

4 Software Structure and Requirements

We decided to use the R programming environment [58] for implementing our framework of generalized implicit indices for estimating indirect control. R is a software tool generally used for statistical computing and graphics. One of the substantial strengths of the R ecosystem is gained through the concept of R packages [60] which are collections of code, data and tests contributed by users. CRAN, the Comprehensive R Archive Network, checks R packages for their quality making successful submissions available as official extensions of the R environment in one central repository [58].

For our concrete task we benefit from the available packages igraph [20] for working with graphs and CoopGame [56] for cooperative game theory. The R package igraph is actually an R interface to an established C++ library with the identical name providing a vast set of tools to create and manipulate graphs and to analyse networks [20]. We use it to create directed graphs of corporate shareholding networks. igraph could also be employed to investigate other attributes of networks such as the existence of cycles. The R package CoopGame [56] offers a collection of tools for cooperative game theory, including power indices and weighted majority games. Functionality in CoopGame for the enumeration of minimal winning coalitions in a simple game proved to be useful for implementing the Karos-Peters method. However, the implementations in CoopGame are meant to be prototypical and are not optimized for efficiency.

Our framework of generalized implicit indices is designed in a modular fashion. It allows us to import power indices from different sources, i.e. we do not need to rely on the prototypical code from CoopGame. Instead, we can alternatively use the package Rcpp [22] to seamlessly integrate efficient C++ implementations of power indices for weighted majority games [57] allowing us to handle the 21-player example in fractions of seconds.

All functions for implicit indices have three arguments in common. The network parameter is expecting a list consisting of the necessary data for igraph to create a graph and retrieve the information on the games. This includes the firms as vertices, the edges with the corresponding weights, the quotas of the games and possible coordinates to visualize the network. Secondly, the user can specify the number of regressions to be calculated in Step 2 of the algorithm with the default set to one regression. The third argument is a parameter allowing for one extra regression for those cases when shareholder-companies of a company only have non-individual shareholders, i.e. companies. When that Boolean parameter is set, the algorithm will calculate another regression for that particular company in order to find an individual shareholder, i.e. an investor. In addition, our function for the generalized Stach-Mercik framework needs users to specify the power index to be used in Step 1 of the algorithm as a function argument.

5   Results and Discussion

5.1   Minimal Winning and Vulnerable Coalitions for Our 21-Player Example

Any power indices introduced in Subsect. 2.2 rely on the knowledge of the distributions of the players in either the minimal winning coalitions or the critical players in the vulnerable coalitions in a simple game. In order to facilitate the understanding of our results for the 21-player problem, we provide Table 2 listing the minimal winning coalitions and the additional vulnerable coalitions (with

Table 2. Minimal winning coalitions and vulnerable coalitions (with critical players underlined) in the 10 weighted voting games for direct control in the 21-player network.

Company	Minimal winning coalitions	Additional vulnerable coalitions
1	$\{3, 4\}$, $\{3, 5\}$, $\{2, 4, 5\}$	$\{2, \underline{3}, \underline{4}\}$, $\{2, \underline{3}, \underline{5}\}$, $\{\underline{3}, 4, 5\}$
2	$\{6, 14\}$	
3	$\{2, 12\}$, $\{2, 20, 21\}$, $\{12, 19, 21\}$, $\{12, 20\}$	$\{2, \underline{12}, 19\}$, $\{2, \underline{12}, 21\}$, $\{2, 19, \underline{20}, \underline{21}\}$, $\{\underline{12}, 19, \underline{20}\}$, $\{\underline{12}, \underline{20}, 21\}$, $\{2, \underline{12}, 21\}$, $\{2, \underline{12}, 19, 21\}$, $\{\underline{12}, 19, 20, 21\}$
4	$\{5, 9\}$	
5	$\{8, 12\}$, $\{9, 12\}$, $\{12, 13\}$, $\{8, 9, 13\}$	$\{8, 9, \underline{12}\}$, $\{8, \underline{12}, 13\}$, $\{9, \underline{12}, 13\}$
6	$\{7\}$	
7	$\{18, 19\}$	
8	$\{14, 15\}$, $\{14, 16\}$, $\{15, 16\}$	$\{\underline{14}, \underline{15}, 17\}$, $\{\underline{14}, \underline{16}, 17\}$, $\{\underline{15}, \underline{16}, 17\}$
9	$\{12\}$	$\{10, \underline{12}\}$, $\{11, \underline{12}\}$, $\{10, 11, \underline{12}\}$
10	$\{4\}$	

critical players underlined). As outlined in Subsect. 3.2, implementing the Karos-Peters index [33] is sophisticated. Our algorithm works out the minimal winning coalitions considering both direct and indirect control. There are 42 such minimal winning coalitions for company 1 alone. Given that we use the Karos-Peters method for comparison only, we do not list these coalitions here. We admit that our current implementation is not efficient as it builds the characteristic functions of the corresponding simple games from the minimal winning coalitions of the companies. The computation for the 21-player network example took more than one day on a standard laptop PC. In the future, we hope to make our Karos-Peters implementation faster using the approach of Lange and Kóczy [36] or the approach of Kirsch and Langner [34] which both show ways to compute Shapley-Shubik indices directly from the set of minimal winning coalitions.

5.2   Comparisons Within the Stach-Mercik Framework

We tested the 12 implicit power indices introduced in Subsect. 3.3 together with the Karos-Peters [33] and Mercik-Lobos [44] approaches. We only report rankings of firms here. For tables with detailed results of implicit index computations and their structure we refer to two previous articles [46, 55] from this series. Tables 3 and 4 report investor and company rankings in ascending order, respectively, with ties indicated via $\equiv$. In both Tables 3 and 4, for any implicit indices the default of one regression was used and there was no extra regression allowed aiming to find an uncontrolled shareholder. Investors 11 and 17 are assigned zero power by any indices apart from the Mercik-Lobos implicit index which lacks the null player property. In Table 3, investors 11 and 17 are tied for last place for all other methods. All methods correctly recognize investors 15 and 16 as symmetrical players despite their different amounts of shares in company 8. Remarkably, the investor rankings for $\pi^\beta = \pi^B$ based on the absolute Banzhaf index and Φ coincide, underpinning the arguments in favour of this implicit index

Table 3. Investor rankings (exactly one regression in implicit indices).

Index	Investor ranking
Φ (Karos-Peters)	$12, 14, 19, 18, 15 \equiv 16, 20, 13, 21, 11 \equiv 17$
π (Mercik-Lobos)	$12, 14, 20, 15 \equiv 16, 19, 21, 13, 18, 11, 17$
$\pi' = \pi^J$ (raw Johnston)	$12, 14, 20, 15 \equiv 16, 19, 21, 13, 18, 11 \equiv 17$
π^j (Johnston)	$12, 19, 18, 14, 15 \equiv 16, 20, 13, 21, 11 \equiv 17$
π^B (raw Banzhaf)	$12, 14, 20, 15 \equiv 16, 21, 19, 13, 18, 11 \equiv 17$
$\pi^\beta = \pi^B$ (abs. Banzhaf)	$12, 14, 19, 18, 15 \equiv 16, 20, 13, 21, 11 \equiv 17$
π^b (rel. Banzhaf)	$12, 19, 14, 18, 15 \equiv 16, 13, 20, 21, 11 \equiv 17$
π^D (raw Deegan-Packel)	$12, 14, 19, 15 \equiv 16, 13, 20, 18, 21, 11 \equiv 17$
π^d (Deegan-Packel)	$12, 19, 14, 18, 15 \equiv 16, 13, 20, 18, 21, 11 \equiv 17$
$\pi^{\mathcal{H}}$ (raw Public Good)	$12, 14, 19, 13 \equiv 15 \equiv 16, 20 \equiv 21, 18, 11 \equiv 17$
π^H (abs. Public Good)	$12, 14, 19, 18, 13, 15 \equiv 16, 20 \equiv 21, 11 \equiv 17$
π^h (rel. Public Good)	$12, 19, 14, 18, 15 \equiv 16, 13, 20 \equiv 21, 11 \equiv 17$
π^σ (Shapley-Shubik)	$12, 19, 14, 18, 15 \equiv 16, 13, 20, 21, 11 \equiv 17$

Table 4. Company rankings (exactly one regression in implicit indices).

Index	Company ranking
Φ (Karos-Peters)	$7, 4, 9, 5, 2, 3, 6, 8, 1 \equiv 10$
π (Mercik-Lobos)	$3, 5, 8, 9, 1, 6 \equiv 7, 4, 2, 10$
$\pi' = \pi^J$ (raw Johnston)	$3, 5, 8, 9, 1, 6 \equiv 7, 4, 2, 10$
π^j (Johnston)	$5, 6 \equiv 7 \equiv 9, 8, 3, 4, 1, 2, 10$
π^B (raw Banzhaf)	$3, 5 \equiv 8, 1, 9, 7, 4, 2 \equiv 6, 10$
$\pi^\beta = \pi^B$ (abs. Banzhaf)	$5 \equiv 8, 3, 6 \equiv 7 \equiv 9, 4, 1, 2, 10$
π^b (rel. Banzhaf)	$5, 6 \equiv 7 \equiv 9, 8, 3, 4, 1, 2, 10$
π^D (raw Deegan-Packel)	$5, 3, 8, 1, 6 \equiv 7 \equiv 9, 4, 2, 10$
π^d (Deegan-Packel)	$6 \equiv 7 \equiv 9, 5 \equiv 8, 3, 4, 2, 1, 10$
$\pi^{\mathcal{H}}$ (raw Public Good)	$3 \equiv 5, 8, 1, 7, 4, 2 \equiv 6 \equiv 9, 10$
π^H (abs. Public Good)	$3 \equiv 5, 8, 7, 4, 1, 2 \equiv 6 \equiv 9, 10$
π^h (rel. Public Good)	$6 \equiv 7 \equiv 9, 5 \equiv 8, 3, 4, 2, 1, 10$
π^σ (Shapley-Shubik)	$5, 6 \equiv 7 \equiv 9, 8, 3, 4, 1, 2, 10$

from [55] where it was first proposed. With the setup for Table 3 allowing for exactly one regression we find it questionable that investor 19 is ranked above investor 14 for the five implicit indices $\pi^j, \pi^b, \pi^d, \pi^h$, and π^σ based on efficient power indices. After all, our setup with only one regression neglects any indirect control investor 19 has in company 2. We see this as further vindication for continuing to use power indices lacking the efficiency property in Step 1 of the implicit index framework and to only scale the implicit indices once in Step 3 at the very end.

As for the company rankings in Table 4, the Karos-Peters index Φ measures only control power. Thus companies 1 and 10 must tie for last place as they are controlled entities without any control in other companies in our network. As pointed out in [46,55], implicit indices measure both control power and position power. The latter means that the implicit indices take the structure and numbers of a company's shareholders into account when calculating the power of companies. As stated in [55], p. 125, the fractions of control power assigned to the investors of a company's shareholders increase the power of a company in the process of estimating a company's power in the entire network. This is reflected whenever companies 3, 5 and 8 are at the top of the company rankings for the implicit indices.

5.3   Investigating More Than One Regression

Our 21-player network example was designed to experiment with more than one regression in Step 2 of the implicit index framework. We amassed plenty of results and pick the three indices $\pi^D, \pi^\beta = \pi^B$, and π^σ to report investor and company rankings which we found to be particularly meaningful and convincing in Tables 5 and 6, respectively. We report rankings in ascending order for 1, 3 and 15 regressions in Step 2 of the algorithm, marked in the column "Steps" in Tables 5 and 6. For one regression we compare results with the Boolean flag for an extra regression trying find an investor both activd and inactived, marked in the column "Extra" in Tables 5 and 6. In our network example no investor exerts any control power in any company that is more than three arcs away. In that sense the maximal path length for measuring control is 4, thus motivating 3 regressions. The investor rankings in Table 5 reveal that 15 regressions distort investor rankings. For the implicit index π^D based on the raw Deegan-Packel index, we see that additional regressions help mapping the indirect control investor 18 exerts in companies 2 and 1. For the company rankings in Table 6, the picture for multiple regressions is more critical. With multiple regressions position power appears to dominate control power. More regressions imply that more frequently fractions of control power are assigned to other firms in the network which directly or indirectly control that company increasing the power of the controlled company itself. Given that company 1 is indirectly controlled by all other players in the network except for company 10 and the null investors 11 and 17, it is no surprise that company 1 leads all company rankings when there are three or more regressions.

5.4   The Null Investor Removable Property

Let us experiment with our 21-player network and divide investor 17, a null player, into five null players, e.g. each of them holding 0.2% of company 8. For the original network, in the weighted majority game for direct control of company 8 the raw Johnston indices of investors 14, 15 and 16 equal 2. Once we divide null investor 17 into five null investors, these indices in the weighted majority game for direct control of company 8 change; the raw Johnston indices of investors 14,

Table 5. Investor rankings for selected indices and various numbers of regressions.

Index	Steps	Extra	Investor ranking
Φ (Karos-Peters)	n.a	n.a	$12, 14, 19, 18, 15 \equiv 16, 20, 13, 21, 11 \equiv 17$
$\pi^\beta = \pi^B$ (abs. Banzhaf)	1	No	$12, 14, 19, 18, 15 \equiv 16, 20, 13, 21, 11 \equiv 17$
$\pi^\beta = \pi^B$ (abs. Banzhaf)	1	Yes	$12, 19, 18, 14, 15 \equiv 16, 13, 20, 21, 11 \equiv 17$
$\pi^\beta = \pi^B$ (abs. Banzhaf)	3	No	$12, 19, 18, 14, 15 \equiv 16, 13, 20, 21, 11 \equiv 17$
$\pi^\beta = \pi^B$ (abs. Banzhaf)	15	No	$12, 13, 14, 15 \equiv 16, 19, 18, 20, 21, 11 \equiv 17$
π^D (raw Deegan-Packel)	1	No	$12, 14, 19, 15 \equiv 16, 13, 20, 18, 21, 11 \equiv 17$
π^D (raw Deegan-Packel)	1	Yes	$12, 14, 19, 18, 13, 15 \equiv 16, 20, 21, 11 \equiv 17$
π^D (raw Deegan-Packel)	3	No	$12, 14, 19, 18, 15 \equiv 16, 13, 20, 21, 11 \equiv 17$
π^D (raw Deegan-Packel)	15	No	$12, 14, 15 \equiv 16, 13, 19, 18, 20, 21, 11 \equiv 17$
π^σ (Shapley-Shubik)	1	No	$12, 19, 14, 18, 15 \equiv 16, 13, 20, 21, 11 \equiv 17$
π^σ (Shapley-Shubik)	1	Yes	$12, 19, 18, 14, 13, 15 \equiv 16, 20, 21, 11 \equiv 17$
π^σ (Shapley-Shubik)	3	No	$12, 19, 18, 14, 15 \equiv 16, 13, 20, 21, 11 \equiv 17$
π^σ (Shapley-Shubik)	15	No	$12, 13, 14, 15 \equiv 16, 19, 18, 20, 21, 11 \equiv 17$

Table 6. Company rankings for selected indices and various numbers of regressions.

Index	Steps	Extra	Company ranking
Φ (Karos-Peters)	n.a	n.a	$7, 4, 9, 5, 2, 3, 6, 8, 1 \equiv 10$
$\pi^\beta = \pi^B$ (abs. Banzhaf)	1	No	$5 \equiv 8, 3, 6 \equiv 7 \equiv 9, 4, 1, 2, 10$
$\pi^\beta = \pi^B$ (abs. Banzhaf)	1	Yes	$1, 2 \equiv 5 \equiv 8, 3, 6 \equiv 7 \equiv 9, 4 \equiv 10$
$\pi^\beta = \pi^B$ (abs. Banzhaf)	3	No	$1, 3, 2 \equiv 5 \equiv 8, 4 \equiv 10, 6 \equiv 7 \equiv 9$
$\pi^\beta = \pi^B$ (abs. Banzhaf)	15	No	$1, 4, 10, 5, 3, 2 \equiv 8, 6 \equiv 7 \equiv 9$
π^D (raw Deegan-Packel)	1	No	$5, 3, 8, 1, 6 \equiv 7 \equiv 9, 4, 2, 10$
π^D (raw Deegan-Packel)	1	Yes	$5, 3, 8, 1, 2, 6 \equiv 7 \equiv 9, 4 \equiv 10$
π^D (raw Deegan-Packel)	3	No	$1, 3, 5, 8, 4 \equiv 10, 2, 6 \equiv 7 \equiv 9$
π^D (raw Deegan-Packel)	15	No	$1, 4, 10, 5, 3, 8, 2, 6 \equiv 7 \equiv 9$
π^σ (Shapley-Shubik)	1	No	$5, 6 \equiv 7 \equiv 9, 8, 3, 4, 1, 2, 10$
π^σ (Shapley-Shubik)	1	Yes	$2, 1, 5, 6 \equiv 7 \equiv 9, 8, 3, 4 \equiv 10$
π^σ (Shapley-Shubik)	3	No	$1, 3, 2, 4 \equiv 10, 5, 6 \equiv 7 \equiv 9, 8$
π^σ (Shapley-Shubik)	15	No	$1, 4, 10, 5, 3, 2, 6 \equiv 7 \equiv 9, 8$

15 and 16 now equal 32. As a consequence, the implicit indices $\pi' = \pi^J$ for the modified network are distorted. Investor 14 ranks highest, investors 15 and 16 tie for second place beating investor 12 to fourth place. As stated at the end of Subsect. 2.2, the raw Johnston index lacks the null player removable property. This is passed on to the implicit index $\pi' = \pi^J$.

In the context of indirect control, the null player removable property was highlighted as a desirable property in [46], p. 76. We formulate a slightly more cautious *null investor removable property* for corporate networks G with distinguishable investors and companies.

Null Investor Removable Property. After removing the null investors, i.e. the investors whose voting rights cannot transform any losing coalition into a winning one, from a corporate shareholding network G with distinguishable investors and companies, the non-null firms' measures of power should remain unchanged. Equivalently, the value of any firm in a corporate shareholding network G is unchanged if G is extended by adding a new null investor.

The generalized implicit indices π^B, π^b, π^D, π^d, π^j, π^H, π^h, $\pi^{\mathcal{H}}$ and π^σ satisfy the null investor removable property, because the absolute Banzhaf, relative Banzhaf, raw Deegan-Packel, Deegan-Packel, Johnston, absolute Public Good, relative Public Good, raw Public Good and Shapley-Shubik indices satisfy the null player removable property. From the implicit indices we investigated only π^B based on the raw Banzhaf index, $\pi^J = \pi'$ based on the raw Johnston index and the original Mercik-Lobos index π lack this property. In conclusion, we have another argument for preferring $\pi^B = \pi^\beta$ based on the absolute Banzhaf index over $\pi^J = \pi'$. If one wants to preserve as many of the features reported on the Stach-Mercik implicit index $\pi^J = \pi'$, then our investigations and experiments show π^D based on the raw Deegan-Packel index as a very viable alternative satisfying the null investor removable property.

We finally note that the Karos-Peters index Φ possesses the null investor removable property, too. We recall that for computing Φ the simple game v_i for an individual firm i is completely determined by the minimal winning coalitions considering both direct and indirect control with indirect control relationships computed from direct control relationships as described in [32]. Obviously, a null investor exerts no direct control and hence no indirect control. As a consequence, any minimal winning coalitions considering both direct and indirect control remain unaffected by the addition or removal of a null investor. Hence adding or removing a null investor does not change the values of Φ for the non-null firms in the corporate network.

6   Conclusions and Further Developments

We introduced and analyzed a framework of implicit power indices generalizing the implicit indices introduced by Mercik and Lobos [44] and Stach and Mercik [46,54,55] via replacing the raw Johnston index with various other power indices. The algorithmic framework appeals due to its modularity. It relies on the computation of power indices for weighted voting games rather than more general simple games. Using efficient software exploiting the special structure of weighted voting games [57] makes it possible handle large corporate network structures. We experimented with more than one regression in Step 2 of that algorithmic framework. The latter deserves further investigations, in particular for measuring the power of investors. Rather than employing a fixed number of regressions throughout the algorithm, we plan to study regressions depending on the individual network taking into account the maximal number of predecessors in each controlled company. We introduced the null investor removable property pointing out that it is not satisfied by the implicit index $\pi^J = \pi'$ based on the raw Johnston index and presented arguments for $\pi^J = \pi'$ to be superseded by $\pi^\beta = \pi^B$ from [55] based on the absolute Banzhaf index and π^D based on the raw Deegan-Packel index. Clearly, further investigation of desirable properties for a good measure of indirect control in the corporate shareholding structures is needed. For example, we note that the power indices we used to modify the approaches by Mercik-Łobos and Stach-Mercik included the Deegan-Packel and Public Good indices. Both these two power indices do not satisfy the local monotonicity property [29]. This carries over to the corresponding implicit indices and warrants further attention in the context of indirect control.

We can use our algorithmic framework and our software for measuring the importance of mutual connections in corporate networks along the lines of [54, 55]. The power of a linkage connecting two entities equals the difference between the implicit power indices before and after removing this link from the network [55]. It will be worthwhile to compare our new implicit power indices with other approaches beyond the Karos-Peters method [33], in particular the approaches by Crama and Leruth [18, 19] and by Levy and Szafarz [39]. Even though we discussed null players in this article, we did not address modelling the float, i.e. the ocean of small shareholders. The various models for the float presented by Crama and Leruth [18, 19] and Levy [38] could be incorporated enhancing our framework of implicit indices by a corresponding component for simulations. A fuzzy logic approach as proposed in [25] may provide another novel research direction.

Further investigations could also take into account a priori unions in the corporate network and consider different connections among the firms, like personal connection of the managements, for example. We strive to incorporate power indices with a pre-coalitions [40, 45] into our framework of implicit indices and note that the sub-coalitional approach introduced in [53] shows promise for investigating a priori unions in shareholding networks as well.

Acknowledgements. The first author thanks the funding of the Bavarian State Ministry of Science and Arts. The third author's contribution to the article was funded under subvention funds for the AGH University of Science and Technology in Krakow, Poland. Moreover, the authors thank two anonymous reviewers for their careful reading of the manuscript and their helpful comments and suggestions.

References

1. Algaba, E., Bilbao, J.M., Fernández Garcıa, J.R.: The distribution of power in the European constitution. Eur. J. Oper. Res. **176**(3), 1752–1766 (2007)
2. Algaba, E., Bilbao, J.M., Fernández Garcıa, J.R., López, J.: Computing power indices in weighted multiple majority games. Math. Soc. Sci. **46**(1), 63–80 (2003)

3. Algaba, E., Fragnelli, V., Sánchez-Soriano, J.: Handbook of the Shapley value. CRC Press (2020). https://doi.org/10.1201/9781351241410
4. Algaba, E., Fragnelli, V., Sánchez-Soriano, J.: The Shapley value, a paradigm of fairness. In: Algaba, E., Fragnell, V., Sánchez-Soriano, J. (eds.) Handbook of the Shapley Value, pp. 17–29. CRC Press (2020). https://doi.org/10.1201/9781351241410
5. Bang-Jensen, J., Gutin, G.Z.: Digraphs: Theory, Algorithms and Applications. Springer, Heidelberg (2008). https://doi.org/10.1007/978-1-84800-998-1
6. Banzhaf, J.F.: Weighted voting doesn't work: a mathematical analysis. Rutgers L. Rev. **19**, 317–343 (1965)
7. Berghammer, R., Bolus, S.: On the use of binary decision diagrams for solving problems on simple games. Eur. J. Oper. Res. **222**(3), 529–541 (2012)
8. Berghammer, R., Bolus, S., Rusinowska, A., De Swart, H.: A relation-algebraic approach to simple games. Eur. J. Oper. Res. **210**(1), 68–80 (2011)
9. Bertini, C., Freixas, J., Gambarelli, G., Stach, I.: Comparing power indices. Int. Game Theory Rev. **15**(02), 1340004 (2013)
10. Bertini, C., Gambarelli, G., Stach, I., Zola, M.: On some applications of the Shapley-Shubik index for finance and politics. In: Algaba, E., Fragnell, V., Sánchez-Soriano, J. (eds.) Handbook of the Shapley Value, pp. 393–418. CRC Press (2020). https://doi.org/10.1201/9781351241410
11. Bertini, C., Mercik, J., Stach, I.: Indirect control and power. Oper. Res. Decis. **26**(2), 7–30 (2016). https://doi.org/10.5277/ord160202
12. Bertini, C., Stach, I.: Banzhaf voting power measure. In: Dowding, K. (ed.) Encyclopedia of Power, pp. 54–55. Sage Publications (2011)
13. Bertini, C., Stach, I.: On public values and power indices. Decis. Making Manuf. Serv. **9**(1), 9–25 (2015). https://doi.org/10.7494/dmms.2015.9.1.9
14. Bilbao, J., Fernández, J., Jiménez Losada, A., Lopez, J.: Generating functions for computing power indices efficiently. TOP **8**(2), 191–213 (2000)
15. Bolus, S.: Power indices of simple games and vector-weighted majority games by means of binary decision diagrams. Eur. J. Oper. Res. **210**(2), 258–272 (2011)
16. Bolus, S.: A QOBDD-based approach to simple games. Ph.D. thesis, Christian-Albrechts Universität Kiel (2012)
17. Chakravarty, S.R., Mitra, M., Sarkar, P.: A Course on Cooperative Game Theory. Cambridge University Press, Cambridge (2015)
18. Crama, Y., Leruth, L.: Control and voting power in corporate networks: concepts and computational aspects. Eur. J. Oper. Res. **178**(3), 879–893 (2007). https://doi.org/10.1016/j.ejor.2006.02.020
19. Crama, Y., Leruth, L.: Power indices and the measurement of control in corporate structures. Int. Game Theory Rev. **15**(03), 1340017 (2013). https://doi.org/10.1142/S0219198913400173
20. Csardi, G., Nepusz, T., et al.: The igraph software package for complex network research. Int. J. Complex Syst. **1695**(5), 1–9 (2006). https://igraph.org/
21. Deegan, J., Packel, E.: A new index of power for simple n-person games. Int. J. Game Theory **7**(2), 113–123 (1978)
22. Eddelbuettel, D., et al.: Rcpp: seamless R and C++ integration. J. Stat. Softw. **40**(8), 1–18 (2011)
23. Gambarelli, G., Owen, G.: Indirect control of corporations. Int. J. Game Theory **23**(4), 287–302 (1994)
24. Gilles, R.P.: The Cooperative Game Theory of Networks and Hierarchies. Springer, Heidelberg (2015)

25. Gładysz, B., Mercik, J., Stach, I.: Fuzzy shapley value-based solution for communication network. In: Nguyen, N.T., Chbeir, R., Exposito, E., Aniorté, P., Trawiński, B. (eds.) ICCCI 2019. LNCS (LNAI), vol. 11683, pp. 535–544. Springer, Cham (2019). https://doi.org/10.1007/978-3-030-28377-3_44

26. Holler, M.J.: Forming coalitions and measuring voting power. Polit. Stud. **30**(2), 262–271 (1982)

27. Holler, M.J.: Public Goods index. In: Dowding, K. (ed.) Encyclopedia of Power, pp. 541–542. Sage Publications (2011)

28. Holler, M.J., Li, X.: From public good index to public value. An axiomatic approach and generalization. Control Cybern. **24**, 257–270 (1995)

29. Holler, M.J., Napel, S.: Local monotonicity of power: axiom or just a property? Qual. Quant. **38**(5), 637–647 (2005)

30. Holler, M.J., Packel, E.: Power, luck and the right index. Zeitschrift Nationalökonomie **43**(1), 21–29 (1983)

31. Johnston, R.: On the measurement of power: some reactions to Laver. Environ. Plan A **10**(8), 907–914 (1978). https://doi.org/10.1068/a100907

32. Karos, D., Peters, H.: Indirect control and power in mutual control structures. Technical report, Maastricht University, Graduate School of Business and Economics (GSBE) (2013)

33. Karos, D., Peters, H.: Indirect control and power in mutual control structures. Games Econ. Behav. **92**, 150–165 (2015). https://doi.org/10.1016/j.geb.2015.06.003

34. Kirsch, W., Langner, J.: Power indices and minimal winning coalitions. Soc. Choice Welfare **34**(1), 33–46 (2010)

35. Kurz, S.: Computing the power distribution in the IMF. 10 p. arXiv preprint, arXiv:1603.01443 (2016)

36. Lange, F., Kóczy, L.Á.: Power indices expressed in terms of minimal winning coalitions. Soc. Choice Welfare **41**(2), 281–292 (2013)

37. Levy, M.: Control in pyramidal structures. Corp. Govern.: Int. Rev. **17**(1), 77–89 (2009)

38. Levy, M.: The Banzhaf index in complete and incomplete shareholding structures: a new algorithm. Eur. J. Oper. Res. **215**(2), 411–421 (2011)

39. Levy, M., Szafarz, A.: Cross-ownership: a device for management entrenchment? Rev. Financ. **21**(4), 1675–1699 (2017). https://doi.org/10.1093/rof/rfw009

40. Malawski, M.: Counting power indices for games with a priori unions. In: Gambarelli, G. (ed.) Essays in Cooperative Games, vol. 36, pp. 125–140. Springer, Boston (2004). https://doi.org/10.1007/978-1-4020-2936-3_10

41. Malawski, M.: A note on equal treatment and symmetry of values. In: Nguyen, N.T., Kowalczyk, R., Mercik, J., Motylska-Kuźma, A. (eds.) Transactions on Computational Collective Intelligence XXXV. LNCS, vol. 12330, pp. 76–84. Springer, Heidelberg (2020). https://doi.org/10.1007/978-3-662-62245-2_5

42. Matsui, T., Matsui, Y.: A survey of algorithms for calculating power indices of weighted majority games. J. Oper. Res. Soc. Jpn. **43**(1), 71–86 (2000)

43. Matsui, Y., Matsui, T.: Np-completeness for calculating power indices of weighted majority games. Theoret. Comput. Sci. **263**(1–2), 305–310 (2001)

44. Mercik, J., Łobos, K.: Index of implicit power as a measure of reciprocal ownership. In: Nguyen, N.T., Kowalczyk, R., Mercik, J. (eds.) Transactions on Computational Collective Intelligence XXIII. LNCS, vol. 9760, pp. 128–140. Springer, Heidelberg (2016). https://doi.org/10.1007/978-3-662-52886-0_8

45. Mercik, J., Ramsey, D.M.: The effect of Brexit on the balance of power in the European union council: an approach based on pre-coalitions. In: Mercik, J. (ed.) Transactions on Computational Collective Intelligence XXVII. LNCS, vol. 10480, pp. 87–107. Springer, Cham (2017). https://doi.org/10.1007/978-3-319-70647-4_7

46. Mercik, J., Stach, I.: On measurement of control in corporate structures. In: Nguyen, N.T., Kowalczyk, R., Mercik, J., Motylska-Kuźma, A. (eds.) Transactions on Computational Collective Intelligence XXXI. LNCS, vol. 11290, pp. 64–79. Springer, Heidelberg (2018). https://doi.org/10.1007/978-3-662-58464-4_7

47. Penrose, L.S.: The elementary statistics of majority voting. J. Roy. Stat. Soc. 109(1), 53–57 (1946). https://doi.org/10.2307/2981392

48. Riker, W.H.: The first power index. Soc. Choice Welfare 3(4), 293–295 (1986)

49. Shapley, L.S.: A value for n-person games. In: Kuhn, H., Tucker, A. (eds.) Contributions to the Theory of Games II, pp. 307–317. Princeton University Press, Princeton (1953). https://doi.org/10.1515/9781400881970-018

50. Shapley, L.S., Shubik, M.: A method for evaluating the distribution of power in a committee system. Am. Polit. Sci. Rev. 48(3), 787–792 (1954). https://doi.org/10.2307/1951053

51. Stach, I.: Shapley-Shubik index. In: Dowding, K. (ed.) Encyclopedia of Power, pp. 603–606. Sage Publications (2011)

52. Stach, I.: Indirect control of corporations: analysis and simulations. Decis. Making Manuf. Serv. 11(1–2), 31–51 (2017). https://doi.org/10.7494/dmms.2017.11.1-2.31

53. Stach, I.: Sub-coalitional approach to values. In: Mercik, J. (ed.) Transactions on Computational Collective Intelligence XXVII. LNCS, vol. 10480, pp. 74–86. Springer, Cham (2017). https://doi.org/10.1007/978-3-319-70647-4_6

54. Stach, I., Mercik, J.: Measurement of control power in corporate networks. Oper. Res. Decis. 31(1), 97–121 (2021). https://doi.org/10.37190/ord210106

55. Stach, I., Mercik, J., Bertini, C.: Some propositions of approaches for measuring indirect control power of firms and mutual connections in corporate shareholding structures. In: Nguyen, N.T., Kowalczyk, R., Mercik, J., Motylska-Kuźma, A. (eds.) Transactions on Computational Collective Intelligence XXXV. LNCS, vol. 12330, pp. 116–132. Springer, Heidelberg (2020). https://doi.org/10.1007/978-3-662-62245-2_8

56. Staudacher, J., Anwander, J.: Using the R package CoopGame for the analysis, solution and visualization of cooperative games with transferable utility (2019). https://cran.r-project.org/package=CoopGame. R Vignette

57. Staudacher, J., et al.: Computing power indices for weighted voting games via dynamic programming. Oper. Res. Decis. 31(2), 123–145 (2021). https://doi.org/10.37190/ord210205

58. The R Core team and others: R: A language and environment for statistical computing. Vienna, Austria (2021). https://www.r-project.org/

59. Uno, T.: Efficient computation of power indices for weighted majority games. In: Chao, K.-M., Hsu, T., Lee, D.-T. (eds.) ISAAC 2012. LNCS, vol. 7676, pp. 679–689. Springer, Heidelberg (2012). https://doi.org/10.1007/978-3-642-35261-4_70

60. Wickham, H.: R Packages: Organize, Test, Document, and Share Your Code. O'Reilly Media (2015). https://r-pkgs.org/

1% Tax in Public Benefit Organizations: Determinants of Its Share in Organizations' Total Revenues – Analysis of 3rd Sector in Poland

Hanna Pyrkosz and Anna Motylska-Kuzma[(✉)] [iD]

WSB University in Wroclaw, Wroclaw, Poland
anna.motylska-kuzma@wsb.wroclaw.pl

Abstract. *Objective:* Identification of variables, which are influencing the share of 1% of income taxes in total revenues of Public Benefit Organizations.

Methodology: Methodology is based on statistical analysis of the data, which have been obtained from (comprehensive) technical reports from year 2018 of 100 Public Benefit Organizations. The organizations have been selected from the official list of Public Benefit Organizations published by Director of the National Institute of Liberty. Using the analysis of correlation and the hierarchical regression, were checked the relations between the 1% tax revenue share in total revenue with such factors like location, legal form, use the website, provide the campaign, area of activity or age of organization.

Results: The analysis shows the importance of the legal form and experience of organizations in attracting the funds from 1% tax mechanism and does not confirm the general opinion about the importance of the promotion and visibility of the PBOs. The research shows also over prioritization the size of the organization as the factor which could significantly attract the possible donors.

Originality/Value: This research can constitute the source of information for non-governmental organizations and non-formal groups, planning to set up NGOs, which features may attract taxpayers in terms of 1% donation as well as signalizes the limitations of 1% tax mechanism.

Keywords: Non-governmental organizations · Public benefit organizations · 1% tax

1 Introduction

Revenues from 1% tax are considered substantial sources of financing activities of Public Benefit Organizations in Poland. According to the research, the possibility of becoming the beneficiary of 1% mechanism have encouraged most of the NGOs to obtain the status of Public Benefit Organization. (Kietlińska 2015, p. 105) Nevertheless, this source of revenue has been proven to be an important, however not the main for the majority of PBOs. (Chojnacka 2020, p. 458). The distribution of revenues from 1% is unequal among organizations and are focused mostly among 10 organizations, which received

© Springer-Verlag GmbH Germany, part of Springer Nature 2021
N. T. Nguyen et al. (Eds.): TCCI XXXVI, LNCS 13010, pp. 94–107, 2021.
https://doi.org/10.1007/978-3-662-64563-5_5

in 2019 40% of all revenues from this source. [https://www.gov.pl/web/finanse/1-pro cent-podatku-dla-opp] This phenomenon shows that 1% mechanism may deepen the inequalities between organizations. The research of Aldashev G. and Navarra C. (2018, p. 11) proved that this dependency not only occur in terms of 1% tax, but in NGOs' revenues in general. According to them the biggest amount of funds is directed to only few organizations as a rule. The other relationship concerning NGOs' funding is the growing competition for the sources of financing (Adashev and Verdier 2010, p. 50), so the organizations having bigger resources are in the better position.

The NGOs' sector is diversified. Organizations may vary in size, legal form, the type of statue activity, its scope and the nature of beneficiaries. There might be many reasons for organizations to be in the less or more favourable situation to obtain revenues from 1% tax. The aim of this article is to identify such variables.

The structure of the paper is as following. The first section describes legal aspects and genesis of Public Benefit Organizations as well as mechanism of 1% tax. The second part focuses on some dependencies, which occur among NGOs' revenues. Following sections describe methodology of research and results of analysis. The last part focuses on conclusions of the research and reflections regarding future courses of the study.

2 Public Benefit Organizations (PBOs) and Mechanism of 1% Tax

The Public Benefit Organizations are often unified with the NGOs. In fact, they are the NGOs, i.e. the entities, which are not the part of public sector and whose goal does not include gaining profit [Law on Public Benefit Activity and Volunteerism article 3.2], but they obtained special status enabling them to get certain benefits. Public Benefit Organizations can act only for the socially useful purposes, [Law on Public Benefit Activity and Volunteerism article 20.1.1] while the goal of regular non-governmental organizations can be discretionary, or more particular, depending on the legal form of organization.

The concept of Public Benefit Organization has been implemented in many European countries, such as Hungary, Slovakia Lithuania, Romania, Croatia, Estonia, Netherlands, France, Germany, Moldova and Latvia (Bullain et al. 2008, pp. 2–25). Receiving the status of Public Benefit Organization is connected to benefits such as tax exemptions, preferential treatment in applying for government contracts and grants, incentives for donors or mechanism enabling donation of some share of income tax. Nevertheless, these forms differ among countries in details. For example, in Hungary, France and Germany donors have a chance to deduct donation dedicated for Public Benefit Organization from tax (Bullain et al. 2008, pp 25). The possibility of income tax donation in favour of PBOs has been implemented in Romania and Lithuania, where individuals can commit 2% of their income tax. Furthermore, in Slovakia both individuals and companies can donate 2% of their income tax. (Bullain et al. 2008, p. 5). Whereas in Hungary, Public Benefit Status is not mandatory to receive 1% tax after meeting certain requirements.

The concept of PBO in Poland was introduced in 2003 by the Law on Public Benefit Activity and Volunteerism. This act regulates, among others, rules of setting up and running Public Benefit Organizations. It specifies also the benefits connected with Public Benefit status and requirements, which these organizations have to fulfil. The status of

PBO can be obtained by non-governmental organizations, such as associations and foundation and other entities specified in the Law of Public Benefit Organizations in article 3.3.1 and 3.3.4 [article 20.1]. In practise, the biggest amount of PBOs occurs among associations and similar social organizations (73,6%), foundations represent 25,8% and religious entities constitute remaining 0,6% as per data from 2017 [Central Statistical Office 2019, p. 2). Public Benefit Activity is one of key concepts in terms of Public Benefit. It is defined in Law of Public Benefit Organizations as activity conducted by non-governmental organizations and entities listed in article 3.3 within the scope of so called "sphere of public tasks", which is listed in article 4.1 [article 7]. Essential feature of Public Benefit Activity is social utility. [article 3.1].

Public Benefit Organizations are registered in Central Court Registry (Bullain et al. 2008, p. 19). To obtain the status of Public Benefit Organization, entitled entities must run public benefit activity ceaselessly for at least two years [article 22.1]. Organizations' actions should include the society as a whole or be directed to the group in particularly difficult life or material situation [art. 20.1.1]. Consequently, business activity cannot be primary for Public Benefit Organisation. Nevertheless, it can be held as supplementary activity [article 20.1.2]. Public Benefit Organizations are obliged to have statutory collective control body, independent from management board [article 20.1.4].

Entities, which obtained the status of Public Benefit Organizations have to follow specific rules, such as submitting technical and financial reports on the webpage of National Institute of Liberty, which is available for the public [article 23.6]. Among benefits can be distinguished exemptions from taxes and charges in the area connected with public benefit activity, which are characterized in article 24.1. Public Benefit Organizations can also gain the rights to utilize the properties belonging to State Treasury or local government units on preferential conditions [article 24.2] and announce free of charge about their activity in public radio and television broadcasting units [article 26]. Specific rules for these conveniences are described in distinct regulations.

Beside the term of PBO, the Law on Public Benefit Activity and Volunteerism have implemented the concept of 1% tax mechanism in Polish legal system. It is one of the benefits of becoming Public Benefit Organizations. Persons, submitting declaration of their PIT can decide whether to donate up to 1% of their income tax to specific Public Benefit Organization [article 27.1]. In practise, they do not donate their private funds to chosen organizations, but they prevent some part of their tax to become public money. Hence, donation of 1% tax cannot be treated as pure philanthropy.

The 1% tax mechanism is one of many possibilities to finance the PBOs activity. The sources of their revenues can be classified in two categories: internal and external (Kusmanto and XuFeng 2013, p. 37). First group contains such revenues as membership fees, income from projects and economic activity. Among external revenue sources can be identified funds from donors and grants (Abou and Trent 2020, pp. 7, 9, 16). Mikołajczak (2019, pp. 113–114) proposed more detailed division of sources of revenues. Among external revenues he identifies: public fundraising revenues, financial and non-financial donations from private individuals, financial and non-financial donations from institutions, companies, revenues from 1% of the income tax, support from other national and foreign NGOs. Whereas membership fees, interests, profits from endowment capital, deposits, shares and stocks, revenues from assets, revenue from commercial activity, revenue from paid-activity of the third sector, punitive damages are qualified as internal sources of revenues. This classification is more oriented on Polish realities, as it includes 1% tax and distinguishes paid-activity from commercial activity, as it is done in Law on Public Benefit Activity and Volunteerism [article 8 and 9].

Organizations' strategies for revenue generation may vary in terms of differentiation or dominant revenue source, what can be observed within the most successful U.S. NGOs (Crittenden 2000, p. 2). Foster and Bradach (2005, pp. 92–100) suggest that choosing commercial activity as a source of revenue may be an advantage, as it makes the organizations pursuing such strategy independent from single donors. According to the resource dependency theories the biggest influence on NGOs' have actors, which are their biggest donors, or in other words, whose support is particularly important (Banaszak-Holl et al. 1996). Government grants have been considered as relatively predictable funding, however smaller organizations have not enough financial resources to obtain and maintain such revenues. (Chang et al. 2018, p. 15) The negative correlation between extent of dependence on revenues from commercial activity and effectiveness in donation generation has been documented. (Ecer et al. 2017, p. 143) Social enterprises have higher efficiency in generating revenues from commercial activity, however traditional non-profit organizations achieve better performance in raising grants and donations. (Ecer et al. 2017, p. 151) It may lead to the conclusion that for certain organizations concentration on particular sources of revenues might be more efficient. When some organizations developed ability to generate specific income, they may present lower effectiveness in raising funds from other sources.

According to the study of Tuckman and Chang (1991), smaller NGOs often have the need to search for more sources of financing, but they might not have enough staff to pursue this action. Such revenue source as 1% tax do not have relevant entry barriers, beside the necessity to operate in the area of Public Benefit Activity, thus for organizations with unstable revenue sources it can be additional diversification and financial support.

Figure 1 shows the revenues from 1% tax gathered each year by all PBOs in Poland (Central Statistical Office 2019, p. 1). Except for year 2010, the constant increase can be observed. This tendency is caused not only by the growing popularity of 1% mechanism, but also the changes in regulations, which made donations of 1% more accessible for taxpayers. Up to year 2007, 1% tax could be transferred to organizations by the bank transfer done by taxpayer, basing on own calculations. Donated amount was returned to the taxpayer by tax authorities. Regulations implemented in 2008 allowed to donate 1% by providing National Court Register number of Public Benefit Organization in tax return and amount, which couldn't be higher than 1% tax. In this way 1% was transferred directed to PBO by tax authorities, not directly by the taxpayer (Chojnacka 2020, p. 455).

Basing on statistics it may be concluded that mechanism of 1% tax is relevant revenue source for Public Benefit Organizations. For example, in 2018 the funds from 1% tax of 761 million PLN were directed to Public Benefit Organizations as an additional source of revenue. Each organization received on average 87,7 thousand PLN. Concededly, the median in the same year amounted to 4,9 thousand PLN, which indicated the inequalities in revenues obtained from 1% among organizations (Central Statistical Office 2019, pp. 1–2). Nevertheless, receival of revenues from 1% tax, does not require any additional expenses from Public Benefit Organizations, so this source of additional funds can be

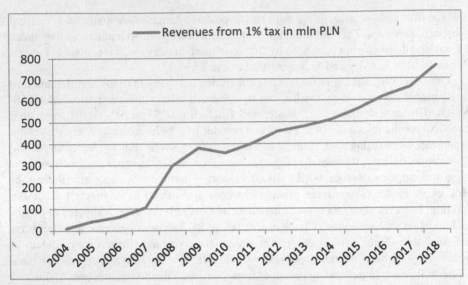

Fig. 1. Sum of all funds transmitted to Public Benefit Organizations in terms of 1% mechanism in years 2004–2018 (dates on figure relate to year in which the funds were transmitted to organizations, not the year to which tax return was related).

considered unquestionably as an advantage. The data concerning revenues shows that 1% tax constitutes on average 2,44% of Public Benefit Organizations' total revenues, which can be considered as a low number, in comparison to the funding from public sources (54,85%). On the other hand, the amount from 1% seems to be almost as significant for organizations as incomes from commercial activity (4,72% of total revenues) and donations from individuals and private entities (3,36% of total revenues).

The aim to implement regulations concerning Public Benefit Organizations in Poland was to promote public benefit activities, enhance the flow of funds to organizations, enable easier cooperation between public bodies and NGOs and make organizations more transparent, which is in favour of tightening relationship between 3rd Sector and society (Bullain et al. 2008, pp. 3–4). It may be observed that these regulations are constructed in a way to support the activities of organizations in scope of public benefit activity and ensure accountability of Public Benefit Organizations.

According to the research made by Kietlińska (2015), the mechanism of 1% tax and the revenue from this mechanism is the most important motivation to have the status of Public Benefit Organizations for NGO's in Poland. However, the benefits of status vary according to the wealth of the organization (see Table 1).

Table 1. Change in financial situation of organization after obtaining the status

Revenue	Definitely improvement	Improvement	No change	Deterioration
1 mln+	100%	–	–	–
300.000 – 1 mln	67%	33%	–	–
100.000–300.000	38%	50%	6%	6%
30.000–100.000	42%	40%	13%	5%
10.000–30.000	40%	52%	4%	4%
2.000–10.000	17%	68%	14%	1%
<2.000	17%	59%	22%	2%
Total	**28%**	**57%**	**12%**	**3%**

Source: (Ratajczak and Chojecki 2012)

Although from the declaration's point of view most of the organizations feel the improvement after obtaining the status of Public Benefit Organization, the higher impact is visible in biggest organizations according to the revenues and smallest one – in the little institutions. In fact, the number of people supporting organizations are increasing from year to year independently from the wealth of the organization, what suggests that the contributors of the little organization could be the less wealthy people (Kietlińska 2015). Another study conducted by Lorentowicz K., Kalinowski S. and Wyduba W. (2020, p. 301) proved strong correlation between revenue size and having the status of PBO. Due to the relative nature of revenues expressed in amounts, above feature should be checked, taking into account the more absolute value as the share of 1% tax's revenue in total revenues. That is why the first hypothesis is formulated as follows:

H1: The size of the organization (measured by the total revenues) has significant impact on the revenues raised from 1% Tax mechanism considered as their share in total revenues.

The size of the organization could be measured not only by the total revenues but also by the geographic area of the activity. Thus next hypothesis is formulated as follows:

H2: The size of the organization (measured by the geographic area of the activity) has significant impact on the revenues raised from 1% tax mechanism considered as their share in total revenues.

According to authors' knowledge there is no significant research concerning the motives of donors, who decide to support the PBO's from the 1% tax mechanism. Therefore, it could be only suppose, that they follow the campaign in media or the popularity of the organization. The organizations are the same opinion (see Table 2).

In fact, the organizations do not prefer the increase of the promotion costs, however the organization's presence in media (26%), support of VIPs or freelancers (22%), charismatic leader of organization (18%) or attractive message of the campaign (15%) are treated as the wide form of promotion and advertisement of organization (Ratajczak

Table 2. Factors influence on increasing the funds raised from 1% tax mechanism in the opinion of PBO's

Factor	Percentage of indication
High prestige and good visibility in the society	46
Attractive line of organization's activity for the donors	34
Organization's experience	32
Long history of organization's activity	27
Organization's presence in media	26
Support of VIPs or freelancers	22
Charismatic leader of organization	18
Attractive message of the campaign	15
Increase of the promotion costs	8

Source: (Ratajczak and Chojecki 2012)

and Chojecki 2012). Adding to this the good visibility in the society push the authors to conjecture, that.

H3: Having the website by the organization has significant impact on the revenues raised from 1% tax mechanism considered as their share in total revenues.

H4: Conducting the campaign by the organization has significant impact on the revenues raised from 1% tax mechanism considered as their share in total revenues.

3   Data and Method

3.1   Sample

The data used for the research have been gathered manually from yearly technical reports of Public Benefit Organizations from year 2018. The registry of all Public Benefit Organizations, which are eligible to receive 1% tax is published on the webpage of National Institute of Liberty. Organizations in this base are ordered ascending according to the National Court Register number. First 100 organizations have been chosen from this registry as a statistical sample intended to the research.

Although, all Public Benefit Organizations are obliged to publish technical reports from their activity, the organizations, which had the revenue below 100 000,00 PLN (22 000,00 EUR) per year, submit the report in simplified form. The essential difference between two types of reports is the level of specificity, e.g. simplified report has fewer types of revenue sources in relation to technical reports for organizations with revenues above 100 000,00 PLN. Nevertheless, the unification of all submitted reports is ensured in the Law on Public Benefit and Volunteerism. Therefore, the data from both types of reports were comparable with each other and could be used in the research.

In Table 3 is gathered basic profile of organisations participating in the study.

Table 3. Profile of PBO's participating in the study

Age	
<5 years	9%
5–10 years	19,0%
10–15 years	49,0%
>15 years	23,0%
Location	
Municipality	84,0%
Countryside	16,0%
Legal form	
Foundation	6,0%
Association	41,0%
Others	53,0%
Geographical area of activity	
Very small (local or within county)	39%
Small (few counties or voivodeship)	22%
Medium (few voivodeship)	6%
Large (whole country)	21%
Very large (abroad)	10%

Source: Own study

The variables applied in analysis have been raised from technical reports of organizations, except the number of citizens of locality, where the residence of organization is placed. The variables have been chosen basing on the potential connection with the share of 1% of tax with total revenues.

3.2 Dependent Variable

Due to the aim and hypothesis, basic dependent variable is the share of 1% tax revenue in total revenues.

3.3 Independent Variables

Following data was gathered from the official reports:

Location   dummy variable answered the question where the organisation has its headquarter – municipality (1) or countryside (2)

Legal form		variable with 3 values, where 1 – foundation, 2 – association, 3 – other. The legal form of organizations has been specified, basing on the names of Public Benefit Organizations, not the actual legal form according to the National Court Registry. Due to knowledge of most taxpayers, which outflows from the name of organization instead of registered legal form, according to authors, this variable is more suitable to show how the legal form of organizations influences taxpayers in terms of 1% tax donation
Website		dummy variable, where 1 – the organisation has his own website, 0 – the organisation has no website
Campaign		dummy variable, where 1 – the organisation used the campaign concerning the 1% tax promotion, 0 – the organisation did not use the campaign
Area		geographical area of activity, where 1 – the organisation works locally within the specific community, 2 – the organisation works within the specific county, 3 – the organisation works within the specific voivodship, 4 – the organisation works within whole country, 5 – the organisation works within Poland and other countries
No_citizens		number of citizens in the place where the organisation is registered
Age		number of years being the Public Benefit Organisation
Total revenue		the total revenue obtained by organisation in the surveyed year

4   Results

The basic characteristics of the gathered data are placed in Table 4.

Table 4. Descriptive statistics of data

	N	Minimum	Maximum	Mean	Std. Deviation
Location	100	1,00	2,00	1,20	0
Legal form	100	1,00	3,00	2,10	1
Website	100	0,00	1,00	0,70	0
Campaign	100	0,00	1,00	0,00	0
Area	100	0,00	5,00	2,30	1
No_citizens	100	347,00	687702,00	129026,10	140232
Age	100	2,00	16,00	12,20	4
Total revenue	100	0,00	12892349	943044,1	2092749
1% share	100	0,00	1,00	0,10	0
Valid N (listwise)	100				

From Table 4 it can be concluded that in the sample more organizations are located in the municipality and their activity is connected with the nearest area (mean of the area is 2.3). They operate as PBO for more than 10 years and are medium organization from the revenue's point of view (around 100th PLN/year). They attract the donations from the 1% tax mechanism, however its share in the total revenue is rather low (mean 10%).

Due to check the relationship between the identified factors and the 1% tax revenue's share, the correlation have been analysed (see Table 5).

Table 5. Correlation between the variables

	Location	Legal form	Website	Campaign	Area	No_Citizens	Age	Total revenue	1% share
Location	1.0000 P = .000								
Legal form	.0590 p = .560	1.0000 p = .000							
Website	−.2020** p= .044	.0110 p = .914	1.0000 p = .000						
Campaign	−.0439 p = .665	−.1170 p = .246	.0642 p = .525	1.0000 P = .000					
Area	−.1415 p = .160	−.0563 p = .519	.0474 p = .640	.1132 p = .262	1.0000 p = .000				
No_citizens	−.3988*** p= .000	−.1377 p = .172	.1297 p = .198	.1213 p = .229	.1879* p= .061	1.0000 p = .000			
Age	−.1585 p = .115	.0478 p = .637	.2307** p= .021	.0213 p = .833	.0891 p = .378	.0968 p = .338	1.0000 p = .000		
Total revenue	.0309 p = .760	.0062 p = .951	.1755* p= .081	.1101 p = .275	.1033 p = .306	.0156 p = .878	.0128 p = .900	1.0000 p = .000	
1% share	−.0895 p = .376	−.2484** p= .013	.0873 p = .388	v.0401 p = .692	−.0966 p = .339	.2369** p= .018	.2047** p= .041	−.2024** p= .043	1.0000 p = .000
Valid N (listwise)	100								

*** $p < 0.01$; ** $p < 0.05$; * $p < 0.1$

The analysis of correlations shows the significant relation between the 1% tax revenue's share and four variables: legal form, no_citizens, age and total revenue. Beside the connection between the 1% share variable and the total revenue, which seems to be obvious, the other relations suggest the real influence of these variables on revenues from 1% tax mechanism. It is worth noticing that such factors as location, website, campaign or area seems to be not important for the taxpayers and possible donators. This is in opposite to the results of previous research (Ratajczak and Chojecki 2012) and does not confirm the opinion of the organisations themselves (see Table 2).

To check the strength of above relation the hierarchical regression analysis has been conducted, which results are gathered in Table 6 and Table 7.

Table 6. Hierarchical regression with dependent variable *1% share*

Step/Predictor	Step 1 (β-factor, p-value)	Step 2 (β-factor, p-value)	Step 3 (β-factor, p-value)	Step 4 (β-factor, p-value)	Step 5 (β-factor, p-value)
(Intercept)	.02762 *** $p = .0000$	.1108 $p = .2401$	.1315 $p = .1584$	.0880 $p = .3499$	.1368 $p = .1649$
Legal form	−.0654 ** $p = .0127$	−.0681 *** $p = .0082$	−.0678 *** $p = .0074$	−.0607 ** $p = .0156$	−.0625 ** $p = .0123$
Age		.0141 ** $p = .0259$	.0142 ** $p = .0218$	.0130 ** $p = .0344$	.0137 ** $p = .0250$
Total revenue			−.0000 ** $p = .0329$	−.0000 ** $p = .0282$	−.0000 ** $p = .0411$
No_citizens				.0000 ** $p = .0473$	.0000 ** $p = .0253$
Area					−.0262 $p = .1114$
R^2	.2484	.3297	.3875	.4299	.4546
ΔR^2	.0616	.1087	.1502	.1848	.2066

*** $p < 0.01$; ** $p < 0.05$; * $p < 0.1$

Table 7. Differences between the models in hierarchical regression

	Res.Df	RSS	Df	Sum of Sq	F	p-value
Model 1/Step1	98	6.0164				
Model 2/Step2	97	5.7149	1	0.30148	5.5707	0.02033 *
Model 3/Step3	96	5.4491	1	0.26583	4.9120	0.02908 *
Model 4/Step4	95	5.2268	1	0.22223	4.1063	0.04556 *
Model 5/Step5	94	5.0871	1	0.13974	2.5821	0.11143

*** $p < 0.01$; ** $p < 0.05$; * $p < 0.1$

The first variable included in the model is the legal form. It explains about 25% of the 1% tax share, which is quite good result and should be surprising for the organizations themselves, because the previous research has not shown this factor as important from their point of view (Ratajczak and Chojecki 2012). This result suggests that the information in the name of organization, is it foundation, association or other could be crucial for the raising funds from taxpayer.

The second variable, which is included in the model, is the age. It adds to the model other 8.13 percentage points of explanation, what is significant difference from the above analyse point of view. The funds from 1% tax mechanism for taxpayer are not the typical donation for organizations because this is the part of the tax, thereby the part of the obligatory payment. The taxpayer could only decide to pay everything to the central budget or to split it and donate the part to the organization. Thus, this is not the renunciation of consumption but more the decision about decreasing the funds for the government. Taking into account this fact, the experience of the organization and the stability connected with it is very important factor for the donors to be sure their funds would be not given to the cheaters.

The third variable added to the model (Total revenue) increases the explanation about next 5.78 percentage points. This figure seems to show that although this factor is important for the raising the funds from the 1% tax mechanism, it is not as crucial as suggests the previous research and the opinion of the organizations themselves. Thus, there is no basis to reject the hypothesis H1. However, there are other factors like age and legal form which are more important for the taxpayers as the possible donors. Analysis of other variable connected with the size of the organization (geographic area) may lead to the conclusion that the size at all is the factor which is over prioritized in the general opinion of the possibility of raising the funds from the 1% tax mechanism. The correlation analysis confirms this finding. Although the area is included in the model in the last step, the hypothesis H2 should be rejected. There is no significant correlation between the area and the 1% tax share and the final model is not significantly different from the previous ones.

The last important factor in our hierarchical analysis is the number of citizens, which included into model increases the $R2$ to 42.00% and this change is significant comparing to the model in the previous step. Therefore, it may be conjectured that the surrounding area of organization's location with more people/citizens gives higher possibility of attracting the funds and potential donors. However, such factors like website or campaign are not significant for these people. Lack of correlation between these factors and the 1% tax share as well the results of the hierarchical analysis suggest that the H3 and H4 hypothesis should be rejected. This means that although the organizations themselves declare and think that promotion and advertisement is important in attracting the funds, this specific mechanism (1% tax) is resistant to such activities. The taxpayers are much more sensitive to experience and "good brand" of the organization or other specific factors which are not included in this research.

5   Discussion

The research was focused on the 1% tax mechanism as the way of raising funds for Public Benefit Organizations in Poland. Although the status of PBO imposes on organizations additional obligations as e.g. preparing and publishing the technical reports from the activity, the possibility of gathering more funds through the 1% tax mechanism is the most important motivation for NGOs to have this status (Kietlińska 2015). Most of the organizations declare that after obtaining the status of PBO their situation improved. However, the share of funds raised from 1% tax mechanism on average is not higher than 10% of total revenues attracted by the organizations. The truth is that from year to year the amount of money transferred via this way to the PBOs is still rising and more taxpayers are willing to split the obligatory payment and donate the organizations. On the other hand, more organizations want to attract these funds for themselves and the knowledge about importance of factors and motives of donors could be crucial in winning this battle. From this study outflow few important findings:

- Size of organization (measured by total revenue or geographical area) is important but there are other factors which are more interesting for the possible donors
- The information in the name of organization about its legal form could be crucial for the decision of taxpayer
- The visible experience and good identity of PBO is very important for possible donors, especially for this from 1% tax mechanism
- The good public relations could influence on the donors, but there is no significant correlation between these factors

This research has also certain limitations. First of all, data is focused only on the one country (Poland) and if the area of analysis is broadened, the results could be different. It is possible because of mentality of people, history, law regulations, tax rates, etc. However, it could be very interesting to check these relations in other communities, where this mechanism works. Second, the data was gathered only from the official technical reports and from 100 organizations. There are a lot of very little foundations set up for only one reason – raising funds for very expensive treatment or surgery. Many families with disable member(s) in Poland have set up such organization to ask the people or companies for help in their daily life. In 2019 and 2020 many of such PBOs have not obtained the money although there were a lot of donors. The tax authorities explain this situation of the formal mistakes in declarations or other accounting problems and regulations. However, such little organizations sometimes are not present in the official reports or the data are very simplified. Besides that, the official technical reports of PBO do not include other data and factors which could show the importance and possible motivations of the taxpayer as e.g. connections with other organizations/companies, specific activity, which taxpayers decided to support, how many taxpayers decided to transfer 1% to certain organization, the basic scope of activity, etc. It will be very interesting to make the more detailed research to know the real motivation of choosing the specific organization, if any.

References

Abou, A., Trent, D.: NGO accountability from an NGO perspective: their perceptions, strategies, and practices. Program on Governance and Local Development Working Paper No. 4 (2020). https://doi.org/10.2139/ssrn.3630087

Aldashev, G., Navarra, C.: Development NGOs: basic facts. ECARES Working Paper 2017-36, Brussels (2018). https://doi.org/10.1111/apce.12188

Aldashev, G., Verdier, T.: Goodwill bazaar: NGO competition and giving to development. J. Dev. Econ. **91**(48–63), 50 (2010). https://doi.org/10.1016/j.jdeveco.2008.11.010

Banaszak-Holl, J., Zinn, J.S., Mor, V.: The impact of market and organizational characteristics on nursing care facility service innovation: A resource dependency perspective. Health Serv. Res. **31**, 97–117 (1996)

Bullain, N., Hadzi-Miceva, K., Moore, D.: A comparative overview of public benefit status In Europe. Int. J. Not-for-Profit Law **11**, 5 (2008)

Chang, C., Tuckman, H., Chikoto-Schultz, G.: Income diversity and non profit financial health. In: Handbook of Research on Nonprofit Economics and Management, pp. 11–34. Edward Elgar Publishing (2018). https://doi.org/10.4337/9781785363528

Chojecki, J., Ratajczak, J.: Wpływ statusu OPP na działalność organizacji. Raport z badań Stowarzyszenie Klon/Jawor, Warszawa (2012)

Chojnacka, E.: One percent of personal income tax as a source of revenue in public benefit organizations. Econ. Law **19**, 449–465 (2020). https://doi.org/10.12775/EiP.2020.030

Crittenden, W.F., Crittenden, V.L.: Relationships between organizational characteristics and strategic planning processes in nonprofit organizations. J. Manag. Issues, 150–168 (2000)

Ecer, S., Margo, M., Sarpca, S.: The relationship between nonprofits' revenue composition and their economic-financial efficiency. Nonprofit Volunt. Sect. Q. **46**, 141–155 (2017). https://doi.org/10.1177/0899764016649693

Foster, W., Bradach, J.: Should nonprofits seek profits? Harv. Bus. Rev. **83**, 92–100 (2005)

Kalinowski, S., Lorentowicz, K., Wyduba, W.: Funding for rural NGOs. Stud. Prawno-Ekon. **115**, 283–305 (2020). https://doi.org/10.26485/SPE/2020/115/16

Kietlińska, K.: Rola 1% w zasilaniu organizacji pożytku publicznego. Wydawnictwo Uniwersytetu Ekonomicznego we Wrocławiu (2015)

Kusmanto, P., XuFeng, F.: An insight into NGO challenges and the need for organisational capacity building for Malaysian NGOs. Indonesian Student Association in Thailand (2013)

Mikołajczak, P.: Diversification of NGO's revenues: implications for the mission changeability. Hum. Soc. Sci. **24**, 113–120 (2019)

Organizacje pożytku publicznego i 1% w 2017 r./2018 r. Główny Urząd Statystyczny/Central Statistical Office (2019). http://stat.gov.pl

Tuckman, H., Chang, C.: A methodology for measuring the financial vulnerability of charitable nonprofit organizations. Nonprofit Volunt. Sect. q. **20**, 445–460 (1991)

Ustawa o działalności pożytku publicznego i o wolontariacie/Law on Public Benefit Activity and Volunteerism. t.j. Dz. U. z 2020 r. poz. 1057 (2003)

Załącznik_nr_2_-_ Wykaz_OPP_2019. https://www.gov.pl/web/finanse/1-procent-podatku-dla-opp. Author, F.: Article title. Journal **2**(5), 99–110 (2016)

Reformulation of Some Indices Using Null Player Free Winning Coalitions

Izabella Stach[1]([⊠]) [iD] and Cesarino Bertini[2] [iD]

[1] AGH University of Science and Technology, Al. Mickiewicza 30, 30-059 Krakow, Poland
istach@zarz.agh.edu.pl
[2] Department of Economics, University of Bergamo, Via dei Caniana, 2, 24127 Bergamo, Italy
cesarino.bertini@unibg.it

Abstract. The proposal of this paper is a new representation for some power indices in a simple game using null player free winning coalitions. Analogously to a set of winning coalitions and minimal winning coalitions, a set of null player free winning coalitions fully captures the characteristics of a simple game. Moreover, expressing indices by winning coalitions that do not contain null players allows us to show the parts of the power that are assigned to null and non-null players in a simple game in a transparent manner.

Keywords: Simple games · Null player free winning coalitions · Power indices

1 Introduction

In simple games, a great variety of power indices that are intended to assess different variations of the notion of power under different conditions have been proposed in the literature. In this paper, we consider the Banzhaf [1, 2], Rae [3], Coleman (to prevent action and to initiate action) [4], Nevison [5], and König and Bräuninger [6, 7] indices. This group of indices has been studied from different points of view. For example, Laruelle et al. [8] analyzed these indices (excluding the Nevison index) from the point of view of the probabilistic interpretation of power by taking the concepts of decisiveness, satisfaction, or success into account. Meanwhile, Stach [9] analyzed these indices as well as others as being well-defined in the social context. Moreover, these indices are closely connected with each other (see Sect. 3.6). More information about these indices as well as their comparisons are provided in [8–11], for example.

The proposal of this paper is a new representation of the above-mentioned power indices in a simple game using null player free winning coalitions. The set of null player free winning coalitions is as important as the sets of winning coalitions or minimal winning coalitions (see Fig. 1). Analogous to the set of winning coalitions and minimal winning coalitions, the set of null player free winning coalitions fully captures the characteristics of a simple game. Thus, the set of null player free winning coalitions states an alternative representation of a simple game (see Sect. 2). To the knowladge of the authors, Álvarez-Mozos et al. [12] were the first to define two power indices that are completely based on a set of null player free winning coalitions. Therefore, the idea to

© Springer-Verlag GmbH Germany, part of Springer Nature 2021
N. T. Nguyen et al. (Eds.): TCCI XXXVI, LNCS 13010, pp. 108–115, 2021.
https://doi.org/10.1007/978-3-662-64563-5_6

express some well-known power indices by a set of null player free winning coalitions appeared. In this way, we can take a new look at the old indices.

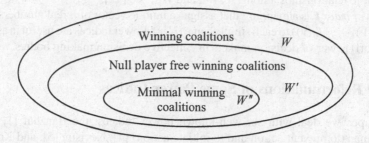

Fig. 1. Set of winning coalitions

The rest of the paper is structured as follows. In Sect. 2, we provide a theoretical background; i.e., the preliminary definitions and concepts of simple games. In Sect. 3, we recall the definitions of all of the power indices and provide formulas based on null player free winning coalitions. Section 4 concludes the paper.

2 Preliminaries on Simple Games

Let $N = \{1, 2, \ldots, n\}$ be a finite set of *players* and 2^N be the set of all subsets of N. Any $S \in 2^N$ is called a *coalition*, and N is called the *grand coalition*. $|S|$ denotes the cardinality of S.

A *simple n-person game* is a pair (N, v) where v is a function $- v : 2^N \rightarrow \{0, 1\}$ – with

– $v(\varnothing) = 0$,
– $v(N) = 1$,
– $v(S) \leq v(T)$ for all coalitions $S \subseteq T \subseteq N$.

If $v(S) = 1$, then S is called a *winning coalition*; otherwise, $(v(S) = 0)$ it is called a *losing coalition*. A player i is *critical* in a winning coalition S if $v(S \setminus \{i\}) = 0$. A winning coalition is called a *minimal winning coalition* if each of its members is critical. For each player $i \in N$, we denote by η_i the set of coalitions in which i is critical. If $\eta_i = \varnothing$ for a player $i \in N$, then i is called a *null player*. A winning coalition S is called a *null player free winning coalition* if none of its members are null players.

In order to state the definitions of the power indices that are considered in this paper, let us introduce the following symbols. Let W, W', and W'' be the sets of winning coalitions, null player free winning coalitions, and minimal winning coalitions, respectively, in a simple game (N, v). Then, by W_i, W_i', and W_i'', we denote the corresponding subsets of W, W', and W'' formed by coalitions that contain player i. Any simple game may be unequivocally described by W, W', or W'' (see [12], for example). So, any simple game (N, v) can be described by its set of null player free winning coalitions W' as W or W'' can be easily obtained from W' as follows:

$$W = \{S \subseteq N : \exists T \in W' | T \subseteq S\}, W'' = \{S \in W' : (\forall T \subset S) \wedge (T \neq S), \ S \notin W'\}$$
$$= \{S \in W' : \forall i \in S \ (S \setminus \{i\}) \notin W'\}.$$

For more relationships among W, W', and W'', see [12].

A *power index* f is a mapping that assigns a unique vector of n real numbers $f(v) = (f_1(v), f_2(v), \ldots, f_n(v))$ to each simple game (N, v). Power indices are useful in assessing the (a priori) power of decision makers in collective decision making bodies.

3 New Reformulations of Some Power Indices

In this paper, we deal with six well-known power indices: the Banzhaf [1, 2], Rae [3], Coleman (to prevent action and to initiate action) [4], Nevison [5], and König and Bräuninger [6, 7] indices. In the following subsections, we recall the definitions of these indices and subsequently introduce our propositions for a new representation of these power indices using null player free winning coalitions. Then, we express the known relationships between the power indices based on null player free winning coalitions in Sect. 3.6.

Consider N' that arises from N by deleting the null players. Then, $N = N' \cup N^{null}$, where N^{null} denotes the set of all null players in (N, v). Since

$$|W| = 2^{|N^{null}|}|W'|, \tag{1}$$

$$|W_i| = 2^{|N^{null}|}|W_i'| \text{ for each } i \in N \setminus N^{null}, \tag{2}$$

and

$$|W_i| = 2^{|N^{null}|-1}|W'| \text{ for each } i \in N^{null}, \tag{3}$$

we can express the power indices that are based on the number of winning coalitions (the Nevison and König and Bräuninger indices) by the number of null player free winning coalitions. Moreover, using the Dubey and Shapley identity [13, p. 127]

$$|\eta_i| = 2|W_i| - |W|, \tag{4}$$

we can formulate the Banzhaf, Rae, and Coleman to prevent action and Coleman to initiate action indices by null player free winning coalitions as well.

3.1 Nevison Index

The Nevison [5] index for each simple game (N, v) and player $i \in N$ is defined as follows:

$$Z_i(v) = \frac{|W_i|}{2^{n-1}}.$$

Proposition 1. $Z_i(v) = \begin{cases} \frac{|W_i'|}{2^{n-|N^{null}|-1}} & \text{if } i \in N' \\ \frac{|W'|}{2^{n-|N^{null}|}} & \text{if } i \in N^{null}. \end{cases}$

Proof. Consider a simple game (N, v). For each $i \in N \setminus N^{null}$, we have $Z_i(v) = \frac{|W_i|}{2^{n-1}}$ $= \frac{2^{|N^{null}|}|W_i'|}{2^{n-1}} = \frac{|W_i'|}{2^{n-|N^{null}|-1}}$ from Eq. (2). Note that, in [5], it was shown that the Z index assigns the same power $Z_i(v) = \frac{|W|}{2^n}$ to each null player $i \in N^{null}$. So, from (1), we immediately obtain $Z_i(v) = \frac{2^{|N^{null}|}|W'|}{2^n} = \frac{|W'|}{2^{n-|N^{null}|}}$ for any null player i,, which is what is needed to be proven.

3.2 König and Bräuninger Index

Introduced in [7] and then reinvented in [6], the König-Bräuninger index (KB) is defined by the following for each (N, v) and player $i \in N$:

$$KB_i(v) = \frac{|W_i|}{|W|}.$$

Proposition 2. $KB_i(v) = \begin{cases} \frac{|W_i'|}{|W'|} & \text{if } i \in N' \\ \frac{1}{2} & \text{if } i \in N^{null}. \end{cases}$

Proof. Consider a simple game (N, v). For each $i \in N'$, we have $KB_i(v) = \frac{|W_i|}{|W|} = \frac{2^{|N^{null}|}|W_i'|}{2^{|N^{null}|}|W'|}$ from (1) and (2). For each $i \in N^{null}$, we have $KB_i(v) = \frac{2^{|N^{null}|-1}|W'|}{2^{|N^{null}|}|W'|} = \frac{1}{2}$ after applying (3); this completes the proof.

3.3 Banzhaf Index

Introduced in [2] and reinvented by the author in [1], the Banzhaf index is given by the following for each (N, v) and $i \in N$:

$$\beta_i(v) = \frac{|\eta_i|}{2^{n-1}}.$$

More information on the Banzhaf index can be found in [11, 14], for example.

Proposition 3. $\beta_i(v) = \begin{cases} \frac{2|W_i'|-|W'|}{2^{n-|N^{null}|-1}} & i \in N' \\ 0 & i \in N^{null}. \end{cases}$

Proof. Consider a simple game (N, v). If $i \in N^{null}$, then the total number of critical defections of i, $|\eta_i|$ is equal to 0 and $\beta_i(v) = 0$. If player $i \in N'$, then we obtain the following from (1), (2), and (4):

$$|\eta_i| = \begin{cases} 2^{|N^{null}|+1}|W_i'| - 2^{|N^{null}|}|W'| & i \in N' \\ 0 & i \in N^{null}. \end{cases} \tag{5}$$

For each $i \in N'$, we have $\beta_i(v) = \frac{2^{|N^{null}|}(2|W_i'|-|W'|)}{2^{n-1}} = \frac{2|W_i'|-|W'|}{2^{n-|N^{null}|-1}}$; this completes the proof.

3.4 Rae Index

The Rae index [3] is defined as follows for each (N, v) and $i \in N$:

$$R_i(v) = \frac{|\{S : i \in S \in W\}|}{2^n} + \frac{|\{S : i \notin S \notin W\}|}{2^n}.$$

Proposition 4. $R_i(v) = \begin{cases} \frac{1}{2} + \frac{2|W_i'|-|W'|}{2^{n-|N^{null}|}} & \text{if } i \in N' \\ \frac{1}{2} & \text{if } i \in N^{null}. \end{cases}$

Proof. There is an affine relationship between the Rae index and the Banzhaf index: $R_i(v) = \frac{1}{2} + \frac{1}{2}\beta_i(v)$ – see [13]. From this and Proposition 3, we immediately obtain the new formula of the Rae index.

3.5 Coleman's Indices

Coleman [4] defined two power indices in terms of different ratios. The Coleman index to prevent action is defined as.

$$C_i^P(v) = \frac{|\eta_i|}{|W|},$$

and the Coleman index to initiate action is given as

$$C_i^I(v) = \frac{|\eta_i|}{2^n - |W|}$$

for each (N, v) and $i \in N$.

Proposition 5. $C_i^P(v) = \begin{cases} \frac{2|W_i'|-|W'|}{|W'|} & \text{if } i \in N' \\ 0 & \text{if } i \in N^{null} \end{cases},$

$$C_i^I(v) = \begin{cases} \frac{2|W_i'|-|W'|}{2^{n-|N^{null}|}-|W'|} & \text{if } i \in N' \\ 0 & \text{if } i \in N^{null}. \end{cases}$$

Proof. The proof follows immediately from (1) and (5).

3.6 Relationships Between Power Indices

There are some known strict relationships between the Banzhaf index and each of the other power indices considered here. Of course, each power index contains important additional information (and not only that of the Banzhaf index). Namely, by applying Eqs. (4) and (1), we can obtain the following relationships that are based on the null player free winning coalitions:

$\beta_i(v) = 2Z_i(v) - \frac{|W|}{2^{n-1}}$, which was also mentioned in [9]. Using (1), we obtain

$$\beta_i(v) = 2Z_i(v) - \frac{|W'|}{2^{n-|N^{null}|-1}}.$$

Using (4), it is not difficult to show the following relationships:

$$\beta_i(v) = |W|\frac{2KB_i(v) - 1}{2^{n-1}} = \frac{|W|C_i^P(v)}{2^{n-1}} = \frac{(2^n - |W|)C_i^I(v)}{2^{n-1}}. \qquad (6)$$

Now, after applying (1), we have

$$\beta_i(v) = |W'|\frac{2KB_i(v) - 1}{2^{n-|N^{null}|-1}} = \frac{|W'|C_i^P(v)}{2^{n-|N^{null}|-1}} = \frac{(2^{n-|N^{null}|} - |W'|)C_i^I(v)}{2^{n-|N^{null}|-1}}. \qquad (7)$$

As is known, Dubey and Shapley [13] established the well-known relationship between the Banzhaf index and the Rae index (see also Sect. 3.4):

$$\beta_i(v) = 2R_i(v) - 1.$$

Then, Lane and Maeland [15] also showed a similar relationship between the König-Bräuninger index and Coleman's index to prevent action indices; namely,

$$KB_i(v) = \frac{1 + C_i^P(v)}{2},$$

which immediately follows from (6) or (7).

The last two relationships do not depend on the number of the null player free winning coalitions, but we put them here to have full pictures of the relationships between the considered indices.

4 Concluding Comments

The novel contributions of this paper is the proposal of a reformulation of some well-known power indices like the Banzhaf [1, 2], Rae [2], Coleman (to prevent action) [4], Coleman (to initiate action) [4], Nevison [5], and König and Bräuninger [6, 7] indices. For these indices, we give a new representation based on the information contained in the set of null player free winning coalitions (see Sect. 3). It is worth noticing that the set of null player free winning coalitions unequivocally defines a simple game (see Sect. 2 and [12]).

The second new contribution is the presentation of the relationships between these indices and the Banzhaf index using the notation of null player free winning coalitions (see Sect. 3.6).

Although these indices can be calculated in other ways. The methods described here could be used to calculate indices in a more optimized manner in games with a lot of null players. In the sense that eliminating the null players from a game give the advantage in lowering the storage issue and improve space efficiency of an algorithm.

It seems plausible to extend the ideas in the present paper to this more general context. Namely, an idea for future research could be extending the notion of null player free winning coalition to games modeling voting rules with abstention as well as the indices considered and relationships found for simple games. To the best of the authors' knowledge, this issue has not been developed in the literatures yet. Some of these indices are already defined for games with abstention but not some others. In [16] some few indices used in this paper appear for games with abstention and some analysis on the Banzhaf index are done in [17] and [18].

References

1. Banzhaf, J.F.: Weighted voting doesn't work: a mathematical analysis. Rutgers Law Rev. **19**(2), 317–343 (1965)
2. Penrose, L.S.: The elementary statistics of majority voting. J. Roy. Stat. Soc. **109**(1), 53–57 (1946). https://doi.org/10.2307/2981392
3. Rae, D.: Decision rules and individual values in constitutional choice. Am. Polit. Sci. Rev. **63**, 40–56 (1969). https://doi.org/10.2307/1954283
4. Coleman, J.S.: Control of collectivities and the power of collectivity to act. In: Liberman, B. (ed.) Social Choice, pp. 269–300. Gordon and Breach, New York (1971)
5. Nevison, Chr.H.: Structural power and satisfaction in simple games. Appl. Game Theory 39–57 (1979). https://doi.org/10.1007/978-3-662-41501-6_3
6. König, T., Bräuninger, T.: The inclusiveness of European decision rules. J. Theor. Polit. **10**, 125–142 (1998). https://doi.org/10.1177/0951692898010001006
7. Nevison, Chr.H., Zicht, B., Schoepke, S.: A naive approach to the Banzhaf index of power. Behav. Sci. **23**(2), 130–131 (1978). https://doi.org/10.1002/bs.3830230209
8. Laruelle, A., Martınez, R., Valenciano, F.: Success versus decisiveness conceptual discussion and case study. J. Theor. Polit. **18**(2), 185–205 (2006). https://doi.org/10.1177/095162980 6061866
9. Stach, I.: Power measures and public goods. In: Nguyen, N.T., Kowalczyk, R., Mercik, J. (eds.) Transactions on Computational Collective Intelligence XXIII. LNCS, vol. 9760, pp. 99–110. Springer, Heidelberg (2016). https://doi.org/10.1007/978-3-662-52886-0_6
10. Bertini, C., Freixas, J., Gambarelli, G., Stach, I.: Comparing power indices. Int. Game Theory Rev. **15**(2), 1340004-1–1340004-19 (2013)
11. Felsenthal, D., Machover, M.: Voting power measurement: a story of misreinvention. Soc. Choice Welfare **25**, 485–506 (2005). https://doi.org/10.1007/s00355-005-0015-9
12. Álvarez-Mozos, M., Ferreira, F., Alonso-Meijide, J.M., Pinto, A.A.: Characterizations of power indices based on null player free winning coalitions. Optim.: J. Math. Program. Oper. Res. **64**(3), 675–686 (2015). https://doi.org/10.1080/02331934.2012.756878
13. Dubey, P., Shapley, L.: Mathematical properties of the Banzhaf power index. Math. Oper. Res. **4**(2), 99–131 (1979). https://doi.org/10.1287/moor.4.2.99
14. Bertini, C., Stach, I.: Banzhaf voting power measure. In: Dowding, K. (ed.) Encyclopedia of Power, pp. 54–55. SAGE Publications, Los Angeles (2011). https://doi.org/10.4135/978141 2994088.n33
15. Lane, J.E., Maeland, R.: Constitutional analysis: the power index approach. Eur. J. Polit. Res. **37**, 31–56 (2000). https://doi.org/10.1111/1475-6765.00503
16. Freixas, J.: Probabilistic power indices for voting rules with abstention. Math. Soc. Sci. **64**(1), 89–99 (2012). https://doi.org/10.1016/j.mathsocsci.2012.01.005

17. Freixas, J., Pons, M.: An appropriate way to extend the Banzhaf index for multiple levels of approval. Group Decis. Negot. **30**(2), 447–462 (2021). https://doi.org/10.1007/s10726-020-09718-7
18. Freixas, J.: The Banzhaf value for cooperative and simple multichoice games. Group Decis. Negot. **29**(1), 61–74 (2019). https://doi.org/10.1007/s10726-019-09651-4

Analysis and Modeling
of Activity-Selection Behavior
in Collaborative Knowledge-Building

Anamika Chhabra[1](✉) [iD], S. R. S. Iyengar[1], Jaspal Singh Saini[2],
and Vaibhav Malik[3]

[1] Department of CSE, Indian Institute of Technology Ropar, Rupnagar, India
[2] Oregon State University, Corvallis, USA
[3] Synaptic Ltd., Gurgaon, India

Abstract. People neither behave uniformly in their social lives nor is
their behavior entirely arbitrary. Rather, their behavior depends on various factors such as their skills, motives, and backgrounds. Our analysis shows that such a behavior also prevails in the websites of Stack
Exchange. We collect and analyze the data of over 5.3 million users from
156 Stack Exchange websites. In these websites, users' diverse behavior
shows up in the form of different activities that they choose to perform
as well as how they stimulate each other for more contribution. Using
the insights gained from the empirical analysis as well as the classical cognitive theories, we build a general cognitive model depicting the
users' interaction behavior emerging in collaborative knowledge-building
setups. Further, the analysis of the model indicates that for any given
collaborative system, there is an optimal distribution of users across its
activities that leads to the maximum knowledge generation. We also
apply the model on Stack Exchange websites and identify the under-
represented activities.

Keywords: Activity-selection · Knowledge-building · Q&A · Stack
Exchange · User-distribution · Triggering · Cognitive model

1 Introduction

Due to the advancements in Internet technology, a collection of websites for
collaboration and interaction are currently available. These websites are extensively helpful in aiding the process of building knowledge over the web. Some
of them include Stack Exchange, Wikipedia, Github, etc. These websites essentially depend on users' contribution for their functioning [15]. Further, these
users - owing to their disparate levels of motivation [18,38,46], skills [1,23,40]
and background [34] - exhibit diverse behavior on these websites. Due to this
behavior, they choose to perform different activities on these websites. This
diversity in the selection of activities is referred to as *role-playing* behavior in

© Springer-Verlag GmbH Germany, part of Springer Nature 2021
N. T. Nguyen et al. (Eds.): TCCI XXXVI, LNCS 13010, pp. 116–160, 2021.
https://doi.org/10.1007/978-3-662-64563-5_7

the literature [10,12,20,22,49]. Here, a role may constitute one or more activities that users generally perform on the website. A decent amount of past work explores the kind of roles that users play in websites such as CoWeb [22], Usenet newsgroups [16,20,48,50], Wikipedia [32,49], Stack Exchange [19,37,52], Yahoo Answers [1] and Naver [38]. These works mostly focus on identifying the kind of roles taken up by the contributors. However, the study of the distribution of users across these roles has been largely absent from the literature. As we will see, an examination of this distribution may provide actionable insights to improve the knowledge-building process in collaborative spaces. For instance, if there are very few users performing a given role, how does it affect the overall knowledge building process? Further, how are the users performing one role affected by the users performing other roles? Knowing that in a collaborative space, people get triggered by each others' contributions, it is natural to think that a variation in the proportion of users in one role may affect the overall knowledge production. This leads to the research aim of exploring the interaction between users of collaborative websites in general and in particular also how the distribution of users across the roles affects the effectiveness of such websites.

In this study, we perform an analysis of the websites of Stack Exchange, which involves examining the activities performed by each user to identify their preferred way of contributing to these websites. The role-playing behavior was accentuated in these websites by the observation that most of the users were inclined towards contributing to *only one* of the primary activities such as questioning, answering, or voting. We refer to this behavior as *Activity-selection Behavior*. This behavior helps in labeling each user, thus enabling the computation of a high-level distribution of users across the activities, termed as *User-distribution*. We also find that the contribution in one activity affects the contribution produced in other activities, thus indicating the triggering behavior among users performing these activities. Triggering among users of collaborative systems has also been endorsed by many classical cognitive theories such as *Luhmann's System Theory* [33] and *Piaget's theory* [42] among others [17,36]. The empirical findings as well as the cognitive theories help in building a model that explains the emerging behavior of the cognitive systems participating in a social system viz., a collaborative knowledge-building system. Using the individual level cognitive mechanisms, we also analyze the group-level dynamics that emerges from these cognitive mechanisms. We further apply this cognitive model to a sample of Stack Exchange websites and identify the activities that are less-represented. The model suggests the need to motivate the users towards the activities that require more contribution through informed strategies.

The work is organized as follows: Sect. 2 discusses the related literature. Section 3 reports the domain analysis, i.e., observations made on Stack Exchange websites with respect to the contributors' behavior. Based on the domain analysis, Sect. 4 presents a cognitive model that emerges from the interaction of users in a collaborative knowledge-building setup. Section 5 analyzes the group-level aspects of the model where we track the knowledge produced by the interaction of cognitive systems. Section 6 computes the model parameters for Stack

Exchange websites and provides insights on improving the knowledge-building process. Finally, Sect. 7 discusses the implications and future directions of the study.

2   Related Work

In this section, we first report the studies performed in examining the role-playing behavior of users. We then discuss the limited amount of work pursued so far in examining the dependency among users of a collaborative system. Finally, we discuss the work on finding the right balance of users in Wikipedia and other collaborative communities in general.

2.1   Role-Playing Behavior

The prevalence of role-playing behavior in online communities has been observed by several past studies. These studies have identified roles considering diverse perspectives. For instance, in Wikipedia, users may perform different activities such as insertion, deletion, or modification of the content. Moreover, they may contribute in different forms such as text, images or references, etc. Considering these diverse forms of contribution, roles have been identified where they consisted of one or more of these activities [4,5]. Studies have also been conducted on identifying the patterns of collaboration among users based on these roles [32]. One more criterion used for identifying roles in Wikipedia is based on users' skills and motivations. This results in roles such as *substantive experts*, *technical editors*, *vandal fighters*, and *social networkers* etc. [49]. Also, access privileges have been used to identify users' roles, which were further examined to study the users making the transition from one role to the other [7]. In addition to this, users have been differentiated based on whether they create an account or not, thus yielding roles such as 'Zealots' for registered users and 'Good Samaritans' for anonymous ones.

Similarly, on Usenet, a few works have studied roles based on the type of contribution made by users [20,50], while a few others have employed the network structure of users' interaction [2,16,48,50]. In the same way, on Q&A websites, roles have been distinguished based on the kind of activities that the users indulge in [1,38] as well as from the perspective of reputation gained by the users [37]. Considering the quantity and quality of users' contribution, Furtado et al. [19] determined ten behavioral profiles with overlapping activities.

A few related studies have been conducted on other Q&A websites such as Yahoo Answers [1] and Naver [38] which is South Korea's popular Q&A portal. On both these websites, the questions are available in diverse categories. It was found that most of the users focus only on one or a few favorite categories rather than across categories. Nam et al. [38] also observed a separation of roles between *askers* and *repliers*.

While the prevalence of contributors' roles has been acknowledged by many studies, the investigation of the implications of this behavior has been largely absent from the literature.

2.2   Triggering/Dependency Among Users

Many existing cognitive theories and empirical studies have highlighted the prevalence of triggering among the users of a collaborative system, whereby they stimulate each other to provide more contribution [29, 39, 44]. Explaining this process, Luhmann's theory of social systems [33] states that the existing content of the system creates perturbations in the cognitive systems of users, which steers them to contribute more content. Piaget's Model of equilibration [41] also supports that users interact with a social system because of cognitive conflicts, which means that when they see some information that is incongruent to their existing knowledge, it creates a disturbance in their minds which leads them to interact with the system. However, there comes a point when the system's information matches with users' knowledge, leading to an equilibration state.

A few empirical studies investigating the presence of triggering among users of collaborative environments have recently been conducted. This kind of triggering among users leads to implicit coordination among Wikipedia users, which is also termed as *Stigmergy* [45]. Rezgui and Crowston [43] studied stigmergy in Wikipedia articles by showing that a majority of edits in these articles are not associated with the discussion that takes place in their talk pages.

While triggering among users has been studied to some extent in Wikipedia, Q&A websites in this direction have rarely been examined.

2.3   Group Composition

In the direction of identifying the optimal group of participants for efficient knowledge building or problem-solving, multiple dimensions such as diversity, familiarity, conflict, etc. have been explored. For example, highlighting the importance of diversity in a group, it has been argued that a group of randomly selected people outperforms a group of best-performing people [26,28]. This is due to the different perspectives that these random people bring into the system. [21] examined the effect of familiarity among the group members on the outcome of the group task. The authors found that when the information was completely shared among the group members, the groups comprising of all-strangers were more likely to perform better than when the members were familiar. On Wikipedia, apart from highlighting the need for diversity and conflict resolution in groups, [6] emphasized on having the right balance of people providing content as well as those performing administrative tasks in the groups. [51] identified the contributors' roles and then suggested the kind of users that should participate based on the existing quality level of the article. For instance, with time, 'Wiki Gnomes', i.e., the users who perform cleanup activities are required more in number than 'Substantive Experts' who provide a good chunk of the raw content that is required more in the initial stages. In the context of task allocation, it has been asserted that different tasks require different kinds of crowds with variable skills and knowledge [15]. In that direction, it is observed that intelligently assigning tasks to the users remarkably increases the value of a crowdsourced system [30].

3 Domain Analysis: Contribution Behavior of Users in Stack Exchange Websites

In this section, we perform a detailed and longitudinal analysis of Stack Exchange websites to investigate the users' contribution behavior. We choose a Q&A portal for this analysis as the activities are clearly delineated in such a system unlike a portal like Wikipedia. It is, therefore, easier to examine users' contribution across different activities. Moreover, a rich collection of websites in Stack Exchange based on a variety of topics provides a comprehensive data set for analysis. The results of our analysis reveal how the users interact differently with the system as well as how they are affected by the contribution made by other users.

3.1 Data Set

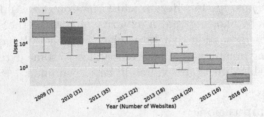

Fig. 1. The number of users in Stack Exchange Websites (excluding Stack Overflow) created in the years 2009 through (July) 2016. Number of websites created in each year have been shown in parenthesis on the X-axis. (Y-axis is log-scaled.)

Stack Exchange is the most popular collection of 156 Q&A websites (at the time of this study), each of which is intended for seeking help on a specific topic. The topics of these websites are quite diverse, ranging from technical subjects like programming, system administration, and operating systems to the general ones like cooking, gardening, and astronomy. Stack Exchange provides a facility to add websites on new topics by submitting a proposal through their interface called *Area51*[1]. It started as a single programming based website, i.e., Stack Overflow in 2008 and has since been adding new websites every year. All these websites operate as standalone websites and use a similar mode of functioning. Users can post questions, answer others' questions, provide comments, and up-vote or down-vote others' questions and answers. Voting leads to an increase or decrease in the reputation of the owner of the corresponding question or answer, which adds a gamification aspect to the websites, encouraging more content. The data set for this study was downloaded in August 2016 from the publicly available archive[2]. It consists of all the data of Stack Exchange websites

---

[1] http://area51.stackexchange.com/.

[2] https://archive.org/download/stackexchange.

from their inception up to July 2016. The data is in XML format storing the historical details of the question threads along with the information about users, tags, links, votes, badges, suggest-edits, deleted posts, timestamps, etc. Due to different starting times as well as diverse topics, the size of the user base across these websites is quite disparate. Figure 1 gives an idea of the number of users in the websites excluding Stack Overflow which has $28,29,352$ users. The Figure also shows the number of websites created each year from January 2009 through July 2016 on the X-axis. Detailed statistics such as the number of questions, answers, votes, users, and the starting year of all the websites are provided as Table 2 in the Appendix A.1.

3.2 Task Vectors and 'Activity-Selection Behavior'

Contribution by users on a Q&A website is primarily made in the form of asking questions or providing answers to them. On Stack Exchange, another activity that is performed extensively is voting. Apart from these, a user may provide a comment or edit another user's question or answer. However, commenting and editing are Stack Exchange-specific secondary activities, and Stack Exchange policies restrict users to perform these activities until they have gained a certain level of reputation through the primary activities. (Appendix A.2 reports these policies in detail.) Therefore, to avoid bias, we consider users' contributions in three primary activities, viz., questioning, answering, and voting for our further analysis.

For analyzing the contribution behavior of users, for each website of Stack Exchange, we processed its data set to compute the number of questions, answers and votes contributed by its users. We then created *Task Vectors* for each user as defined below:

Task Vector. V_i^w for a user i on website w is a vector that contains the percentage contribution of user i in the activities questioning, answering and voting with respect to their total contribution on w, i.e.,

$$V_i^w = \left[\frac{q_i^w}{T_i^w} \times 100, \ \frac{a_i^w}{T_i^w} \times 100, \ \frac{v_i^w}{T_i^w} \times 100 \right]$$

where q_i^w, a_i^w and v_i^w are the number of questions, answers and votes posted by the user i on the website w and T_i^w is the sum of their total contribution on the website w, i.e., $T_i^w = (q_i^w + a_i^w + v_i^w)$.

For instance, if a user A posts 20 questions, 170 answers, and 10 votes on a website, then his task vector will be [10, 85, 5]. The analysis focuses on the computation of percentages rather than the actual numbers as the motive is to identify the primary traits of users from the perspective of which activity they are more inclined to contribute to. In this context, we define three types of users: *Uni-C*, *Bi-C* and *Tri-C*. Uni-C are the users whose entire contribution is in *only one* activity. Similarly, Bi-C and Tri-C users contribute in two and all three of the activities respectively.

122   A. Chhabra et al.

Given the three activities under consideration, we were interested in finding how many of them behaved as Uni-C, i.e., the users who contributed precisely in one activity only. For each Stack Exchange website, we computed the proportion of task vectors belonging to Uni-C, Bi-C and Tri-C[3]. Remarkably, despite the above definition of Uni-C where they do not make even a slight contribution in any activity other than their favorite one, there was quite a high proportion of users exhibiting such behavior in almost all the websites. Figure 2(a) shows a box-plot depicting the proportion of Uni-C, Bi-C and Tri-C on the websites. The average proportion of Uni-C, Bi-C, and Tri-C on these websites was found to be 68.51% ($\sigma = 6.01$), 22.19% ($\sigma \doteq 4.14$) and 9.29% ($\sigma \doteq 3.54$) respectively, with the maximum fraction of Uni-C being 85.57% for the website 'patents'. Table 3 in the Appendix A.3 shows the proportion of Uni-C, Bi-C and Tri-C found in all the websites.

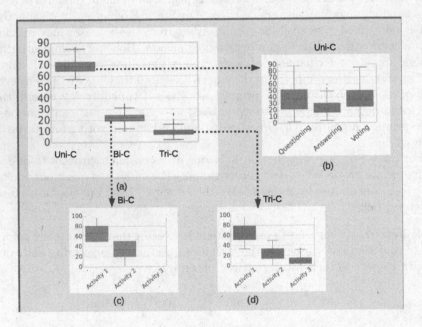

Fig. 2. (a) Fraction of Uni-C, Bi-C and Tri-C observed across the websites. A large proportion of users is observed to be Uni-C (b) Uni-C: Proportion across the activities. (c) Bi-C: Relative contribution across the two activities (Sorted). (d) Tri-C: Relative contribution across the three activities (sorted as per each user's contribution across them. The contribution in the second and third activity by Bi-C and Tri-C users was very small.

---

[3] The analysis does not consider those users who created their account but never contributed to the website in any way. There is a large number of users on these websites that create an account, however, they remain passive knowledge consumers. On Stack Exchange websites, the average fraction of users who did not contribute at all in questioning, answering or voting was found to be 54.10%.

We further examined these Uni-C to examine their distribution across the activities. Figure 2(b) shows the proportion across questioning, answering and voting. Apparently, in questioning (38.33% ± 19.73) and voting (37.36% ± 19.10), there were more users than in answering (24.29% ± 10.68). We also observed a high standard deviation of the proportion of users in the activities across different websites. This is an important observation and is discussed more in the next Subsection, where we report the variability in the users' distribution obtained for different websites. Table 4 in Appendix A.4 reports the proportion of Uni-C across the activities for all the websites.

Additionally, we examined the task vectors of Bi-C and Tri-C to see how their contribution was spread across the two and three activities respectively. That is, whether it was evenly spread across the activities or were they inclined towards one or a subset of these activities. For this, we sorted their task vectors from their most contributed activity ('Activity 1') to the least contributed activity ('Activity 3'). The aggregated behavior of Bi-C is shown in Fig. 2(c) and Tri-C is shown in Fig. 2(d). Figure 2(c) shows that the contribution of Bi-C was found to be higher in one of the two activities than the other, i.e., it was not equally spread across the two activities. Similarly, Fig. 2(d) shows that the contribution of Tri-C is very less in the second and third activities. Together with the observations in Fig. 2(a), this shows that firstly, the websites have a small proportion of Bi-C and Tri-C. Secondly, their contribution to the second and third activities is very less. This depicts that most of the users on Q&A websites mainly contribute to one of the activities. We call this behavior 'Activity-selection Behavior'. Observed across a variety of websites on different topics, this observation points towards a general prevalence of this behavior in Q&A websites.

3.3 'User-Distribution' Across Activities

The activity-selection behavior observed in the previous Subsection revealed the users' inclination towards performing mainly *one* of the primary activities in Q&A websites. This is indeed a stronger case of role-playing behavior, where a role may contain a collection of activities. This allows us to label users based on the activity they are most inclined to perform. This labeling further provides a rough distribution of users across the activities, which we refer to as '*User-distribution*'. Through this distribution, one can get an idea of a high-level composition of a Q&A website in terms of the kind of users that are contributing to it. To compute this distribution, we need to be able to handle the presence of the small proportion of Bi-C and Tri-C, especially those having a comparable contribution in two or three activities. Since the proportion of such users is small, we use clustering technique to group users into clusters where the users in each cluster behave similarly.

We use *K-means clustering* to divide the set of task vectors for a given website into clusters. This is a preferred technique to cluster users in similar contexts in the past literature [19,32]. Knowing that the users are performing in mainly one of the three activities, it is justified to take the value of k as three. Nevertheless, to further confirm whether or not three is the optimal value of k for the given data, we follow the method given by [24] for finding the ideal k. The best k is the one for which intra-cluster distances for the data points are minimum and the inter-cluster distances are maximum. The authors provide measures to compute these two parameters. The details of the method are given in Appendix A.5. We performed K-means clustering on the task vectors of each website, with the value of k varying from 2 to 10. For each value of k, we applied the method by He et al. on the obtained clusters. The optimal k was found to be 3 for 73.71% of the websites (More details in Appendix A.5). This further supplies extra validation that the users are inclined to contribute in mainly one of the three activities and that the decision of proceeding with $k = 3$ in k-means is reasonable. The reason behind some of the websites showing optimal k other than 3 maybe the presence of a small proportion of Bi-C and Tri-C. Nevertheless, given the observations from the previous Subsection, this approach can provide a high-level estimate of the group composition of the websites.

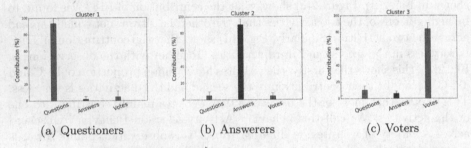

(a) Questioners   (b) Answerers   (c) Voters

Fig. 3. Average of centroids of the clusters obtained for 156 websites. The main contribution of users falling in the three clusters is questioning, answering and voting respectively. Small values of SD indicate the behavior is observed across all the websites.

Figure 3 shows the mean of the centroids of the three clusters obtained for the websites. The centroids depict a clean division of users with each cluster grouping users contributing in the form of either questioning, answering or voting respectively with a very little contribution in the rest of the activities. We, therefore, call the corresponding clusters as *Questioners*, *Answerers* and *Voters* accordingly. For instance, for the users belonging to the Questioners cluster, the contribution in questioning was as high as 93.3%, while in answering and voting, it was only 1.90% and 4.71% respectively. Similarly, for the users belonging to the Answerers cluster, the contribution in answering was as high as 90.57% and for the users who belonged to Voters cluster, their contribution in voting was 83.84%. This confirms that the users who were asking questions were rarely providing answers. Similarly, the values obtained for the answerers' cluster shows that the users who were providing answers were hardly asking questions. Small values of σ further confirm the phenomenon prevailing across all the websites. The relative sizes of the three clusters for each website provide us the user-distribution for the website. This distribution provides insights into the website's user base composition as well as enables comparison across websites. For instance, it may tell whether a website has more users inclined towards questioning as compared to answering or vice-versa. If very few users are doing a particular activity, it may indicate that either the activity is unnecessary or the administrators should take measures to encourage participation in this activity. Table 6 in Appendix A.6 shows the user-distribution for each website. The following are some of the observations made on these distributions.

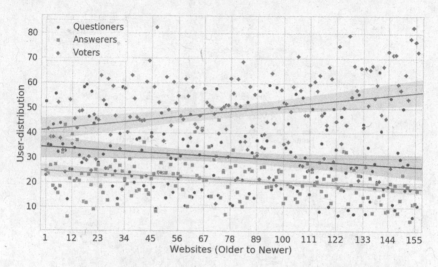

Fig. 4. Percentage of *Questioners*, *Answerers*, and *Voters* varying for the websites (ordered as per their creation time). Newer websites exhibit more voters and fewer questioners and answerers as compared to the older websites.

1. In most of the websites, the size of the voters' cluster is the maximum. The average sizes of the questioners, answerers and voters clusters are 29.7% (σ = 14.38), 20.64% (σ = 7.49) and 49.66% (σ = 15.06) respectively.
2. All the Stack Exchange websites do not exhibit a similar distribution of users, rather it widely varies across the websites. The percentage of questioners varies from 6.13% to 64.73%, the percentage of answerers varies from 4.64% to 43.16% and the percentage of voters varies from 11.47% to 82.55%. This leads to a few websites exhibiting a peculiar distribution where some of the activities are under-represented, which calls for further exploration. This variability in the distributions of the websites also explains the reason for high σ values obtained in the Fig. 2(b).
3. On a high-level, the proportion of answerers and questioners in the new websites was found to be lesser as compared to the old websites. Alternatively, the proportion of voters in the new websites was more than in the old websites. Figure 4 shows how the proportion of questioners, answerers, and voters varies on the websites. The X-axis contains the websites sorted by their creation time from the oldest to the newest.

Overall, these observations depict that different websites of Stack Exchange exhibit different distributions of users across the activities. In the next Subsection, we observe how the contribution of users performing one activity may affect the contribution of users from other activities.

3.4   Triggering/Dependency Among Users of a Q&A System

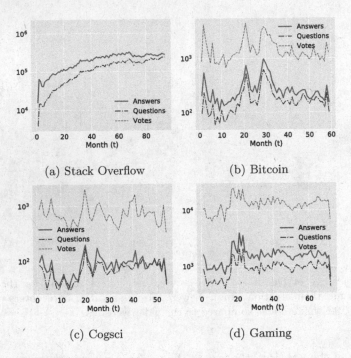

(a) Stack Overflow

(b) Bitcoin

(c) Cogsci

(d) Gaming

Fig. 5. Number of questions, answers and votes produced in each month in four websites. (Y-axis is log-scaled.)

Collaborative setups are perceived to exhibit the phenomenon of triggering that takes place among their contributors, whereby, the users are instigated to contribute more due to the contribution made by each other [9,27,35]. While the empirical validation of this phenomenon has been done in a few portals such as Wikipedia [43], hardly any work is done in Q&A portals in this direction so far. In this subsection, we examine the temporal growth of contribution made across different activities in Stack Exchange websites that provides evidence of triggering in Q&A settings. In particular, we computed the number of questions, answers and votes produced in each month for each of the websites. It was found that on a few websites, the growth rate was increasing with time, while in the others, it was either reducing or kept fluctuating. However, quite remarkably, in all the websites, questions, answers and votes exhibited a similar growth rate with respect to each other. That is, for a given website, the three entities showed patterns of growth that were highly correlated. For representation, Fig. 5 shows the number of questions, answers and votes produced in each month in the websites Stack Overflow, Bitcoin, Cogsci and Gaming. It can be seen that the three entities are moving very much parallel to each other. This reflects that any change in one entity quickly affects the rest two, making them move correspondingly. The same observation was made on other Stack Exchange websites as well. The average Pearson correlation coefficient between the growth of questions and answers per month across the websites was found to be 0.886 (SD = 0.138), between answers and votes it was 0.844 (SD = 0.161) and between questions and votes it was 0.778 (SD = 0.199) (See Fig. 6). The value of correlation for the websites was statistically significant with $p < .001$ for 145 websites and $p < .01$ for 11 websites. The reason for this high correlation is the fact that the knowledge units of different types in a collaborative environment are not independent contributions. Rather, they are highly dependent pieces of knowledge such that the production of one directly affects the production of the other. One may argue that in this particular case, the high correlation might also be bécause for every question asked on the portal, an average number of answers and votes are produced. While we agree that correlation merely conveys coexistence rather than causation, it should, however, be noted that although the triggering of answers due to questions, and the triggering of votes due to questions and answers are apparent and direct, the triggering takes place in the other way around as well. In other words, receiving answers to the questions asked by themselves or others motivates users to ask more questions, thus resulting in answers indirectly triggering more questions. Similarly, votes obtained on the questions and answers instigate users to post more questions and answers, thus resulting in votes indirectly triggering questions and answers. This is depicted by a sudden change in any one type of knowledge units leading to a correlated change in the growth of the rest two types of knowledge units in Fig. 5. Knowing that the users in Stack Exchange websites contribute mainly in one of the activities, the observation of triggering among questions, answers and votes further implies that the users contributing in these activities trigger each other and are dependent on each other for their contribution.

Additionally, Fig. 5 shows a small ratio between the number of answers and questions produced in each month, while a large ratio between the votes and questions; and votes and answers respectively. Note that the Y-axis is log-scaled. This shows that the knowledge units of different types are dependent on each other with varying degrees. This variability in triggering among knowledge units of different kinds is captured by the triggering matrix, as defined in the next section, where we model the emerging cognitive behavior of users in a collaborative environment.

4   A Cognitive Model for the Interactive User Behavior in Collaborative Knowledge-Building

The domain analysis highlights the following two important observations:

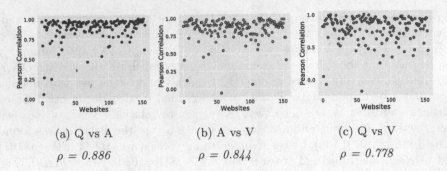

(a) Q vs A   (b) A vs V   (c) Q vs V

$\rho = 0.886$ $\rho = 0.844$ $\rho = 0.778$

Fig. 6. Pearson Correlation Coefficient (ρ) between (a) questions and answers (b) Answers and votes (c) questions and votes produced in each month. Most of the websites showed a high value of correlation, depicting the growth of knowledge units of one type affecting the growth of knowledge of the other type.

- **Activity-selection behavior of Users:** We observed in StackExchange websites that by virtue of their internal characteristics, the users tend to choose one of the available activities. These findings corroborate with similar observations made in a few other portals such as Wikipedia [32]. The categories observed in Wikipedia include *copy editors, watchdogs, starters* and *cleaners*. These findings point towards a general prevalence of activity-selection behavior among the users of a collaborative knowledge-building portal.

- **Triggering among Users:** Another observation made in the domain analysis was the presence of triggering among the users performing different activities. The phenomenon of triggering in collaborative environments is also supported by the classical theories [36,39] highlighting the process of existing knowledge leading to the creation of more knowledge. Triggering is defined as a procedure by which an idea or a comment spearheads the generation of another idea or thought [29,44]. A few classical theories on cognition also explain the interaction of users with social systems. One of them is Luhmann's theory [33] that describes a social system as an Autopoietic system. An Autopoietic system refers to a system which once started, keeps recreating and maintaining itself. The theory states that the existing ideas of the system create perturbations in the cognitive systems of users, which steer them to produce more ideas. A collaborative knowledge building system is no different from a social system where the knowledge added by some users leads to perturbations in the cognitive systems of other users and hence makes the system autopoietic. As an instance, in a Q&A system, the questions lead to perturbations in the minds of answerers which triggers them to provide answers, thus leading to an autopoietic execution of the system.

  A question that arises is whether this phenomenon of triggering goes on indefinitely or it stops after a while. In that context, Piaget's Model of equilibration [42] states that people interact with the system because of cognitive conflicts, which means that when they see some information that is incongruent to their existing knowledge, it creates a disturbance in their mind which leads them to interact with the system. However, there comes a point when the system's information matches with people's knowledge, leading to an equilibration state which in turn stops the process. In the context of a Q&A system, after an equilibration state, the answers to a given question cease being added to the system. This state of equilibration is again disturbed as new questions are asked, thus making the system highly dynamic.

Types of Contribution in a Social System: We can classify all the knowledge generated in the system on the basis of whether it is an outcome of the interaction with among cognitive systems or not, in the following two types:

1. **Internal Knowledge:** It is a subset of the user's knowledge which is added to the system independent of the effect of group dynamics. This is precisely the knowledge that the user would have added to the system if they had been participating in the knowledge building process individually (and not in a group). As a very simplistic example, consider the following experiment: If a user is asked to name all the countries in the world, assume, s/he is able to come up with 40–50 of these countries. These generated knowledge units are what we consider as his/her internal knowledge. It should be noted that in this case, it may happen that the user knows some more countries' names, but currently s/he does not recall them. These names are not a part of internal knowledge since they never got added to the social system.
2. **Triggered Knowledge:** This is the kind of knowledge that gets added to the system as a result of interaction among users. When users participate in the knowledge building process as a group, they get triggered on seeing each others' contribution and hence, provide more contribution. This knowledge is called triggered knowledge. In the countries' example, if coming across a few country names stated by other users, if a user gets triggered to provide a few more countries' names, they will constitute his/her triggered knowledge.

Relevant to the process of triggering, Cress et al. [14] propose two processes explaining the interaction of the cognitive systems with a social system, viz., *externalization* and *internalization*. From a cognitive system's point of view, externalization is a process by which users add their knowledge to the system. On the other hand, internalization is the process of taking the information from the system. Clearly, addition of internal knowledge to the system consists of only the process of externalization. On the other hand, the addition of triggered knowledge to the system is a process, in which first internalization and then externalization takes place. The users first internalize the knowledge from the system, and then externalize their own knowledge to the system.

Using the insights from the domain analysis backed by the cognitive theories, we build a cognitive model of contributors' behavior in collaborative knowledge building. In what follows, we first explain the setup of StackExchange and then provide its generalization:

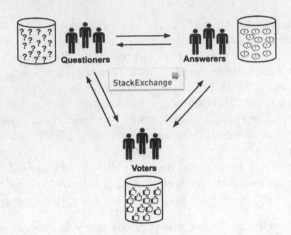

Fig. 7. A reflection of the outcomes of the domain analysis of StackExchange: Activity-selection behavior and triggering among Users

The activity-selection behavior gives rise to a labeling of the users as Questioners, Answerers and Voters as shown in Fig. 7. This indicates that the users in such portals have an internal state that distinguishes them from others. For instance, the questioners have characteristics of asking questions, the answerers mainly tend to provide answers to others' questions. The voters do not ask questions or provide answers. They merely consume the existing content and provide up-votes or down-votes for the content. This is by virtue of their backgrounds, motivations and experiences that the users behave in such a way in the system. Further, due to the triggering effect, these users instigate each other to contribute on the portal. For instance, questions asked by the questioners trigger the answerers to provide answers. Similarly, when users see that the questions receive answers through the system, they are instigated to ask more questions. The contribution by both answerers and questioners triggers the voters to consume their content and thus provide votes. Also, receiving votes on their content further triggers questioners and answerers to contribute more in the system. This presents an example of how users with different internal characteristics are stimulated through each others' contribution. This results in the emergence of an ecosystem of different kinds of users communicating with each other and producing valuable content. Further, the amount of triggering among the users contributing to different activities may be variable. For instance, the extent of triggering that an answerer produces for a questioner may be different from how much a questioner may trigger an answerer. This is also empirically depicted by the parallel but variable trends of questions, answers and votes produced with time as observed in Fig. 5. This variability is an important aspect that may help in understanding the internal dynamics of users' interaction.

We now describe a general cognitive model depicting the emerging behavior of users in collaborative knowledge-building setups. Consider a system with n

users and m activities in which these users can contribute[4]. Each of these users possesses different internal characteristics due to which they choose one of the m activities to contribute as well exhibit varying levels of triggering.

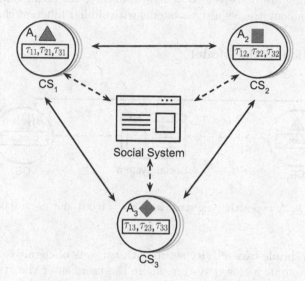

Fig. 8. A general cognitive model for a system containing three activities (A_1, A_2 and A_3). CS_1, CS_2 and CS_3 represent sets of cognitive systems inclined towards performing activities A_1, A_2 and A_3 respectively. The values of the three tau's for each user represent the inherent personal cognitive characteristics of that particular user; they determine that user's posting behavior upon encountering the content posted by the others.

Figure 8 shows a model describing a system where the users tend to contribute to one of the activities A_1, A_2 or A_3. Each user represents a cognitive system which interacts with other cognitive systems via the social system, which is a knowledge-building system in this case. The Figure shows three sets of cognitive systems CS_1, CS_2 and CS_3, each containing the users contributing to the corresponding activity. Further, these cognitive systems are triggered to varying degrees upon encountering the contribution made by other systems, which we capture using τ_{ij} values. Here, τ_{ij} represents the number of knowledge units of activity i that will be triggered *per cognitive system* of the set CS_i due to one knowledge unit (KU) contributed by the cognitive systems belonging to the set CS_j. Here, KU represents knowledge such as questions, answers or votes etc.

---

[4] To particularly focus on the effect of user-distribution on the amount of knowledge produced, we assume that the number of users remains fixed over time. Nevertheless, the outcomes of the model may be used even for the cases where the number of users keeps changing, by evaluating the given system at small time windows considering the average number of users present in that time window.

in the case of a Q&A system. We call triggering among cognitive systems contributing to the same activity as *Intra-triggering* and across the categories as *Inter-triggering*. In Fig. 8, τ_{11}, τ_{22} and τ_{33} represent intra-triggering. The values of intra-triggering are perceived to be less than inter-triggering due to the similarity of traits among the cognitive systems with similar inherent characteristics.

4.1 Simulation of the Model

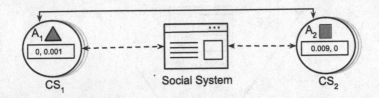

Fig. 9. A two-activity system with $\tau_{12} = 0.001$ and $\tau_{21} = 0.009$

We simulate a simple two-activity setup with two sets of cognitive systems CS_1 and CS_2. We assume a closed system where the users enter the system with an initial amount of knowledge that they wish to contribute, referred to as their *internal knowledge*. Let's assume this to be 100 units per cognitive system belonging to both CS_1 and CS_2. Further, let us assume that each unit of contribution made by the cognitive systems belonging to CS_2 to the social system triggers each user of CS_1 by 0.001, i.e., $\tau_{12} = 0.001$. Similarly, each unit of contribution made by the cognitive systems belonging to CS_1 to the social system triggers each user of CS_2 by 0.009, i.e., $\tau_{21} = 0.009$. We assume intra-triggering to be zero for simplicity. Let the total number of users be 100, i.e., $n = 100$. Out of these 100 users, a few have the characteristics such that they contribute to activity A_1 and hence belong to CS_1, while the rest contribute to A_2 and hence belong to CS_2.

We discuss two cases of divisions of cognitive systems across CS_1 and CS_2 to depict the kind of behavior that emerges. The two cases are- Case 1: $n_1 = 20$, $n_2 = 80$ and Case 2: $n_1 = 50$, $n_2 = 50$. In case 1, 20 cognitive systems contribute to A_1 (hence belong to CS_1), while the rest 80 contribute to A_2 (hence belong to CS_2). At time $t = 0$, each of them contribute their internal knowledge to the social system, which we assume to be 100 units per cognitive system. Therefore, total number of KU's contributed at $t = 0$ by CS_1 are $20 \times 100 = 2000$ and by CS_2 are $80 \times 100 = 8000$. Subsequently, as a result of the interaction among these systems, more knowledge gets produced in the social system, i.e., triggered knowledge. At time $t = 1$, the knowledge generated at time $t = 0$ instigates the cognitive systems belonging to CS_1 and CS_2 as per their tau values as shown in Fig. 9. As an example, at time $t = 1$, a total of 2000 units of CS_1 instigate each cognitive system of CS_2 by 0.009 triggering, while a total of 8000 units of CS_2 instigate each cognitive system of CS_1 by 0.001 triggering. The amount

Table 1. Knowledge produced by the cognitive systems CS_1 and CS_2 with time. Blue values represent internal knowledge ($t = 0$) and red values represent the triggered knowledge ($t = 1$ through 5) emerged out of the interaction among the cognitive systems.

Time (t)	#KU's produced by CS_1	#KU's produced by CS_2
$t = 0$	$20 \times 100 = 2000$	$80 \times 100 = 8000$
$t = 1$	$20 \times (8000 \times 0.001) = 160$	$80 \times (2000 \times 0.009) = 1440$
$t = 2$	$20 \times (1440 \times 0.001) = 28.8$	$80 \times (160 \times 0.009) = 115.2$
$t = 3$	$20 \times (115.2 \times 0.001) = 2.3$	$80 \times (28.8 \times 0.009) = 20.7$
$t = 4$	$20 \times (20.7 \times 0.001) = 0.414$	$80 \times (2.3 \times 0.009) = 1.656$
$t = 5$	$20 \times (1.656 \times 0.001) = 0.033$	$80 \times (0.414 \times 0.009) = 0.29$

Table 1: *

(a) Case 1: $n_1 = 20$, $n_2 = 80$

Time (t)	#KU's produced by CS_1	#KU's produced by CS_2
$t = 0$	$50 \times 100 = 5000$	$50 \times 100 = 5000$
$t = 1$	$50 \times (5000 \times 0.001) = 250$	$50 \times (5000 \times 0.009) = 2250$
$t = 2$	$50 \times (2250 \times 0.001) = 112.5$	$50 \times (250 \times 0.009) = 112.5$
$t = 3$	$50 \times (112.5 \times 0.001) = 5.625$	$50 \times (112.5 \times 0.009) = 50.625$
$t = 4$	$50 \times (50.625 \times 0.001) = 2.53$	$50 \times (5.625 \times 0.009) = 2.53$
$t = 5$	$50 \times (2.53 \times 0.001) = 0.1265$	$50 \times (2.53 \times 0.009) = 1.138$

Table 2: *

(b) Case 2: $n_1 = 50$, $n_2 = 50$

of knowledge thus emerged is reported in the Table. Similarly, more knowledge gets produced in the social system as a result of interaction among the cognitive systems, thus making the system autopoietic as per Luhmann's theory. Subsequently, the amount of knowledge thus emerged reduces with time, as a result of Piaget's theory of equilibration as the cognitive conflicts among the cognitive systems reduce. Based on the τ values, Table 1(a) systematically tracks the amount of internal and triggered knowledge produced. In the Table, the blue values represent internal knowledge while the red values represent triggered knowledge emerged out of the interaction of the cognitive systems with each other. Similarly, Table 1(b) shows the case 2 with a different division of users across CS_1 and CS_2. We observe varying amounts of knowledge triggered as a result. In case 1, a total of 1769.39 units are triggered while in case 2, a total of 2787.57 units are triggered in the subsequent 5 timestamps. This depicts the effect of change in the relative distribution of cognitive systems with different characteristics - i.e., user-distribution (refer to Sect. 3.3)- resulting in a change in the dynamics. This aspect is further analyzed in detail in the next Section.

5   Analysis of the Model

In this Section, we analyze the model with a focus on (a) delineating the effect of changing the user-distribution on the amount of knowledge produced, and (b) investigating whether or not there is a particular distribution of n users across m categories that leads to the maximum knowledge.

In the forthcoming analysis, we refer to the users performing the activity i as belonging to the set of cognitive systems referred to as CS_i. We also use the term CS for a set of cognitive systems in general. We also store the τ values in the form of a matrix which we refer to as *triggering matrix* as shown below:

$$T = \begin{bmatrix} \tau_{11} & \tau_{12} & \cdots & \tau_{1m} \\ \tau_{21} & \tau_{22} & \cdots & \tau_{2m} \\ \vdots & & & \vdots \\ \tau_{m1} & \tau_{m2} & \cdots & \tau_{mm} \end{bmatrix} \tag{1}$$

The values in this matrix may be low, high or zero, depending on whether or not contribution by one cognitive system is a prerequisite for the generation of KU's of another cognitive system. For example, in a Q&A website, a question may trigger an answer with a different extent than how much an answer may trigger another question.

We track the knowledge generated in the system by using one simplifying assumption that the knowledge produced in the system at time t is triggered by the knowledge produced at time $t - 1$ only. This is not an unreasonable assumption as we observe in Stack Exchange websites that when a question is asked, most of the answers are received in the first month. In particular, in Stack Overflow, on an average, 91% of the answers were received in the first month, only 6% were received in the 2nd to 12th month, and only 3% were received in beyond one year. Similar values were obtained for the rest of the Stack Exchange websites as well. We, therefore, consider t to be a period of one month and define $k_i(t)$ to be the number of KUs of CS_i produced at time t. We see that $k_i(t)$ depends on the following parameters:

1. The number of KUs of all CS that get added to the system at time $t - 1$, i.e., $k_j(t - 1)$, $\forall 1 \leq j \leq m$. (This includes CS under consideration, due to some amount of intra-triggering.)
2. The triggering factors from all other CS to the CS_i, i.e. τ_{ij}, $\forall 1 \leq j \leq m$. (See Fig. 8)
3. The number of users in CS_i, i.e. n_i.

Therefore, $k_i(t)$ can be computed as (See Fig. 10):

$$k_i(t) = n_i(\tau_{i1}k_1(t - 1) + \tau_{i2}k_2(t - 1) + \cdots + \tau_{im}k_m(t - 1))$$

Alternatively, $\forall 1 \leq i \leq m$, we can write,

$$k_i(t) = n_i \left(\sum_{j=1}^{m} \tau_{ij}k_j(t - 1) \right) \tag{2}$$

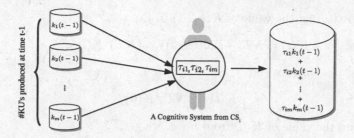

Fig. 10. Number of knowledge Units (KU's) generated by one user from CS_i at time t are triggered by the knowledge produced by other cognitive systems at time $t-1$. (Here CS_i is a set of cognitive systems having the characteristic of contributing to the activity i.)

To start the system, let r_i be the average initial knowledge entered into the system by each user of CS_i. Therefore, the amount of initial knowledge of CS_i into the system, i.e., $k_i(0)$ will be:

$$k_i(0) = n_i r_i \tag{3}$$

Let $K(t)$ be the column vector consisting of the knowledge generated by different CS_i at time t as its elements, N be a diagonal matrix storing the number of users n_i in each CS_i, and R be a column vector storing the average internal knowledge of each CS *per user* as shown below:

$$K(t) = \begin{bmatrix} k_1(t) \\ k_2(t) \\ \vdots \\ k_m(t) \end{bmatrix} \quad N = \begin{bmatrix} n_1 \\ & \ddots \\ & & n_m \end{bmatrix} \quad R = \begin{bmatrix} r_1 \\ r_2 \\ \vdots \\ r_m \end{bmatrix}$$

Using these definitions of $K(t)$, N, R and T, the Eqs. (3) and (2) respectively can be written as,

$$K(0) = NR \tag{4}$$

$$K(t) = NTK(t-1) \tag{5}$$

5.1   Total Knowledge Generated in the System

Equation (5) gives a recursive formula for computing the total number of KU's produced in the system at time t. The following theorem provides a closed form of the formula for the knowledge built in the system at time t.

Theorem 1. *The vector representing the knowledge generated in various categories at time t, i.e. $K(t)$ is given by:*

$$K(t) = (NT)^t NR \tag{6}$$

Proof. Substituting the value of $K(t-1)$ in Eq. (5),

$$K(t) = NT(NTK(t-2)) = (NT)^2 K(t-2)$$

Continuing like this, we get,

$$K(t) = (NT)^t K(0)$$

Substituting the value of $K(0)$ from Eq. 4, we get,

$$K(t) = (NT)^t NR$$

□

Equation (6) gives the amount of knowledge generated in the system at time t. To get the total knowledge generated *upto* time t which we call $K_c(t)$, we have the following theorem:

Theorem 2. *The vector representing the total knowledge generated in each CS 'upto' time t is given by:*

$$K_c(t) = ((NT)^t - I)((NT) - I)^{-1} NR \tag{7}$$

Proof. We know that,

$$K_c(t) = \sum_{j=0}^{t} K(j) \tag{8}$$

Therefore, from Theorem 1,

$$K_c(t) = \sum_{j=0}^{t} (NT)^j NR$$

$$K_c(t) = ((NT)^0 + (NT)^1 + (NT)^2 + \cdots + (NT)^t) NR$$
$$K_c(t) = ((NT)^t - I)((NT) - I)^{-1} NR$$

where I is an $m \times m$ identity matrix.   □

From Eq. (8), we can also compute the total knowledge that ever gets added to the system, i.e. $K_c(\infty)$, as given by the following corollary:

Corollary 1. *The vector representing the total knowledge ever produced in each CS in the system is given by:*

$$K_c(\infty) = \sum_{t=0}^{\infty} K(t) \tag{9}$$

$$K_c(\infty) = \sum_{t=0}^{\infty} (NT)^t NR \tag{10}$$

$$K_c(\infty) = ((NT)^0 + (NT)^1 + (NT)^2 + \cdots + \infty) NR \tag{11}$$

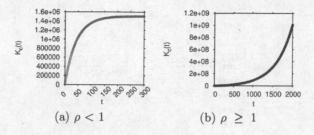

Fig. 11. Total knowledge produced upto time t for (a) $\rho < 1$ and (b) $\rho \geq 1$ respectively.

There can be two cases depending on the value of the spectral radius of NT, i.e. $\rho(NT)$ which is equal to $max\{|\Lambda_1|, \ldots, |\Lambda_e|\}$ where Λ_i's are the eigenvalues of the matrix NT. As per the Eq. (11), if $\rho(NT) \geq 1$, the knowledge keeps on increasing exponentially with time and reaches infinity [8] (See Fig. 11(b)). In this case, a bound on the total knowledge produced in the system can not be computed. However, if $\rho(NT) < 1$, then initially the knowledge production rate is high, which keeps decreasing with time and eventually converges (See Fig. 11(a)). In this case, the total knowledge produced in the system is bounded. This is because $(NT)^0 + (NT)^1 + (NT)^2 + \cdots + \infty$ converges to $(I - NT)^{-1}$. Therefore, we get the following closed form for the total knowledge produced in the system.

$$K_c(\infty) = (I - NT)^{-1}NR \tag{12}$$

Equation (11) shows that whether a system keeps growing its knowledge base or stops after a while, largely depends on the division of users in the diagonal matrix (N) as well as the amount of triggering among them (T).

5.2   Computing the Optimal User-Distribution

The optimal user-distribution is the distribution of users across the activities of the system such that it leads to the maximum knowledge generation. The values in the diagonal matrix N, i.e., $\{n_1, n_2, \ldots n_m\}$ represent the number of users in the categories 1, 2, ... m. Therefore, from the matrix N corresponding to the maximum $K_c(\infty)$, one can find the distribution of users $\mathcal{D} = \{d_{n_1}, d_{n_1}, \ldots, d_{n_m}\}$, as shown below:

$$d_{n_i} = \frac{n_i}{\sum_{j=1}^{m} n_j}$$

This distribution provides an estimate of the kind of users that should be present in the system to facilitate optimal knowledge generation. We now examine the effect of change in the user-distribution on the amount of knowledge produced in the systems with two ($m = 2$) and three ($m = 3$) categories. We also compute the optimal user-distribution in these systems considering different model parameters.

5.3 $m = 2$

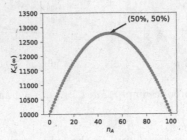

Fig. 12. The best distribution in a 2-activity system leading to the maximum knowledge comes out to be (50%, 50%)

Let us re-consider the 2-activity system discussed previously (Sect. 4.1). If the system is supposed to contain only 100 users (i.e., $n = 100$), what should be its composition in terms of the cognitive systems belonging to CS_1 and CS_2? Intuitively, since CS_1 users do not get triggered much to add more content, the system might do better by keeping a lesser proportion of the users of this type. However, we also note that these users highly trigger CS_2 users to add more content. To find the solution, we need to compute the amount of knowledge produced in the system for each possible division of 100 users across CS_1 and CS_1, based on their inherent triggering characteristics. As before, we consider the initial knowledge in the system to be [100, 100] and then using Eq. 12, compute the amount of knowledge produced, i.e., $K_c(\infty)$. Figure 12 shows the value of $K_c(\infty)$ for all possible divisions of 100 into CS_1 and CS_2. The maximum knowledge (i.e., 12787.72 units) is produced at the distribution $\mathcal{D} = (50, 50)$. We see that although the users of type A are triggered to a lesser extent, they are nevertheless required in a good number in the system, as they trigger the users of the other type (i.e., CS_2) to a high extent. This simple example shows that the triggering among the knowledge units plays an important role in deciding the right distribution of users across the categories. It may explain why a system requires a good number of users asking questions in a Q&A system as they trigger the *answerers* to a good extent to provide the answers.

5.4 $m = 3$

To examine how $K_c(\infty)$ varies as we change the distribution in three categories' case, we simulated the model while taking random values for the triggering matrix such that $\rho(NT)$ is less than 1. We do this, as when $\rho(NT)$ is greater than 1, the knowledge in the system becomes unbounded. Moreover, as per many existing studies [47], the knowledge growth in practical settings follows *Heap's law* [25,27] which follows a sub-linear power-law growth rather than exponential,

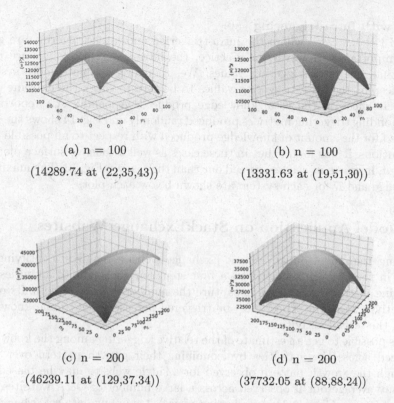

(a) n = 100

(14289.74 at (22,35,43))

(b) n = 100

(13331.63 at (19,51,30))

(c) n = 200

(46239.11 at (129,37,34))

(d) n = 200

(37732.05 at (88,88,24))

Fig. 13. Total knowledge produced $(K_c(\infty))$ with respect to all possible distributions (n_1, n_2, n_3) in 3-activity systems. (*Note: Here* $n_3 = 100 - n_1 - n_2$). The optimal user-distribution is shown below each plot.

suggesting that given sufficient time in a closed system, the rate of knowledge growth decreases with time.

For simplicity, we kept the initial knowledge in the system to be [100, 100, 100]. We varied the value of N by checking all possible distributions of users across the three categories and computed the total knowledge produced in the system with respect to each distribution. Figure 13 shows the amount of knowledge produced in four different knowledge-building systems. The X and Y axes show the values of n_1 and n_2. The value of n_3 is $(n - n_1 - n_2)$. The Z-axis shows the amount of knowledge produced with respect to (n_1, n_2, n_3). The triggering matrices used for each case are reported in Appendix A.7. The plots show that the amount of knowledge produced keeps varying with the change in the users' distribution. Further, there is always a particular distribution at which, the maximum knowledge is produced. The maximum knowledge produced in the four systems along with the distribution $\mathcal{D}$ is shown below each plot.

Cases with Intra-triggering = 0:
Figure 13 shows cases where the intra-triggering and inter-triggering are given equal importance. However, in practice, the intra-triggering values are quite lesser than the inter-triggering values. We, therefore, simulate more systems while keeping the intra-triggering values to be zero to check the extreme cases and their effect on the total knowledge produced. Appendix A.7 reports the corresponding triggering matrices produced randomly and Fig. 14 shows the plots obtained for the amount of knowledge produced with respect to all possible user-distributions. It was found that in these cases as well a concave surface plot was obtained, however, it was less spread out than the cases in Fig. 13. The maximum knowledge and $\mathcal{D}$ for each system are shown below each plot.

6   Model Application on StackExchange Websites

Applying the model on any Stack Exchange website requires identifying the values in the triggering matrix as a first step. For each pair of activities, the triggering matrix is supposed to capture the number of knowledge units of the first activity that are expected to be triggered per user, due to one knowledge unit of the second activity.

It is possible to get an estimate of the relative triggering among the knowledge produced across the activities by examining their growth pattern over time. Although the growth pattern observed for a single website may be biased, the bias may average out if observed across a large number of Q&A websites from different genres. Given a large collection of websites in our data set, we can find the general relationship among the knowledge units from different activities. In Fig. 5, we observed that triggering from questions to answers is higher than from answers to questions. Similarly, the triggering from questions to votes as well as answers to votes is very high as compared to that in the reverse direction.

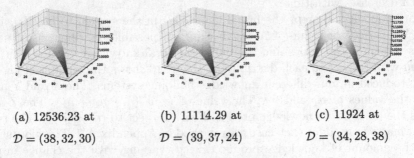

(a) 12536.23 at   (b) 11114.29 at   (c) 11924 at

$\mathcal{D} = (38, 32, 30)$ $\mathcal{D} = (39, 37, 24)$ $\mathcal{D} = (34, 28, 38)$

Fig. 14. Cases with intra-triggering = 0

To know the exact relationship, we computed the average association among the values of questions, answers and votes produced in each month by the websites, which was found to be the following:

$$\frac{a}{q} = 1.89, \qquad \frac{v}{q} = 13.26, \qquad \frac{v}{a} = 7.09 \qquad (13)$$

These relationship values represent the general association among the knowledge produced across activities in Q&A portals. Using these, we can estimate the values of the triggering matrix for Stack Exchange websites. Therefore, respecting these associations, we have the following triggering matrix for Stack Exchange websites with $n = 1000$.

$$\begin{array}{ccc} \mathbf{q} & \mathbf{a} & \mathbf{v} \end{array}$$
$$\begin{bmatrix} 0 & 0.00189 & 0.01326 \\ 0.000529 & 0 & 0.00709 \\ 0.0000754 & 0.000141 & 0 \end{bmatrix} \begin{array}{c} \mathbf{q} \\ \mathbf{a} \\ \mathbf{v} \end{array}$$

We thus compute the amount of knowledge produced for all possible distributions as per Eq. 12. While computing the amount of knowledge, we also computed the value of $\rho(NT)$, which was found to be less than 1 for each distribution examined corresponding to this triggering matrix and n. In total, we examined $\binom{1002}{2}$, i.e. 501501 cases of user-distributions. The surface plot obtained for these parameters is shown in Fig. 15. We find that the maximum knowledge is produced with respect to the distribution (35.4%, 25.2%, 39.4%). This shows $\mathcal{D}_{1000} = (35.4, 25.2, 39.4)$ to be the distribution that may lead to the maximum knowledge in Stack Exchange websites with $n = 1000$.

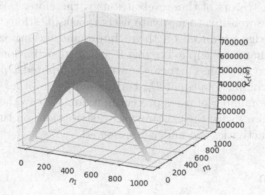

Fig. 15. Surface plot obtained for Stack Exchange (n = 1000) leading to an optimal number of questioners, answerers and voters to be (354, 252, 394) resulting in $\mathcal{D}_{1000} = (35.4, 25.2, 39.4)$

We now examine Stack Exchange websites having the number of users close to 1000 and compare their user-distributions with respect to $\mathcal{D}_{1000}$. We find that six websites, i.e. 'Italian' ($n = 927$), 'Hardware' ($n = 998$), 'music' ($n = 1025$), 'beer' ($n = 1042$), 'Tridion' ($n = 1047$) and 'wood' ($n = 1069$) have the number of users closest to 1000 (For details on the number of users in each website, refer to Table 2 in Appendix A.1). Figure 16 compares their distributions with respect to the reference line of $\mathcal{D}_{1000}$. The Figure shows that many of these

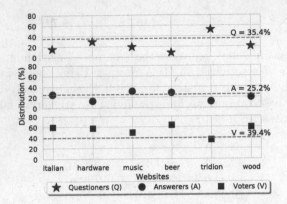

Fig. 16. Distribution of Stack Exchange websites with around 1000 users as compared to the reference distribution. For example, the website 'Italian' has only 15.31% questioners while the optimal distribution suggests it to be 35.4%.

websites have a smaller proportion of users inclined towards asking questions (the top plot), while the proportion of users who are only voting (the bottom plot) is higher compared to the reference line. In particular, the website 'beer' was found to be having only 8.38% of users engaged in asking questions. Notably, these websites are among the newly created websites, hence a lack of publicity may be one of the reasons for a smaller proportion of users asking questions on them. The administrators of these websites may, therefore, take measures such as promoting these websites to motivate users to ask questions and increase the amount of knowledge produced on them. Improving incentivization policies is another measure that may help in keeping a healthy distribution. We discuss this measure in the next Section. Further, the way we computed $\mathcal{D}_{1000}$ for $n = 1000$, we can similarly compute optimal $\mathcal{D}_n$ corresponding to other Stack Exchange websites as per the number of users present in them. We can then compare these reference distributions with the existing user-distributions on these websites and find which of the activities are under-represented.

7 Discussion

The empirical findings and the subsequent cognitive model underpin one simple idea that the distribution of users performing different activities affects the knowledge generation process. In case this distribution is not healthy, the website may not be expected to produce optimal knowledge. We find that certain distributions of users across the activities of a website may be a catalyst while some others may be a hindrance to effective knowledge production. An extreme case to understand this may be a hypothetical Q&A based knowledge-building portal where all the users like to provide answers and do not ask questions. Another similar case would be that of a portal where all the users only ask questions. We obviously can not expect such portals to be doing even a mediocre job of building knowledge. This example also indicates why a group formed out of only experts in an area - who might feel reluctant to ask basic questions - might not be as good as another group formed out of a mixture of experts as well as non-experts for a Q&A website. Therefore, it is important to examine the user-distribution on these websites and attempts should be made to maintain them well.

The model helps in discerning that many of the websites of Stack Exchange exhibit extreme cases of user distribution (See Table 6 in the Appendix A.6), where there is a scope for improving the knowledge generation process by motivating users to contribute to the less-represented activities. For instance, *languagelearning* (**6.13%, 11.32%**, 82.55%) has very few users who are asking questions; *latin* (17.3%, **4.64%**, 78.06%) has a very small bunch of users mainly providing answers and very few users are voting the content in *rus* (57.83%, 30.7%, **11.47%**). These extreme distributions certainly point towards a possibility of improvement in the knowledge generation process by motivating the users to contribute to under-represented activities.

The study suggests periodically monitoring the proportion of users across the activities of the portal and taking steps in case of unfavorable distributions. The steps may be taken by either updating the incentivization policies or by using task allocation strategies. Incentivization strategies using a point system and badges [3, 31] are known to steer the users towards a particular activity or feature. Therefore, incentivization policies as well as the interface should be such that the users are motivated to contribute to all the activities [22]. As an instance, realizing that the presence of voters is also important, passive lurkers may be encouraged to upvote or downvote the content by providing them points for their valuable judgment. Further, measures should be taken to periodically identify whether there are a sufficient number of users participating in a particular activity and taking corrective measures by appropriately changing the incentivization policies. A *dynamic incentivization system* that involves moderating the policies based on the functioning of the website is one of the measures that may help. Currently, the incentivization strategies used by crowdsourced websites are mostly static. Monitoring the functioning of the websites and based on that, incorporating changes in the rewarding schemes may help in motivating the users to turn to under-provisioned activities. This may enable a change in the user-distribution and hence aid in improved knowledge-building. A dynamic incentivization system may also help in customized rewarding policies based on the specific requirements of a website. Research already indicates that collaborative websites have a varying requirement of the kind of users that should contribute based on the phase that the websites are currently in [51]. Having the same incentivization policies across all websites at different levels may not always produce the desired engagement.

There are many future directions of this work. To keep the model simplistic, the current model controls for a few parameters in the form of assumptions. For example, given the observation of the activity-selection behavior, a user belonging to a cognitive system contributes only in one of the activities and the small amount of contribution made by any user in other activities, if any, is ignored. This was primarily required to get a high-level view of a website's distribution. However, as an extension, the small amount of contribution made by the users in other activities may also be accounted for, to get a refined distribution. Also, another assumption that the model uses is that the knowledge produced at time t is triggered by the knowledge produced at time $t - 1$ only. To account for the knowledge produced at time t due to all the knowledge produced so far, the model may use a weighted knowledge function that gives reducing weightage to older knowledge. Further, in this model, an activity such as voting is given equal importance as answering and questioning. Although votes constitute an important piece of qualitative meta-data about other knowledge units, this decision was taken to focus on different traits of users rather than the amount of effort dispensed in the activity. The model may be extended by assigning unequal weights to different activities of the system. Finally, although the current study examines the websites of Stack Exchange, the proposed model is simplified enough to be extendable to other cases of collaboration. Therefore, the analysis may be conducted to investigate the implications of user distribution on other kinds of collaborative websites with similar settings.

8 Conclusion

The work examined the tendency of users of a Q&A website to exhibit inclination towards contribution in one of the activities and the effect of this behavior on the ability of the website to produce knowledge. The domain analysis performed on a comprehensive data set of Stack Exchange websites enabled understanding the emerging cognitive behavior of users through a generalized model. The model showed that the distribution of users performing different activities on Q&A websites may catalyze or hamper the knowledge building process on these websites. Given the large-scale participation of users on modern online websites, our work provides a useful measure to gauge the health of collaboration among these users. The monitoring of the user-distribution of users with respect to their contribution type should, therefore, be considered as a necessary maintenance parameter for optimal output. As future work, we plan to alleviate some of the assumptions made in the model as well as apply this model to domains other than knowledge-production.

Acknowledgments. This work was supported by WOS-A (Women Scientists - A), Department of Science and Technology, India [SR/WOS-A/ET-1058/2014] and CSRI (Cognitive Science Research Initiative), Department of Science and Technology, India [SR/CSRI/344/2016].

Author contributions. A.C. and S.R.S.I. designed the project. A.C. and V.M. collected the data and performed the experiments. A.C. analyzed the results. A.C. and J.S.S. worked on the model. A.C. wrote the manuscript. A.C. and S.R.S.I. reviewed the manuscript.

Note. A preliminary version of this work is published as a poster in The Web Conference 2020 [13] and is published in the proceedings of the 12th International Conference on Computational Collective Intelligence (ICCCI) 2020 [11].

A   Appendix

A.1   Stack Exchange Data Set Statistics

Table 2. Data Set Statistics (The websites are sorted as per their creation time)

Site name	Questions	Answers	Votes	No of users	Starting date
stackoverflow	11846517	19090959	83047749	2829352	2008-07-31
serverfault	222504	382582	1436660	150860	2009-04-30
superuser	315759	474594	2235024	248741	2009-07-15
mathoverflow	71827	111820	1248241	29288	2009-09-28
sharepoint	62869	78697	171576	23785	2009-10-06
money	14499	28382	199722	14656	2009-10-06
electronics	61690	114841	551612	38377	2009-10-28
judaism	19277	31639	227474	4303	2009-12-06
sound	7365	21841	55801	5149	2010-02-22
stackapps	2175	2222	21030	4173	2010-05-19
webapps	19946	29256	191639	29521	2010-06-30
gaming	67255	113040	947722	54297	2010-07-07
webmasters	23966	39323	152670	23024	2010-07-08
cooking	14946	37583	224029	18860	2010-07-09
gamedev	32399	53283	317113	28678	2010-07-14
photo	16278	41259	255801	16424	2010-07-15
stats	81776	79723	481460	49026	2010-07-19
math	621163	886172	3931799	174347	2010-07-20
diy	24105	42733	171918	22194	2010-07-21
gis	69044	83124	379400	35731	2010-07-22
tex	114589	150690	1469577	51588	2010-07-26
askubuntu	230177	301894	1558290	203312	2010-07-28
english	71773	180215	1091092	67902	2010-08-05
ux	20271	56171	351102	29299	2010-08-09
unix	93209	141921	822791	80747	2010-08-10
wordpress	68455	84980	246515	35976	2010-08-11
cstheory	7957	12239	181917	7959	2010-08-16
apple	72499	107053	455924	77925	2010-08-17
rpg	16943	43308	478052	10484	2010-08-19
bicycles	8132	21409	124398	9240	2010-08-25
programmers	39930	129353	1705012	71001	2010-09-01

(*continued*)

Table 2. (*continued*)

Site name	Questions	Answers	Votes	No of users	Starting date
android	38321	45750	234326	45051	2010-09-13
ru	95029	127712	350933	28326	2010-10-10
boardgames	6892	13691	112301	6395	2010-10-19
physics	77380	115463	674552	42582	2010-11-02
homebrew	4364	10378	42622	3264	2010-11-08
security	30548	60662	524112	41672	2010-11-11
writers	4184	12280	58665	5431	2010-11-18
avp	3732	5131	29379	4638	2010-12-07
dba	46286	60769	305335	40578	2011-01-03
graphicdesign	17126	30942	143067	22680	2011-01-04
scifi	31984	64059	926666	30236	2011-01-11
codereview	34891	58649	411869	36611	2011-01-19
codegolf	5580	54741	385641	16377	2011-01-27
quant	6952	9895	55203	5534	2011-01-31
pm	3299	10882	47299	5581	2011-02-07
skeptics	6643	8347	239736	10452	2011-02-24
fitness	6055	12637	68487	6510	2011-03-01
drupal	61502	79598	278989	21802	2011-03-02
mechanics	8682	14759	84121	8395	2011-03-07
parenting	4146	14045	107826	8305	2011-03-29
music	8002	22186	134892	9768	2011-04-26
sqa	4447	10009	33907	5552	2011-05-03
german	6763	16089	120088	5698	2011-05-24
japanese	9271	14755	119715	4111	2011-05-31
philosophy	6513	15860	76569	6609	2011-06-07
gardening	5762	9798	74317	4231	2011-06-08
travel	17485	29986	316588	17316	2011-06-21
productivity	2122	7810	39291	4952	2011-06-22
crypto	9870	13111	90354	9956	2011-07-12
dsp	9597	12158	51231	7205	2011-08-16
french	4172	9791	67404	3587	2011-08-17
christianity	8086	19935	179350	6384	2011-08-23
bitcoin	10826	16805	91559	10082	2011-08-30
linguistics	4092	6625	38961	3538	2011-09-13
hermeneutics	3452	7140	53725	2510	2011-10-04
history	5407	10758	121458	5745	2011-10-11

(*continued*)

Table 2. (*continued*)

Site name	Questions	Answers	Votes	No of users	Starting date
bricks	1689	3029	25592	2351	2011-10-25
spanish	3105	7554	39721	2980	2011-11-15
scicomp	5363	7490	49680	4437	2011-11-29
movies	11759	18488	201265	12989	2011-11-30
rus	9540	20877	41045	3606	2011-12-13
chinese	3489	9220	40681	3318	2011-12-13
biology	12393	14920	118519	8368	2011-12-14
poker	999	2368	10951	1223	2012-01-10
mathematica	34226	51714	459933	13269	2012-01-17
cogsci	3881	4647	40966	3427	2012-01-18
outdoors	2813	6798	71248	3266	2012-01-24
martialarts	1023	3758	21017	1681	2012-01-31
sports	2904	4677	37586	2885	2012-02-08
academia	14320	35459	478434	17296	2012-02-14
cs	14911	19282	138636	13955	2012-03-06
workplace	11079	35565	454801	18830	2012-04-10
windowsphone	2851	3754	19903	3013	2012-04-24
chemistry	15550	17785	126746	9581	2012-04-25
chess	2750	6486	39116	3082	2012-05-01
raspberrypi	13061	17780	78924	17104	2012-06-12
russian	1997	5408	30407	2333	2012-06-13
islam	5242	9127	55210	4259	2012-06-19
salesforce	43522	53208	201223	13529	2012-07-31
patents	2416	3846	14037	4032	2012-09-05
genealogy	1581	3046	23214	1209	2012-10-09
robotics	2631	4129	16275	2802	2012-10-23
expressioneng.	11221	14276	35617	3310	2012-11-15
politics	2478	4247	35984	2820	2012-12-04
anime	6485	9105	98390	4965	2012-12-11
magento	39013	45965	114886	15897	2013-01-22
ell	26680	47320	217833	13714	2013-01-23
sustainability	947	1911	16639	1157	2013-01-29
tridion	4293	6876	44868	1047	2013-02-19
reverseengineering	2999	4177	28611	3402	2013-03-19
networkengineering	6860	10100	47304	6833	2013-05-07
opendata	2509	3622	22823	3095	2013-05-08

(*continued*)

Table 2. (*continued*)

Site name	Questions	Answers	Votes	No of users	Starting date
freelancing	1038	2590	13331	2061	2013-05-21
blender	18653	20322	119201	10107	2013-05-22
space	4119	6793	84397	4335	2013-07-16
astronomy	3386	5138	35623	3253	2013-09-24
tor	2780	3388	14433	3037	2013-09-25
pets	2988	4742	37246	2712	2013-10-08
ham	1281	2248	11712	1176	2013-10-22
italian	1304	2313	17177	927	2013-11-05
pt	45307	58750	276945	15496	2013-12-11
aviation	6220	12553	155098	5821	2013-12-17
ebooks	780	1281	8162	1196	2013-12-18
beer	524	1244	8694	1042	2014-01-21
softwarerecs	9390	9333	58241	9101	2014-02-04
arduino	7264	10032	29399	6631	2014-02-11
expatriates	2012	2426	17285	2161	2014-03-12
matheducators	1458	4967	45451	2374	2014-03-13
earthscience	1848	2573	33416	1804	2014-04-15
joomla	3775	5400	20462	2039	2014-04-22
datascience	2877	3901	19243	3624	2014-05-13
puzzling	6194	17333	194049	8766	2014-05-14
craftcms	5210	6436	30499	1699	2014-06-12
buddhism	2831	8600	36825	1764	2014-06-17
hinduism	3288	3965	28528	1803	2014-06-18
moderators	386	902	9612	767	2014-07-29
startups	1996	3624	16569	2678	2014-07-30
worldbuilding	6221	28576	205714	9366	2014-09-16
emacs	6930	8639	52853	3651	2014-09-23
ja	8495	10428	37246	4012	2014-09-29
hsm	1022	1468	14193	1183	2014-10-28
economics	3178	3952	23080	2301	2014-11-18
lifehacks	1375	4982	35465	3692	2014-12-09
engineering	2359	3443	23921	2475	2015-01-20
coffee	565	1061	8347	811	2015-01-27
vi	2631	3822	29850	2539	2015-02-03
musicfans	889	1169	9608	1025	2015-02-24
woodworking	1104	2739	20787	1069	2015-03-17

(*continued*)

Table 2. (*continued*)

Site name	Questions	Answers	Votes	No of users	Starting date
civicrm	4258	5570	20172	1640	2015-03-24
health	1941	1617	17161	1601	2015-03-31
mythology	524	685	9898	496	2015-04-28
law	3580	4232	22080	3077	2015-05-26
opensource	849	1631	16642	1451	2015-06-23
elementaryos	2278	2319	11389	2060	2015-06-30
portuguese	800	1336	13057	443	2015-07-14
arabic	122	208	1217	176	2015-07-14
computergrap.	621	765	7851	676	2015-08-04
hardwarerecs	853	897	10283	998	2015-09-09
es	4161	5862	19600	2543	2015-10-29
3dprinting	359	681	3848	410	2016-01-12
ethereum	1883	2560	18738	1128	2016-01-20
latin	373	530	6103	245	2016-02-23
languagelearn.	193	311	3256	215	2016-04-05
retrocomputin.	220	409	4866	505	2016-04-19
crafts	244	364	3236	228	2016-04-26

A.2   Stack Exchange Policies Regarding Commenting and Editing

As per StackExchange rules, users require at least 50 reputation points to be able to unlock the feature of commenting on questions and answers that they don't own. This policy has indeed been laid in order to discourage spam comments by casual users as well as to emphasize that Stackexchange restricts itself to a Q&A portal rather than a discussion forum such as 'ubuntuforums.org' where even comments such as '*Thanks, that was useful*', '*I agree*', '*I have the same problem*' are allowed as answers. Moreover, commenting is done to better understand a question or an answer. It basically adds a small discussion thread along with a question or an answer, which Stack Exchange community discourages. However, one may ask the reason for having encountered some number of Uni-C in commenting in such a scenario. The reason for that are two more StackExchange policies, whereby if a user gets 200 reputation points on any one Stack Exchange site, then that user automatically gets an association bonus of 100 on every site, enabling him to contribute across any activity on any of the StackExchange websites. Also, StackExchange automatically converts trivial answers containing a link to another question in the network to comments on the question. Due to these reasons, we could find some, although small, number of Uni-C in commenting. On the other hand, the reason for having less number of Uni-C in editing is supposed to be the requirement that until a user gathers 2000 reputation points, their edits are likely to be rejected, i.e. they can not actually edit the content; they can only suggest the edits. Additionally, there is an upper limit of the reputation points that can be gained by editing others' content viz. 1000 points. Beyond this, a user can not earn more reputation by editing. This further discourages the users to become an Uni-C in editing.

A.3   Uni-C, Bi-C and Tri-C in Stack Exchange Websites

Table 3. Percentage of Uni-C, Bi-C and Tri-C across websites. (The websites are sorted as per their creation time.)

Site name	Uni-C (%)	Bi-C (%)	Tri-C (%)	Site name	Uni-C (%)	Bi-C (%)	Tri-C (%)
stackoverflow	60.64	19.48	19.89	serverfault	65.46	22.38	12.16
superuser	71.06	18.67	10.27	mathoverflow	64.6	20.64	14.77
sharepoint	71.9	16.38	11.72	money	70.02	23.2	6.79
electronics	69	22.63	8.37	judaism	70.9	16.67	12.43
sound	71.8	17.29	10.91	stackapps	80.9	13.82	5.28
webapps	77.88	15.99	6.13	gaming	76.11	14.56	9.33
webmasters	69.12	23.58	7.3	cooking	75.64	17.23	7.13
gamedev	66	23.72	10.28	photo	71.2	20.7	8.1
stats	73.61	18.58	7.82	math	69.36	20.03	10.61
diy	77.13	17.25	5.63	gis	70.18	18.47	11.35
tex	60.68	27.6	11.72	askubuntu	76.77	15.66	7.57
english	71.24	21.44	7.32	ux	68.52	22.85	8.63
unix	70.62	21.08	8.31	wordpress	68.03	21.07	10.9
cstheory	70.51	20.31	9.18	apple	77.4	15.35	7.25
rpg	60.75	24.27	14.98	bicycles	70.77	20.48	8.74
programmers	67.6	25.03	7.37	android	79.18	14.95	5.87
ru	66.75	18.77	14.48	boardgames	66.74	23.16	10.1
physics	67.53	22.46	10.01	homebrew	64.72	22.09	13.19
security	73.02	21.06	5.92	writers	66.56	24.86	8.58
avp	72.79	21.63	5.58	dba	70.97	22.17	6.85
graphicdesign	75.59	19.17	5.25	scifi	75.07	16.65	8.28
codereview	58.54	34.25	7.22	codegolf	69.47	24.13	6.4
quant	68.21	22.31	9.47	pm	72.33	20.85	6.83
skeptics	75.25	19.08	5.67	fitness	65.72	26.08	8.2
drupal	63.12	20.88	16	mechanics	70.47	22.51	7.02
parenting	73.65	19.85	6.5	music	68.85	22.94	8.22
sqa	75.48	17.8	6.72	german	61.16	30.43	8.41
japanese	60.04	29.32	10.64	philosophy	67.63	23.49	8.88
gardening	62.87	28.04	9.09	travel	74.74	18.76	6.5
productivity	69.28	23.48	7.25	crypto	72.96	21.43	5.62
dsp	70.68	22.11	7.2	french	59.62	31.13	9.26

(continued)

Table 3. (*continued*)

Site name	Uni-C (%)	Bi-C (%)	Tri-C (%)	Site name	Uni-C (%)	Bi-C (%)	Tri-C (%)
christianity	72.93	18.15	8.92	bitcoin	74.67	17.65	7.68
linguistics	68.31	22.88	8.81	hermeneutics	73.58	17.17	9.26
history	69.21	22.49	8.3	bricks	76.26	16.73	7.01
spanish	64.56	27.34	8.1	scicomp	65.31	24.03	10.66
movies	74.83	18.32	6.85	rus	84.42	10.64	4.94
chinese	65.76	26.1	8.14	biology	63.57	27.47	8.96
poker	67.93	22.22	9.85	mathematica	64.56	24.43	11.01
cogsci	65.77	25.2	9.03	outdoors	68.86	22.73	8.4
martialarts	69.17	21.83	8.99	sports	64.22	25.35	10.43
academia	69.34	23.93	6.73	cs	70.93	22.96	6.11
workplace	72.61	22.18	5.2	windowsphone	76.1	16.03	7.86
chemistry	70.36	22.16	7.48	chess	68.02	21.66	10.32
raspberrypi	74.84	18.38	6.78	russian	66.5	26.18	7.31
islam	77.16	15.87	6.97	salesforce	66.5	19.49	14.01
patents	85.57	12.2	2.23	genealogy	73.46	17.83	8.7
robotics	69.18	22.47	8.35	expressionengine	59.82	20.18	20
politics	66.97	24.61	8.42	anime	73.4	17.85	8.75
magento	69.18	18.79	12.03	ell	69.08	26.81	4.11
sustainability	64.17	22.92	12.91	tridion	51.46	24.07	24.46
reverseeng.	74.16	19.09	6.75	networkeng.	73.27	20.16	6.58
opendata	72.16	20.93	6.91	freelancing	72.27	23.02	4.71
blender	69.8	20.41	9.79	space	73.27	20.27	6.47
astronomy	64.4	27.64	7.97	tor	82.22	12.4	5.37
pets	66.51	24.02	9.46	ham	67.97	23.24	8.79
italian	59.27	31.92	8.81	pt	61.62	22.85	15.52
aviation	72.62	20.65	6.73	ebooks	73.07	20.16	6.78
beer	67.89	23.42	8.69	softwarerecs	69.81	21.54	8.65
arduino	73.38	20.78	5.84	expatriates	72.13	21.79	6.09
matheducators	67.19	23.24	9.57	earthscience	62.66	29.53	7.81
joomla	64.8	22.59	12.61	datascience	70.66	22.99	6.36
puzzling	67.56	22.84	9.59	craftcms	49.37	25.13	25.49
buddhism	67.77	20.91	11.32	hinduism	69.13	19.92	10.96
moderators	69.42	21.76	8.82	startups	68.21	24.88	6.91
worldbuilding	67.13	24.07	8.79	emacs	57.2	27.13	15.67
ja	68.01	21.32	10.67	hsm	62.98	28.55	8.47
economics	68.03	23.92	8.05	lifehacks	73.68	19.25	7.08
engineering	67.61	26.15	6.24	coffee	65.55	22.88	11.57
vi	63.32	25.99	10.69	musicfans	62.54	27.72	9.75
woodworking	63.55	27.09	9.36	civicrm	62.11	20.56	17.34
health	63.64	29.14	7.22	mythology	66.81	21.78	11.42
law	68.64	25.99	5.37	opensource	69.4	24.45	6.15
elementaryos	74.21	17.9	7.9	portuguese	52.12	30.19	17.69
arabic	59.88	28.49	11.63	computergraphics	64.32	26.03	9.65
hardwarerecs	62.13	27.64	10.23	es	68.81	20.43	10.76
3dprinting	62.06	26.63	11.31	ethereum	58.85	24.93	16.22
latin	58.05	29.66	12.29	languagelearning	51.66	32.23	16.11
retrocomputing	72.83	18.91	8.26	crafts	57.67	25.58	16.74

A.4   Proportion of Uni-C Across the Activities in Stack Exchange Websites

Table 4. Percentage of Uni-C across the activities. (The websites are sorted as per their creation time.)

Site name	Questioning	Answering	Voting	Site name	Questioning	Answering	Voting
stackoverflow	72.51	27.15	0.34	serverfault	44.9	25.36	29.74
superuser	44.11	30.92	24.97	mathoverflow	59.83	23.38	16.79
sharepoint	66.47	27.24	6.29	money	43.25	18.88	37.87
electronics	57.09	20.99	21.92	judaism	44.8	39.09	16.11
sound	42.05	47.01	10.94	stackapps	10.55	4.41	85.04
webapps	28.77	25.67	45.55	gaming	29.17	48.9	21.93
webmasters	43.68	22.35	33.97	cooking	25.46	46.22	28.32
gamedev	40.01	19.82	40.17	photo	36.91	28.16	34.93
stats	72.7	11.61	15.68	math	77.17	12.1	10.73
diy	57.41	25.85	16.73	gis	70.07	17.89	12.04
tex	63.22	10.46	26.32	askubuntu	55.33	24.57	20.1
english	36.81	33.38	29.81	ux	19.16	19.49	61.35
unix	35.67	19.4	44.93	wordpress	64.28	21.16	14.56
cstheory	26.74	12.89	60.36	apple	38.61	31.71	29.68
rpg	26.64	34.2	39.16	bicycles	32.58	35.09	32.34
programmers	13.44	14.11	72.44	android	46.86	28.27	24.87
ru	75.08	22.68	2.24	boardgames	29.3	28.97	41.73
physics	52.5	22.41	25.08	homebrew	31.77	39.4	28.83
security	28.48	14.23	57.29	writers	28.36	32.05	39.59
avp	47.98	13.71	38.32	dba	46.75	15.05	38.2
graphicdesign	40.93	24.11	34.96	scifi	22.08	46.35	31.57
codereview	33.6	18.28	48.13	codegolf	1.75	20.11	78.15
quant	52.3	22.66	25.04	pm	23.75	27	49.25
skeptics	7.93	10.48	81.59	fitness	31.93	31.62	36.44
drupal	61.26	28.87	9.87	mechanics	52.86	27.59	19.55
parenting	17.18	29.01	53.81	music	25.91	40.47	33.62
sqa	36.3	28.36	35.34	german	23.71	33.17	43.11
japanese	42.87	24.87	32.26	philosophy	28.93	28.21	42.86
gardening	45.33	30.75	23.92	travel	48.22	19.8	31.98
productivity	13.69	34.37	51.94	crypto	43.24	9.1	47.67
dsp	60.67	14.13	25.21	french	20.1	40	39.9
christianity	19.76	52.02	28.21	bitcoin	43.19	25.05	31.76
linguistics	42.48	26.66	30.87	hermeneutics	19.93	54.06	26
history	20.92	28.4	50.67	bricks	33.49	23.61	42.91
spanish	20.58	46.2	33.22	scicomp	47.42	16.28	36.3
movies	27.26	37.74	35	rus	64.81	29.86	5.32
chinese	19.3	59.08	21.62	biology	50.73	17.18	32.09
poker	34.82	29.74	35.44	mathematica	71.01	5.64	23.35
cogsci	42.06	22.11	35.83	outdoors	10.86	35.41	53.73
martialarts	15.12	42.44	42.44	sports	30.4	36.23	33.37
academia	29.32	21.1	49.58	cs	45.99	11.26	42.75
workplace	28.15	11.92	59.93	windowsphone	47.94	26.23	25.83
chemistry	68	15.64	16.37	chess	21.03	30.41	48.56

(continued)

Table 4. (*continued*)

Site name	Questioning	Answering	Voting	Site name	Questioning	Answering	Voting
raspberrypi	38.94	22.41	38.65	russian	18.91	41.72	39.37
islam	45.56	36.12	18.32	salesforce	72.43	21.13	6.44
patents	45.02	27.01	27.97	genealogy	43.79	32.64	23.58
robotics	49.31	19.71	30.98	expressionengine	80.11	13.29	6.59
politics	23.68	23.28	53.04	anime	25.86	45	29.14
magento	71.79	19.72	8.48	ell	30.49	30.17	39.34
sustainability	16.88	34.6	48.52	tridion	79.55	12.31	8.14
reverseeng.	36.08	12.67	51.25	networkeng.	54.78	19.54	25.68
opendata	42.22	19.8	37.98	freelancing	24.29	22.48	53.23
blender	71.2	10.05	18.75	space	15.31	13.76	70.93
astronomy	37.66	15.85	46.5	tor	63.67	18.08	18.25
pets	42.22	28.8	28.98	ham	33.93	35.34	30.73
italian	16.41	36.49	47.1	pt	68.95	26.28	4.77
aviation	19.64	24.32	56.04	ebooks	29.61	23.31	47.09
beer	12.05	34.79	53.16	softwarerecs	47.61	17.5	34.89
arduino	59.87	20.08	20.04	expatriates	54.92	17.48	27.6
matheducators	11.15	24.98	63.87	earthscience	36.64	16.15	47.21
joomla	65.37	20.16	14.47	datascience	42.79	19.57	37.64
puzzling	7.24	24.33	68.44	craftcms	71.03	8.85	20.12
buddhism	21.5	42.31	36.19	hinduism	29.42	40.28	30.3
moderators	8.33	14.68	76.98	startups	35.69	21.74	42.57
worldbuilding	7.84	32.62	59.55	emacs	34.98	15.22	49.8
ja	71.66	23	5.34	hsm	20.96	12.46	66.57
economics	58.76	15.44	25.8	lifehacks	6.87	31.78	61.34
engineering	46.04	16.53	37.43	coffee	16.67	29.02	54.31
vi	20.91	10.68	68.41	musicfans	42.53	21.59	35.88
woodworking	21.63	23.2	55.17	civicrm	88.53	7.08	4.39
health	58.63	13.65	27.71	mythology	17.41	18.35	64.24
law	63.03	7.62	29.35	opensource	17.83	7.28	74.89
elementaryos	67.66	14.65	17.69	portuguese	10.86	29.41	59.73
arabic	9.71	20.39	69.9	computergraphics	30.95	10	59.05
hardwarerecs	44.65	14.09	41.26	es	62.46	22.96	14.58
3dprinting	25.91	21.05	53.04	ethereum	40	19.21	40.79
latin	10.95	3.65	85.4	languagelearning	11.93	11.93	76.15
retrocomputing	2.09	14.63	83.28	crafts	11.29	24.19	64.52

It should be noted that as per StackExchange policies, users require atleast 15 reputation points to be able to vote. The reason for the presence of uni-C in voting is the *association bonus*[5], whereby users who have atleast 200 reputation points on any of the StackExchange websites, get a bonus of 100 on each new StackExchange website that they register, in addition to the 1 reputation point that they normally get upon registering. This leads to a total of 101 reputation points automatically provided to them, enabling them to upvote or downvote content on the new website despite no contribution in questioning or answering on these new websites.

---

[5] https://meta.stackexchange.com/questions/141648/what-is-the-association-bonus.

Further, the presence of less than 1% (i.e., 0.34%) uni-C in voting on Stack-Overflow depicts the possibility of users gaining bonus reputation points on other websites due to their contribution on StackOverflow rather than the other way around, as it is the oldest website.

A.5   Method Used for Finding the Optimal k

To verify the optimal value of k, we use a method provided by He et al. [24]. In their method, the authors compute two parameters '*Cluster compactness (CMP)*' and '*Cluster separation (SEP)*', where CMP captures the intra-cluster distances and SEP captures the inter-cluster distances. The formulae for CMP and SEP are given as below:

Cluster Compactness (CMP):

$$CMP = \frac{1}{C} \sum_i^C \frac{v(c_i)}{v(X)}$$

where,

$$v(X) = \sqrt{\frac{1}{N} \sum_{i=1}^N d^2(x_i, \bar{x})}$$

Cluster Separation (SEP):

$$SEP = \frac{1}{C(C-1)} \sum_{i=1}^C \sum_{j=1, j \neq i}^C \exp\left(-\frac{d^2(x_{ci}, x_{cj})}{2\sigma^2}\right)$$

The formula for SEP is such that a smaller value of SEP indicates a larger inter-cluster distance. Further, the clusters should also be compact (measured by CMP). Therefore, for the optimal value of k, the values of both CMP, as well as SEP, should be minimum. The authors suggest using another parameter *OCQ (Overall Cluster Quality)* which is given as:

$$OCQ(\alpha) = \alpha * CMP + (1 - \alpha) * SEP$$

where α indicates the relative weight assigned to inter-cluster and intra-cluster distances and lies between 0 and 1. A value of $1/2$ for α indicates equal weight for both CMP and SEP. For our analysis, we considered α to be $1/2$.

We used this method to compute the optimal k for all the websites. The Table in Fig. 5 shows the value of k along with the number of websites for which that value of k was found optimal. For most of the websites, $k = 3$ was the optimal value of k.

Table 5. Number of websites with the given ideal k. For 73.71% of the websites, ideal k value was found to be 3.

Value of k	Number of websites
2	0
3	115
4	26
5	9
6	5
7	0
8	1
9	0
10	0

A.6   User-Distribution Obtained For Stack Exchange Websites

Table 6. Percentage Distribution of questioners, answerers and voters for each website.

Website	Questioners (%)	Answerers (%)	Voters (%)	Website	Questioners (%)	Answerers (%)	Voters (%)
stack overflow	52.45	24.69	22.86	serverfault	35.06	23.48	41.46
superuser	34.88	26.91	38.2	mathoverflow	43.28	18.5	38.21
sharepoint	55.58	27.17	17.25	money	32.25	15.62	52.13
electronics	43.83	18.37	37.79	judaism	35.24	31.93	32.83
sound	32.72	43.16	24.12	stackapps	13.1	6.1	80.8
webapps	25.24	21.52	53.23	gaming	25.15	39.32	35.53
webmasters	33.91	20.52	45.57	cooking	21.17	36.98	41.84
gamedev	30.82	20.54	48.63	photo	27.81	23.38	48.82
stats	58.44	12.05	29.5	math	59.44	11.68	28.88
diy	46.54	23.11	30.35	gis	56.45	18.78	24.77
tex	43.7	9.03	47.28	askubuntu	45.7	25.04	29.27
english	27.97	26.92	45.11	ux	18.75	18.2	63.06
unix	31.26	15.74	53.0	wordpress	51.28	23.12	25.6
cstheory	25.63	12.74	61.63	apple	34.65	26.28	39.07
rpg	18.38	22.91	58.72	bicycles	24.45	28.68	46.88
programmers	13.33	10.9	75.77	android	39.58	26.88	33.54
ru	58.42	24.43	17.15	boardgames	20.56	21.52	57.93
physics	40.44	19.29	40.27	homebrew	24.09	29.49	46.42
security	22.46	14.43	63.1	writers	19.94	26.29	53.77
avp	37.31	16.44	46.25	dba	37.8	17.0	45.21
graphicdesign	33.03	22.1	44.88	scifi	18.62	36.25	45.12
codereview	22.59	16.87	60.54	codegolf	15.75	15.26	68.98
quant	40.0	21.49	38.51	pm	17.96	23.52	58.51
skeptics	9.32	8.3	82.38	fitness	23.74	24.04	52.22
drupal	47.96	28.02	24.02	mechanics	39.48	23.79	36.72
parenting	13.69	23.8	62.52	music	19.35	31.25	49.39
sqa	29.74	27.23	43.04	german	15.98	23.53	60.49
japanese	29.41	18.6	52.0	philosophy	21.44	23.55	55.01
gardening	30.79	22.3	46.91	travel	37.43	17.03	45.54
productivity	10.63	27.58	61.79	crypto	34.77	10.38	54.85

(continued)

Table 6. (*continued*)

Website	Questioners (%)	Answerers (%)	Voters (%)	Website	Questioners (%)	Answerers (%)	Voters (%)
dsp	47.55	14.38	38.07	french	14.15	27.16	58.68
christianity	15.95	40.45	43.6	bitcoin	34.86	22.88	42.25
linguistics	31.18	21.84	46.98	hermeneutics	17.04	41.85	41.11
history	21.22	20.84	57.93	bricks	26.58	21.06	52.36
spanish	14.47	34.44	51.09	scicomp	34.94	14.51	50.56
movies	22.93	29.31	47.76	rus	57.83	30.7	11.47
chinese	14.87	45.32	39.81	biology	36.39	13.91	49.7
poker	24.98	24.39	50.63	mathematica	51.38	7.03	41.59
cogsci	30.43	18.32	51.25	outdoors	11.63	26.38	61.99
martialarts	10.82	33.19	55.99	sports	21.14	26.99	51.87
academia	22.03	16.21	61.76	cs	36.65	12.43	50.92
workplace	21.09	10.28	68.63	windowsphone	38.85	24.54	36.61
chemistry	52.52	14.01	33.48	chess	15.75	25.46	58.79
raspberrypi	32.28	24.79	42.93	russian	13.82	30.58	55.6
islam	37.09	31.83	31.08	salesforce	57.04	21.44	21.52
patents	39.28	26.29	34.43	genealogy	33.93	26.43	39.64
robotics	37.09	18.32	44.59	expressionengine	59.33	18.45	22.21
politics	17.32	18.53	64.15	anime	21.39	34.65	43.96
magento	58.52	22.42	19.06	ell	24.48	25.21	50.31
sustainability	17.76	24.71	57.53	tridion	52.39	11.88	35.74
reverseeng.	34.26	13.8	51.95	networkeng.	43.98	19.54	36.48
opendata	32.61	18.66	48.72	freelancing	18.2	23.06	58.75
blender	55.85	13.6	30.55	space	16.72	12.34	70.94
astronomy	27.09	15.67	57.24	tor	54.35	18.84	26.81
pets	30.23	22.51	47.26	ham	24.78	27.91	47.3
italian	15.31	25.14	59.54	pt	49.86	24.61	25.53
aviation	20.03	19.26	60.71	ebooks	22.48	20.49	57.03
beer	8.38	28.4	63.23	softwarerecs	36.04	16.7	47.25
arduino	48.3	21.68	30.03	expatriates	41.67	15.02	43.31
matheducators	10.33	23.0	66.67	earthscience	26.02	12.0	61.98
joomla	49.9	21.32	28.78	datascience	33.54	21.75	44.71
puzzling	6.83	18.1	75.08	craftcms	46.71	17.34	35.94
buddhism	16.93	32.86	50.21	hinduism	24.26	32.43	43.32
moderators	9.08	11.69	79.23	startups	26.12	19.21	54.68
worldbuilding	7.37	25.48	67.15	emacs	26.37	16.28	57.35
ja	55.76	23.1	21.13	hsm	22.82	11.05	66.13
economics	43.59	14.05	42.36	lifehacks	7.48	26.43	66.09
engineering	34.32	14.38	51.31	coffee	12.58	21.95	65.47
vi	24.97	7.85	67.18	musicfans	27.79	18.05	54.16
woodworking	20.6	19.9	59.5	civicrm	64.73	14.6	20.67
health	41.0	11.43	47.57	mythology	17.72	15.4	66.88
law	45.71	8.27	46.02	opensource	18.36	8.71	72.93
elementaryos	54.18	19.89	25.94	portuguese	11.29	17.18	71.53
arabic	9.25	19.08	71.68	computergraphics	32.42	7.8	59.79
hardwarerecs	29.61	12.96	57.43	es	50.02	23.18	26.8
3dprinting	17.04	19.3	63.66	ethereum	27.78	18.52	53.7
latin	17.3	4.64	78.06	languagelearning	6.13	11.32	82.55
retrocomputing	11.5	11.71	76.79	crafts	10.65	16.67	72.69

A.7   Model Parameters for the Systems Studied in Chapter 3

The values in the matrix T were chosen uniformly at random between 0.00007 and 0.005 making sure that $\rho(NT) < 1$.

System 1: $n = 100$, $K_c(\infty) = 14289.74$, $\mathcal{D} = (22, 35, 43)$

$$T = \begin{bmatrix} 0.00045596 & 0.00435622 & 0.00287159 \\ 0.00382782 & 0.00076362 & 0.00499575 \\ 0.00399529 & 0.00348565 & 0.0018039 \end{bmatrix}$$

System 2: $n = 100$, $K_c(\infty) = 13331.63$, $\mathcal{D} = (19, 51, 30)$

$$T = \begin{bmatrix} 0.00078797 & 0.00359952 & 0.00363374 \\ 0.00194002 & 0.0018636 & 0.00456399 \\ 0.0026924 & 0.00233821 & 0.00057316 \end{bmatrix}$$

System 3: $n = 200$, $K_c(\infty) = 46239.11$, $\mathcal{D} = (64.5, 18.5, 17)$

$$T = \begin{bmatrix} 0.00257957 & 0.00330136 & 0.00199484 \\ 0.0033283 & 0.00098843 & 0.00397102 \\ 0.00491812 & 0.0016636 & 0.00101264 \end{bmatrix}$$

System 4: $n = 200$, $K_c(\infty) = 37732.05$, $\mathcal{D} = (44, 44, 12)$

$$T = \begin{bmatrix} 0.00025509 & 0.00491508 & 0.00236663 \\ 0.00365481 & 0.00047938 & 0.00425228 \\ 0.0033825 & 0.0004316 & 0.00066393 \end{bmatrix}$$

Systems with Self-triggering − 0: $n = 100$ in all three systems.

System 1: $K_c(\infty) = 12536.23$, $\mathcal{D} = (38, 32, 30)$

$$T = \begin{bmatrix} 0. & 0.00265766 & 0.00448791 \\ 0.00400489 & 0. & 0.00111834 \\ 0.00194009 & 0.00390131 & 0. \end{bmatrix}$$

System 2: $K_c(\infty) = 11114.29$, $\mathcal{D} = (39, 37, 24)$

$$T = \begin{bmatrix} 0. & 0.00299839 & 0.00122855 \\ 0.00070994 & 0. & 0.00168737 \\ 0.00149221 & 0.00082065 & 0. \end{bmatrix}$$

System 3: $K_c(\infty) = 11924.27$, $\mathcal{D} = (34, 28, 38)$

$$T = \begin{bmatrix} 0. & 0.00264557 & 0.00119586 \\ 0.00115856 & 0. & 0.00398131 \\ 0.00448212 & 0.00097011 & 0. \end{bmatrix}$$

References

1. Adamic, L.A., Zhang, J., Bakshy, E., Ackerman, M.S.: Knowledge sharing and Yahoo answers: everyone knows something. In: Proceedings of the 17th International Conference on World Wide Web, pp. 665–674. ACM (2008)
2. Agrawal, R., Rajagopalan, S., Srikant, R., Xu, Y.: Mining newsgroups using networks arising from social behavior. In: Proceedings of the 12th International Conference on World Wide Web, pp. 529–535. ACM (2003)
3. Anderson, A., Huttenlocher, D., Kleinberg, J., Leskovec, J.: Steering user behavior with badges. In: Proceedings of the 22nd International Conference on World Wide Web, pp. 95–106. ACM (2013)
4. Anthony, D., Smith, S.W., Williamson, T.: Explaining Quality in Internet Collective Goods: Zealots and Good Samaritans in the Case of Wikipedia. Dartmouth College, Hanover (2005)
5. Arazy, O., Lifshitz-Assaf, H., Nov, O., Daxenberger, J., Balestra, M., Cheshire, C.: On the 'how' and 'why' of emergent role behaviors in Wikipedia. In: Conference on Computer-Supported Cooperative Work and Social Computing, vol. 35 (2017)
6. Arazy, O., Nov, O., Patterson, R., Yeo, L.: Information quality in Wikipedia: the effects of group composition and task conflict. J. Manag. Inf. Syst. **27**(4), 71–98 (2011)
7. Arazy, O., Ortega, F., Nov, O., Yeo, L., Balila, A.: Functional roles and career paths in Wikipedia. In: Proceedings of the 18th ACM Conference on Computer Supported Cooperative Work & Social Computing, pp. 1092–1105. ACM (2015)
8. Aubin, J.P.: Applied Functional Analysis, vol. 47. Wiley, Hoboken (2011)
9. Chhabra, A., Iyengar, S.S.: Characterizing the triggering phenomenon in Wikipedia. In: Proceedings of the 14th International Symposium on Open Collaboration, p. 11. ACM (2018)
10. Chhabra, A., Iyengar, S.: How does knowledge come by? arXiv preprint arXiv:1705.06946 (2017)
11. Chhabra, A., Iyengar, S.R.S., Saini, J.S., Malik, V.: Activity-selection behavior and optimal user-distribution in Q&A websites. In: Nguyen, N.T., Hoang, B.H., Huynh, C.P., Hwang, D., Trawiński, B., Vossen, G. (eds.) ICCCI 2020. LNCS (LNAI), vol. 12496, pp. 853–865. Springer, Cham (2020). https://doi.org/10.1007/978-3-030-63007-2_67
12. Chhabra, A., Iyengar, S., Saini, P., Bhat, R.S.: Presence of an ecosystem: a catalyst in the knowledge building process in crowdsourced annotation environments. In: Proceedings of the 2015 International Conference on Advances in Social Networks Analysis and Mining (ASONAM 2015) (2015)
13. Chhabra, A., RS Iyengar, S.: Activity-selection behavior of users in stackexchange websites. In: Companion Proceedings of the Web Conference 2020, pp. 105–106 (2020)
14. Cress, U., Kimmerle, J.: A systemic and cognitive view on collaborative knowledge building with wikis. Int. J. Comput.-Support. Collab. Learn. **3**(2), 105–122 (2008). https://doi.org/10.1007/s11412-007-9035-z
15. Erickson, L., Petrick, I., Trauth, E.: Hanging with the right crowd: matching crowdsourcing need to crowd characteristics (2012)
16. Fisher, D., Smith, M., Welser, H.T.: You are who you talk to: detecting roles in usenet newsgroups. In: Proceedings of the 39th Annual Hawaii International Conference on System Sciences, HICSS 2006, vol. 3, pp. 59b–59b. IEEE (2006)

17. Fisher, K., Lipson, J.I.: Information processing interpretation of errors in college science learning. Instr. Sci. **14**(1), 49–74 (1985)
18. Fugelstad, P., et al.: What makes users rate (share, tag, edit...)?: predicting patterns of participation in online communities. In: Proceedings of the ACM 2012 Conference on Computer Supported Cooperative Work, pp. 969–978. ACM (2012)
19. Furtado, A., Andrade, N., Oliveira, N., Brasileiro, F.: Contributor profiles, their dynamics, and their importance in five Q&A sites. In: Proceedings of the 2013 Conference on Computer Supported Cooperative Work, pp. 1237–1252. ACM (2013)
20. Golder, S.A., Donath, J.: Social roles in electronic communities. Internet Res. **5**, 19–22 (2004)
21. Gruenfeld, D.H., Mannix, E.A., Williams, K.Y., Neale, M.A.: Group composition and decision making: how member familiarity and information distribution affect process and performance. Organ. Behav. Hum. Decis. Process. **67**(1), 1–15 (1996)
22. Guzdial, M., Rick, J., Kerimbaev, B.: Recognizing and supporting roles in CSCW. In: Proceedings of the 2000 ACM Conference on Computer Supported Cooperative Work, pp. 261–268. ACM (2000)
23. Hanrahan, B.V., Convertino, G., Nelson, L.: Modeling problem difficulty and expertise in stackoverflow. In: Proceedings of the ACM 2012 Conference on Computer Supported Cooperative Work Companion, pp. 91–94. ACM (2012)
24. He, J., Tan, A.H., Tan, C.L., Sung, S.Y.: On quantitative evaluation of clustering systems. In: Wu, W., Xiong, H., Shekhar, S. (eds.) Clustering and Information Retrieval. NETA, vol. 11, pp. 105–133. Springer, Boston (2004). https://doi.org/10.1007/978-1-4613-0227-8_4
25. Heaps, H.S.: Information Retrieval, Computational and Theoretical Aspects. Academic Press, Cambridge (1978)
26. Hong, L., Page, S.E.: Groups of diverse problem solvers can outperform groups of high-ability problem solvers. Proc. Natl. Acad. Sci. U.S.A. **101**(46), 16385–16389 (2004)
27. Iacopini, I., Milojević, S., Latora, V.: Network dynamics of innovation processes. Phys. Rev. Lett. **120**(4), 048301 (2018)
28. Jehn, K.A., Northcraft, G.B., Neale, M.A.: Why differences make a difference: a field study of diversity, conflict and performance in workgroups. Adm. Sci. Q. **44**(4), 741–763 (1999)
29. Just, M.A., Carpenter, P.A.: A theory of reading: from eye fixations to comprehension. Psychol. Rev. **87**(4), 329 (1980)
30. Kobren, A., Tan, C.H., Ipeirotis, P., Gabrilovich, E.: Getting more for less: optimized crowdsourcing with dynamic tasks and goals. In: Proceedings of the 24th International Conference on World Wide Web, pp. 592–602. International World Wide Web Conferences Steering Committee (2015)
31. Kriplean, T., Beschastnikh, I., McDonald, D.W.: Articulations of WikiWork: uncovering valued work in Wikipedia through barnstars. In: Proceedings of the 2008 ACM Conference on Computer Supported Cooperative Work, pp. 47–56. ACM (2008)
32. Liu, J., Ram, S.: Who does what: collaboration patterns in the Wikipedia and their impact on article quality. ACM Trans. Manag. Inf. Syst. (TMIS) **2**(2), 11 (2011)
33. Luhmann, N.: Social Systems. Stanford University Press (1995)
34. Mamykina, L., Manoim, B., Mittal, M., Hripcsak, G., Hartmann, B.: Design lessons from the fastest Q&A site in the west. In: Proceedings of the SIGCHI Conference on Human Factors in Computing Systems, pp. 2857–2866. ACM (2011)
35. Marengo, L., Zeppini, P.: The arrival of the new. J. Evol. Econ. **26**(1), 171–194 (2016)

36. Minsky, M.: Frame-System Theory. Thinking: Readings in Cognitive Science, pp. 355–376 (1977)
37. Movshovitz-Attias, D., Movshovitz-Attias, Y., Steenkiste, P., Faloutsos, C.: Analysis of the reputation system and user contributions on a question answering website: stackoverflow. In: 2013 IEEE/ACM International Conference on Advances in Social Networks Analysis and Mining (ASONAM), pp. 886–893. IEEE (2013)
38. Nam, K.K., Ackerman, M.S., Adamic, L.A.: Questions in, knowledge in?: a study of Naver's question answering community. In: Proceedings of the SIGCHI Conference on Human Factors in Computing Systems, pp. 779–788. ACM (2009)
39. Norman, D.A.: Categorization of action slips. Psychol. Rev. **88**(1), 1 (1981)
40. Pal, A., Chang, S., Konstan, J.A.: Evolution of experts in question answering communities. In: ICWSM (2012)
41. Piaget, J.: Piaget's Theory. Springer, Heidelberg (1976)
42. Piaget, J.: The Development of Thought: Equilibration of Cognitive Structures. (Trans A. Rosin). Viking (1977)
43. Rezgui, A., Crowston, K.: Stigmergic coordination in Wikipedia. In: Proceedings of the 14th International Symposium on Open Collaboration, p. 19. ACM (2018)
44. Rumelhart, D.E.: Understanding Understanding. Memories, Thoughts and Emotions: Essays in Honor of George Mandler, pp. 257–275 (1991)
45. Secretan, J.: Stigmergic dimensions of online creative interaction. Cogn. Syst. Res. **21**, 65–74 (2013)
46. Tausczik, Y.R., Pennebaker, J.W.: Participation in an online mathematics community: differentiating motivations to add. In: Proceedings of the ACM 2012 Conference on Computer Supported Cooperative Work, pp. 207–216 (2012)
47. Tria, F., Loreto, V., Servedio, V.D.P., Strogatz, S.H.: The dynamics of correlated novelties. Sci. Rep. **4**, 5890 (2014)
48. Turner, T.C., Smith, M.A., Fisher, D., Welser, H.T.: Picturing usenet: mapping computer-mediated collective action. J. Comput.-Mediated Commun. **10**(4), JCMC1048 (2005)
49. Welser, H.T., et al.: Finding social roles in Wikipedia. In: Proceedings of the 2011 iConference, pp. 122–129. ACM (2011)
50. Welser, H.T., Gleave, E., Fisher, D., Smith, M.: Visualizing the signatures of social roles in online discussion groups. J. Soc. Struct. **8**(2), 1–32 (2007)
51. Yang, D., Halfaker, A., Kraut, R.E., Hovy, E.H.: Who did what: editor role identification in Wikipedia. In: ICWSM, pp. 446–455 (2016)
52. Yang, J., Tao, K., Bozzon, A., Houben, G.-J.: Sparrows and owls: characterisation of expert behaviour in stackoverflow. In: Dimitrova, V., Kuflik, T., Chin, D., Ricci, F., Dolog, P., Houben, G.-J. (eds.) UMAP 2014. LNCS, vol. 8538, pp. 266–277. Springer, Cham (2014). https://doi.org/10.1007/978-3-319-08786-3_23

Author Index

Printed in the United States
by Baker & Taylor Publisher Services